Public Libraries
AN ECONOMIC VIEW

MALCOLM GETZ is Associate Professor of Economics at Vanderbilt University. He is the author of *The Economics of the Urban Fire Department*, also published by The Johns Hopkins University Press.

Public Libraries

AN ECONOMIC VIEW

Malcolm Getz

THE JOHNS HOPKINS UNIVERSITY PRESS
BALTIMORE AND LONDON

This study and its publication were supported by grants to the National Bureau of Economic Research, Inc., from the Book-of-the-Month Club, Inc., and the Scherman Foundation. The author is solely responsible for the views expressed.

The Johns Hopkins University Press, Baltimore, Maryland 21218
The Johns Hopkins Press Ltd., London

Library of Congress Cataloging in Publication Data

Getz, Malcolm,
Public libraries.

Bibliography: p. 207
1. Public libraries—United States—Administration.
2. Public libraries—United States—Finance.
I. Title.
Z678.G46   027.473   80-10651
ISBN 0-8018-2395-1

For Wystan and Kiesa

Contents

Tables

Preface and Acknowledgments

This is a study of the strategic decisions that shape the provision of public library services in the United States. The basic choices in public services are how many facilities to operate, how many materials to put in each, and how many hours to operate. These are the issues addressed here. The character of public library services provided by large library systems is described, and sources of variation in services are investigated. The pattern of change in technical operations is examined. A variety of public policies toward libraries are discussed.

This study should be of interest both to scholars concerned with local government, and to officials responsible for the quality of library services. While standard statistical methods are applied throughout, an appendix is provided to explain the use of the statistics in general terms for readers unfamiliar with the techniques.

The support of this investigation by the Book-of-the-Month Club, Inc., the Scherman Foundation, and the National Bureau of Economic Research, Inc., is gratefully acknowledged, as are the support of a research leave during 1977–78 by the National Science Foundation and Vanderbilt University. The leave was spent at the Joint Center for Urban Studies of the Massachusetts Institute of Technology and Harvard University, and the hospitality of the Joint Center is much appreciated. John R. Meyer of Harvard University brought me to this research, provided invaluable advice as the study took shape, and made the whole study possible. While none of the above bear responsibility for remaining faults or the views expressed, each has been important in bringing it about.

This study would not have been possible without the encouragement and support of library officials across the country. Librarians are inundated with surveys and requests for information. It is, therefore, especially noteworthy that so many participated. Richard Couper, John MacKenzie Cory, and Edwin Holmgren of the New York Public Library have been especially supportive from beginning to end. They taught me a good deal about libraries. David Marshall Stewart, Director of the Public Library of Nashville and Davidson County and past president of the Public Library Association, commented on a draft of this work and provided several helpful insights. I very much appreciate the thoughtfulness and cooperation of the many librarians who participated in the study.

Several people assisted in the study, including Amar Bhide, Susan Collins, Hatti Myers, Darryl Mikami, and John Vahaly. Ray Palmer conducted a substantial part of the interviews and his role is especially appreciated. The typescript was very competently prepared by Edda Leithner at Vanderbilt.

Preliminary versions of several chapters in this book appeared as working papers of the Joint Center for Urban Studies and of the National Bureau of Economic Research, Inc. These essays were discussed in seminars at the Joint Center, at Yale University, and at Vanderbilt. Remaining faults are the responsibility of the author.

Public Libraries
AN ECONOMIC VIEW

1

An Introduction to the Public Library Industry

This chapter reviews the nature of the public library industry. It presents a background that serves as a basis for policy toward public libraries. The history of public libraries is discussed briefly and is followed by a discussion of the book trade. The character of library users and the nature of the library production process are described. The purpose of this chapter is to provide a background for the more detailed investigations made in subsequent chapters.

The demand for public library services seems to be changing. Recently, public libraries have suffered from increasing costs and municipal budget cuts. Consequently, library services in many cities have been restricted. In most central cities, circulation of library materials has been falling in per capita terms for over a decade. This is primarily because of declines in city population. On the other hand, in many suburban library systems circulation has grown, even in per capita terms.

Library managers are seeking ways to alleviate the problems caused by increasing costs and municipal budget cuts. Changes in the way libraries operate, such as charging for services, cutting costs, and looking for new techniques, as well as the possibility of more direct support from state and federal government and private sources, may alleviate the fiscal problems of public libraries.

At the same time, computer and telecommunication advancements may reshape library operations to some extent beyond the control of individual libraries. Historically, each library has operated autonomously. An individual library was responsible for all the operations that range from book purchase to book loan to the public. Skilled effort went into each operation from selecting books to leading library users to the materials and information they seek.

A revolution may be taking place such that individual libraries may now be able to buy many services externally more cheaply than they can produce them in-house. Changes in the production process for supplying library services may have implications for the structure and organization of the industry.

The public library, then, is at a critical time. The need for an informed electorate, an educated work force, and information to manage complex institutions in a changing world is greater than ever. However, the public library's position in helping to meet this need may be changing. Public policy toward libraries, especially at the national level, should be reexamined for two reasons: one, to clarify the philosophical objectives of policy; and two, to design the policy to take into account a full understanding of the changing nature of the public library industry.

In many ways it is useful to think of the institutions providing public library services as an industry, similar to other industries dominated by nonprofit service oriented institutions. The public library service is an industry in that a variety of inputs are hired, including labor, buildings, and materials. The inputs are bundled together in ways that make a service available to patrons more valuable than the sum of the parts. This bundling may be thought of as a production process. In many respects, then, the public library industry shares concerns with other service sector industries such as the higher education, medical care, and recreation industries. For example, the public library industry must be concerned about changes in the demand for its services, as with changes in the number of children and in reading habits. Also, the library industry experiences changes in technology, as with the introduction of nonprint materials. On the other hand, of course, the public library industry is different from some other service industries. Most public libraries are financed primarily by local property taxes, and make significant services available to all comers without charge. This study deals with the public library industry in all its particularity.

A BRIEF HISTORY AND DESCRIPTION
OF THE PUBLIC LIBRARY

The short history of public libraries,[1] though presented in rough chronological order, incorporates several themes that are relevant to later parts of this study. One such theme identified in this chapter is the relationship between government and public libraries. A second theme is the nature and growth of library services. A third theme is the impact of competition—for example, book clubs and paperback books. Finally, recent trends in library use are examined.

The first book-lending services were privately financed. Shares in these formal institutions were sold and annual subscription fees were charged. In 1731, Benjamin Franklin helped found the Philadelphia Library Company on this basis. The Boston Library began in 1792 with shares at $25 and annual subscriptions at $3. The Boston Athenaeum was founded in 1806 when shares sold for $300 and annual subscriptions for $10.

In many cases, the collections of these private institutions were developed through book contributions by members. The Yale College Library was founded in this way in 1700. The early library companies were public in the same sense that General Motors is a publicly held corporation: shares were traded, and subscriptions were sold publicly. The Boston Athenaeum continues to operate in this manner.

The first libraries also received support from government on occasion. Two examples of this are the Harvard College Library and the Philadelphia Library Company. Several state legislatures in New England voted to make contributions to the Harvard College Library after it burned in 1764. The Philadelphia Library Company was housed in the Pennsylvania State House. Moreover, public officials by virtue of their office were allowed access to some library company facilities without charge. Yet even the government library benefited from private support. The Library of Congress was founded in 1800; it was burned by the British in 1814. After the burning it was improved substantially by the contribution of Jefferson's personal library. For more than their first 100 years the line between private and government support of libraries was never crisp.

In the United States in 1850, 694 libraries, outside the public schools, held 2,201,632 volumes. Five libraries held over 50,000 books each: Harvard had 84,200; Philadelphia had 60,000; Yale had 50,481; the Library of Congress had 50,000; and the Boston Athenaeum had 50,000.

In the second half of the nineteenth century, library services began to be provided as a direct item of government budgets. The Boston Public Library was founded in 1852 as a department of the city government. It received its budget from the city government and all citizens could borrow books free of charge. The public in the library's title took on added meaning once governments began to finance them.

The character of public libraries of the nineteenth century was similar to that of their antecedents, the library companies. The books were for adults and could usually be used only on the premises. The collections emphasized the classics and works of philosophy and science.

Public libraries spread through the beneficence of Andrew Carnegie. His gifts provided enough funds to build over 1,500 public library buildings in the United States and about a thousand more in Canada, Great Britain, and elsewhere. Carnegie's donations for library construction began in 1886 and extended to 1917. Private philanthropy, such as Carnegie's, led many local governments into the public library industry.

Public library services changed dramatically in the first two decades of the twentieth century. Many services identified with public libraries today were offered for the first time. For example, works of popular fiction were included in the collection. By 1920, libraries began to supply the reading material the public wanted rather than what librarians and trustees thought was good for the public. At the time, many librarians viewed popular fiction as a deviation from their main function, but the new view prevailed.[2] Public libraries were thus important sources of recreation. (One extreme example of this is the public library service in Jefferson Parish, Louisiana, which is operated by the recreation department.)

Another change that took place in the early 20th century was that library materials began to circulate and libraries extended their hours and were open on Sundays. A third example of change was that branches and rural systems were developed which extended services beyond the central city. A fourth example of change was that public libraries began to cater to children by acquiring children's books and housing them in separate rooms.

Finally, libraries began to develop reference collections. The increase in the size of collections required that more attention be paid to cataloging and to preparing guides and indexes. Thus, in addition to being sources of just reading material in general, libraries also provided access to specific information. The period when the character of service expanded was the heyday of the public library.

The library is not simply a warehouse for reading material. In selecting materials for purchase, libraries make quality judgments. In placing materials in the collection, librarians sort and label materials so that not only can they be easily found, but similar materials are placed together, which makes for easy browsing. Librarians help readers find suitable materials and answer readers' specific questions. Many libraries operate telephone reference services. A questioner may ask questions that range from whether a particular book is available, to the name of a Congressman or a telephone number in Tokyo. The question-answering function is related to, and a direct outcome of, handling books. The quality of library service reflects librarian skills as well as the size of the acquisition budget.

In the 1920s, public libraries, as a source of recreation, faced competition from movies, radio, rental libraries, and book clubs. Thus, the importance of the public library as a source of recreation probably declined. During the 1930s, however, the use of public libraries increased because services were supplied without charge and public libraries were used for self-education.

Whereas local and state governments were involved in financing libraries in the nineteenth century, the federal government did not get involved until 1956, with the passage of the Library Services Act. The act followed a period of advocacy by the American Library Association. The act's central mission was to supply library services to people who were not being served, mainly those in rural areas. In 1964, the act was amended and renamed the Library Services and Construction Act. Funds became available to build libraries in any area without facilities, not just rural areas. The federal act also included funds to encourage library services for the handicapped. The central objective of universal availability of public library services has almost been achieved: over 95 percent of the population now live in areas served by public libraries.

In the 1960s the public library faced competition from three sources. First, the sales of mass market paperback books increased dramatically. This had a devastating effect on rental libraries and possibly decreased the use of public libraries as sources of recreation.

Second, the number of special libraries, libraries operated within businesses and government agencies, grew rapidly. Third, schools have improved the quality of their library services. Title II of the Elementary and Secondary Education Act of 1965 has substantially improved the quality of school libraries. As a consequence, the use of the public library by students may have been reduced. Also, because the birth rates in the 1960s were smaller, the total demand by children for books has gone down.

Recent Trends

Recent circulation trends for selected libraries are reported in table 1.1. Central city library systems have typically experienced substantial declines in circulation. The San Diego Public Library was an exception for most of the period, but recently its circulation has also experienced declines.

Metropolitan systems have generally maintained a balanced circulation: presumably suburban growth has offset central city decline. Birmingham, Alabama, is a clear exception: library use has fallen dramatically.

Suburban library systems generally have had substantial increases in circulation. Montgomery County is an example of a suburban area where circulation appears to have leveled off. The changes in circulation are due not only to changing population totals in the different jurisdictions, but also to changes in the per capita circulation. Circulation averages about 5.0 books per person nationwide but has fallen to 1.75 books per capita in Detroit; it is over 9.0 in Montgomery County and Baltimore County, Maryland. Change in library use may be caused, in part, by changing library operations and budgets. The recent decline in use in Buffalo followed a severe budget cut.

The relative growth in numbers of libraries is illustrated in table 1.2. From 1964 to 1978, the number of public library systems has grown 78 percent. The number of branches operated by library systems had increased by 77 percent in the same period. Financial assistance provided by the Library Services and Construction Act probably played some role in the expansion of the number of library systems. The expansion of suburbs may also be an important factor in the expanded number of library systems. The recent decline in the number of systems may reflect consolidation of smaller systems rather than loss of service.

Table 1.1. Circulation Trends in Selected Library Systems

	Thousands of Books Loaned per Year			Average Annual Percentage Change	
	1963	1975	1977	1963-75	1975-77
Central City Systems					
Boston Public Library	3,275	2,624	2,278	−1.8	−7.1
New York Public Library	13,696	9,272	9,250	−3.3	−0.1
San Diego Public Library					
(California)	3,059	4,377	4,203	3.0	−2.0
Metropolitan Systems					
Buffalo and Erie County					
Public Library (New York)	6,594	6,199	4,647	−0.5	−14.4
Public Library of Cincinnati					
and Hamilton County (Ohio)	5,636	5,752	5,437	0.2	−2.8
Multnomah County Libraries					
(Oregon)	3,485	2,793	2,808	−1.8	0.2
Public Library of Birmingham					
and Jefferson County					
(Alabama)	3,225	2,142	2,034	−3.4	−2.6
Suburban Systems					
Contra Costa County Library					
(California)	2,285	2,860	3,012	1.9	2.7
Montgomery County Depart-					
ment of Public Libraries					
(Maryland)	3,293	5,422	5,347	4.2	−0.7
San Diego County Libraries					
(California)	1,603	2,388	2,927	3.3	10.2

Source: American Library Directory (New York: R. R. Bowker, biennial).
Note: The 1964, 1976-77, and 1977-78 volumes used here report figures for 1963, 1975, and 1977, respectively.

The main growth in the number of college libraries has been among junior colleges, where the number of libraries increased 58 percent. School libraries are not included in these figures. The number of special libraries has grown faster than any other group: from 1964 to 1976-77 it grew by 66 percent. However, from 1977 to 1978, the number declined by 19 percent. I have no explanation for this decline.

In recent years libraries have increased the services provided. Recordings, works of art, films, and games are often held and circulated by libraries. Public libraries sponsor cultural events (e.g., lectures, concerts, and puppet theatre). Libraries have also tried to provide services to nonreaders. (Many consider libraries as a possible tool for socially uplifting the poor. For example, adult literacy classes are held in some libraries.) Libraries sometimes provide other formal adult continuing education opportunities (e.g., courses in a foreign language or in how to grow plants). Librarians disagree about which nonreading services are appropriate for public libraries.

Table 1.2. *Number of Libraries*

American Library Directory Year	Number of Public Library Systems	Number of Public Library Branches	Number of University and Four Year College Library Systems	Number of Junior College Library Systems	Number of Special Libraries
1978	8,455	5,963	1,708	1,142	5,287
1976-77	8,504	5,477	1,696	1,129	6,563
1974-75	7,652	5,538	1,605	1,081	4,449
1972-73	7,109	4,881	1,667	1,056	4,200
1970-71	7,190	4,855	1,896	1,072	4,277
1968	6,922	3,833	1,870	1,024	4,030
1966	6,783	3,676	1,810	858	4,011
1964	6,141	3,376	1,442	721	3,948

Source: American Library Directory (New York: R. R. Bowker, biennial).
Note: To be included a library must have a book acquisition budget of more than $500 per year and meet certain other standards. Information from earlier years does not seem to use the same definitions. National Center for Educational Statistics, *Library Statistics of Colleges and Universities Fall 1975: Institutional Data* (Washington, D.C.: National Center for Educational Statistics, 1977) reports a total of 2,980 libraries in universities, colleges, and junior colleges. Preliminary data from a 1974 survey of public libraries by the National Center for Educational Statistics indicate a universe of 8,307 public libraries at that time.

Special, nontraditional services are of substantial importance in many public library and may increase in importance. Films and recordings are of growing importance. Public libraries may provide talking books for the blind and large print materials for people with limited sight. The Nashville Public Library has organized a teletype network with weather and news information for the deaf. Many public libraries provide information about careers, training programs, and jobs. Some public libraries take special pains to make information about government programs available to patrons in need of assistance. Some public libraries have special materials and personnel for Spanish language persons. Outreach programs seek out nontraditional users of the library. About 25 percent of the budget of the branches of the New York Public Library are devoted to such special services. Nontraditional services are a large, varied, and growing part of many public library systems.

The Archive Function

The public library may also perform an archive function and operate as a research tool. Most public libraries maintain collections of materials relating to the history of their state and local area. The public library may be a repository for local government documents. Libraries maintain back issues of local and national newspapers. Public libraries may also maintain archives of materials relating to an industry, an ethnic group, or other subjects. These materials are useful for writers and scholars for a variety of purposes.

Many public libraries are depositories for federal government documents. Official depositories receive such documents as they choose free of charge, but receive no endowment for cataloging and maintaining the collections. Thus, accessibility to government documents depends in part on the budget and talents of the public library.

Some public libraries attempt to maintain collections of materials for research purposes. For readers seeking information in more depth than that offered by encyclopedias or popular works, the usual library collections will most likely be inadequate. Since the demand for scholarly works is likely to be small, and since the frontier of knowledge continually advances, the development of a research collection on a broad range of topics is expensive. Maintaining research capabilities is the primary mission of major university libraries and of a small group of private libraries. Only a few public libraries participate in this activity. The research libraries of the New York Public Library are privately financed and operated; they are not part of the city government. The Boston Public Library, a department of the city government, maintains a substantial noncirculating collection of research materials.

In recent years, new knowledge from scholarly research is primarily reported in periodicals. Thus, the commitment to a research function requires a library to maintain expensive subscriptions to a large number of scholarly journals and other serial publications. The Boston Public Library demonstrates a substantial commitment to supporting research by maintaining 11,000 subscriptions to serials. The Sacramento City-County Library serves a larger population with subscriptions to only 1,160 serial publications and so demonstrates a much smaller research capacity.

Libraries in the United States and Canada that maintain collections of sufficient depth and breadth to sustain researchers on a wide variety of topics are included among the 105 members of the Association of Research Libraries.[3] Of these, 94 are university libraries, 6 are maintained by national governments, 3 are private research libraries, and only 2 operate a branch library system in addition to maintaining a substantial commitment to meeting research needs. Of these two, the research function of the New York Public Library is privately operated. Only the City of Boston operates branch libraries and a major research facility. Most public libraries do not have the collections of materials in depth, nor do they subscribe to a sufficient number of periodicals to support scholarly work on a broad scale. The central library of many systems, however, has subject specialists and serial subscriptions like those of better college libraries. The appropriate role of public libraries in providing extensive archives for research relative to the similar activities of academic and some special libraries is open to debate. The focus of this work is on the popular services of the public library.

The Public Library versus Other Libraries

The services performed by the public library have changed since their emergence in modern form at the turn of the century. The public library once was a major source of reading material for a variety of readers. Now, the public library often seems to perform a backstop function: when the library service of the schools is inadequate, readers seek help at the public library. While businesses and government agencies have increasingly developed their own special libraries, businesses use the resources of the public library (e.g., materials too expensive or little used for special libraries to maintain). While the main source of recreational reading is now mass market paperback books, many readers borrow such books from the public library. As a research institution, the public library may hold extensive collections, more varied in a few areas than a university library, newspaper morgue, or special library. For many reading needs, the public library may serve as the source of last resort in a local area. From a national perspective, few public libraries aspire to collect materials in depth as archives for future researchers.

The demands placed on the public library, then, may differ from community to community. These demands are based not only on the reading habits of the residents, but also on the quality of school, university, and special libraries. Sharing responsibilities among the different institutions has both good and bad features.

On the positive side, competing institutions may complement each other. When one institution atrophies, the vigor of another may compensate. Moreover, different institutions, with different philosophies, may serve disparate clients better than a monolith. When the public library is organized as a separate department or agency, it often assumes an advocacy role for books and reading for their own sake. Librarians may try to develop collections of materials from a holistic perspective, making an effort to encompass most of the fields of written expression and knowledge of the times. Such a perspective may create serendipitous uses that are unlikely when reading materials are collected for specific purposes.

On the negative side, competing institutions may duplicate expensive fixed costs (for example, the costs of subscriptions to journals and indexing services). As competitors for funds, the different institutions may find that success for one may be at the cost of others. The growth of school libraries may cause diminished support for the public library. When the public library is operated by the school department of a city, as in Kansas City, the coordination of school and public library services is likely to be facilitated. However, both the independent orientation of the library, in developing a holistic perspective to collection development, and the supply of services to nonschool users are likely to be poorer with this arrangement. The attitude of librarians is illustrated by the success of the Vigo County Public Library in

Terre Haute, Indiana, in achieving independence from the school system in the early 1970s.

The Spatial Character of Service

Public library services may also have a geographic dimension. While in one sense the entire nation is served by the 18 million volumes of the Library of Congress, the ordinary reading needs of even the people in Washington, D.C., are better met by the 2 million volumes of the Public Library of the District of Columbia, which is dispersed over twenty-three branches. For children, for readers of popular fiction, and for other general readers, proximity is more important than the number of volumes held over some minimum amount. Berelson reports several studies that indicate that two-thirds to three-quarters of library users live within one mile of the library.[4] Therefore, the greater the density of residents, the greater will be the library use, other things equal.

The lower cost of putting library service within a mile of residents might be termed an economy of density. When 50,000 people live on each square mile, the cost of putting a branch within one mile of all residents is much lower than when only 1,000 people live on each square mile because one-fiftieth as many branches are needed per 50,000 people. Of course, actual transportation patterns and the fact that branches may become crowded modify this simple arithmetic somewhat, but the general principle of economies of density seems of substantial importance in comparing urban and rural library services. While there has been sustained effort to bring library service to rural areas, public library services are likely to remain better in urban areas. County library systems were created at the turn of the century in an effort to supply library services to rural areas. Bookmobile service began before 1920 and continues to bring books to places without branches. The Library Service Act originally was designed to bring library services to communities with populations under 10,000.

The quality of service provided by bookmobiles, however, does not match that of branch libraries. Among over fifty of the largest public library systems in the country, only the St. Louis County Library system operates more than seven bookmobiles—St. Louis County operates twenty-three. While bookmobiles offer the prospect of bringing books to every street corner on a fixed schedule, in fact, the greater visibility of the fixed location of the branch, the somewhat larger collection at even a small branch, and the opportunity to scan a periodical, or sit and sample a book, apparently make the branch substantially more attractive than bookmobiles for most systems.

Some libraries maintain subbranches or stations. A jail, a hospital, a nursing home, and even schools in some systems, may have small collections of books, and regular pickup and delivery of books from the public library system. While the extent of such stations is hard to judge, libraries seem to be moving to more formal branches. The station lacks the supervision of materials that a bookmobile provides, but shares the small selection problem of the bookmobile.

Branches that hold at least 10,000 volumes usually are the front line of the public library service. Bookmobiles and stations are merely skirmishers.

The heavy artillery of specialized reference collections and collections of greater depth and breadth are typically housed in the central library. In recent years, some library systems have developed the concept of superbranches as library centers. A few branch libraries in the system maintain substantially larger reference collections, receive more serial publications, and house collections of more breadth and depth then regular branches. The New York Public Library maintains a library center in each of the three boroughs it serves. The Atlanta Public Library has a center in the northern part of the county, and is considering one in the southwestern part of the county.

An important issue for the operation of the libraries may be whether smaller branches should be consolidated. Perhaps the public would be better served by fewer, somewhat larger, branches than by more smaller ones. Greater affluence over the last century has increased the public's mobility. With increased numbers of automobiles, parking has become a greater concern than being within walking distance. Moreover, the typical user of the public library may now be better educated and more sophisticated, and may want to use the public library for more specialized reading than mass market paperback books provide. The larger branch may be becoming more valuable. (The relationship between branch size and library use is the subject of chapter 4.)

The character of library service may also be influenced by the relationship between the local library and the central library. The local library service may be performed by a local government or by the branch library of a larger governmental unit. In New England, each town typically maintains its own library. Library revenues come mainly from the local property tax, and library use may be limited to residents of the town. Interinstitutional cooperation among libraries is required in the lending of materials and in the development of an acquisitions policy.

In several cities—San Diego, Cleveland, St. Louis, and Baltimore—there are two major library systems, one in the central city and a second in the suburbs. The suburban system may be larger than the central city system in number of volumes held and in circulation rate. Over the last decade, both total and per capita circulation has declined in most central city libraries. Alternatively, in many suburbs total and per capita circulation has increased. The shift of library use from city to suburb is an important phenomenon in the library industry.

In some areas, however, the library service may be a countywide operation with all local service supplied by branches of the metropolitan system. Buffalo, Cincinnati, and Sacramento are examples of such metropolitan services. In these cases, the finance of the service is countywide; interlibrary loans and the financial support for the diversified holdings of the central library come from the whole area. Circulation in many metropolitan systems has remained steady over the last decade.

One possibility for achieving some of the advantages of a metropolitan system among separate local libraries is the establishment of formal networks. Routine pickup and delivery can so improve interlibrary loans of materials that the resources of the large central city library can be brought, in part, to local libraries, just as if these libraries were branches of the central system. Several states support such networks, notably Massachusetts, Illinois, and California. Such networks may be of value to metropolitan libraries: even large libraries cannot maintain access to all the printed material produced annually. Even the Boston Public Library's 11,000 serial publications represent less than half the number of periodicals produced worldwide.

A network system does not provide financial support of the development of the specialized collections of the central library. Networking does not provide the same character of access to materials as does having the materials in the library's or branch's own collection. While networks have been created as institutions, it is not clear to what extent rapid interlibrary loans and coordinated acquisitions policies have developed. Whether a library participates in a network or not is probably of little significance to most users. Improvements in coordination may develop, however, so that network participation may be important in the future.

Sources of Finance

The sources of finance also shape library services. While Carnegie's philanthropy was significant in launching the industry, Carnegie's funds were for construction, not for endowment. The New York Public Library, a private research library, operates the branch library system in Manhattan, the Bronx, and Staten Island under contract from the City of New York. The New York Public Library depends on endowment income and private contributions to operate its central research facilities. Some other public libraries depend on financial contributions and donations of collections. For the most part, however, the activities of public libraries are financed by local taxes.

In many states (e.g., New Jersey and Texas) property tax revenues are earmarked for library activities. Sometimes libraries are operated as special districts, but most often libraries are agencies of local governments and compete for funds with other agencies such as public works and the police department. As a consequence, the fiscal health of libraries is a reflection of the fiscal health of local governments. The fiscal crisis that local governments encountered in the 1970s has caused cutbacks in library operations. Primarily the hours of operation of branches have been reduced, as has acquisition of new materials.

Some state governments provide aid for the operation of libraries. Maryland, New York, Pennsylvania, and Illinois provide the most support. Pennsylvania and Maryland provide capitation grants to local public libraries; both states support a small number of regional library centers. Some states support local library services by providing services in kind through the state library, as in Georgia. Only Hawaii operates the whole library service as a branch of state government. Several states (e.g., Indiana) provide little or no support for libraries. The federal program of grants to libraries has required state or local matching support, a feature that has induced some states to grant aid to local libraries.

The public library industry, then, operates primarily through agencies of local government. The central function of the public library is providing access to reading material for local residents. Popular fiction, juvenile books, and general reference works are the standard fare offered in main libraries and branches. The quality of library services depends on the librarians' skill in selecting materials and in organizing the libraries' resources. Only a few public libraries maintain the breadth and depth of collections required for research, including a large number of periodical subscriptions, as well as specialized book collections.

THE BOOK TRADE

Since the main function of libraries is providing books, it is instructive to examine developments in the book trade for clues to the function of libraries. Books have grown in importance over the last decade. The number of new titles produced has increased much more rapidly than the population. In 1964, 20,542 new book titles were published. In 1977, 33,292 new titles appeared.[5] There has been a less marked increase in the number of new editions. The increase in new titles has held for most categories of books. Fiction titles grew by 36.1 percent from 1,703 to 2,317. Social science and economics titles grew by 129.1 percent from 2,445 to 5,602. The juvenile category changed from 2,533 to 2,626 over the period, with a dip to 2,098 in 1975. This dip was probably caused by both declining birth rates and changing federal support for libraries. Overall, books seem to have increased in importance as vehicles for the dissemination of knowledge and culture.

Income from book sales has also increased, but the increase is largely a consequence of increases in prices. Table 1.3 reports total book sales and the average prices of books in selected categories. Book prices seem to have increased faster than total dollar sales of books; therefore, the total number of books sold has probably decreased. Given the large increase in the number of book titles produced and the decrease in unit sales the average number of

Table 1.3.   Trends in Book Sales and Prices

	Sales (in millions of dollars)			Average Annual Percent Change	
	1964	1975	1977	1964–75	1975–77
Book Sales					
Total all books	1,808.7	3,850.7	4,605.5	6.9	8.9
Adult hardcover trade books	117.0	313.4	370.1	9.0	8.3
Adult paperback trade books	20.0	111.2	132.8	15.6	8.9
Juvenile books	112.0	124.6	128.9	0.9	1.7
Book clubs	139.0	303.4	374.3	7.1	10.5
Mass market paperback books	99.0	339.6	515.9	14.9	20.9
Book Prices (average)					
All hardcover	$6.93	$16.19	$19.22	7.7	8.6
Hardcover fiction	4.14	8.31	10.09	6.3	9.7
Hardcover juvenile	3.06	5.82	6.65	5.8	6.7
Hardcover history	7.73	15.85	17.12	9.5	3.8
Mass market paperback	0.59	1.46	1.72	8.3	8.2
Trade paperback	2.41	5.24	5.93	7.0	6.2

Source: The Bowker Annual of Library and Book Trade Information (New York: R. R. Bowker, annual). Volumes for 1979, 1976, and 1966 are used here.

books sold per title has decreased substantially. The smaller number of units sold per title, along with the large increase in titles, probably reflects improved productivity and technological change in the printing and publishing industry that allows a publisher to break even on smaller press runs than in the past. Books, then, can be tailored for more specialized audiences.

The decline in the number of books sold is not uniform across all categories of books. The number of mass market paperback books sold has more than tripled from 1964 to 1977. Unit sales of adult paperback trade books have also tripled. Book clubs may have registered a slight increase in the number of units sold. A new category, books by mail, has grown rapidly and may soon surpass book club sales. The number of juvenile books sold has been cut almost in half. (Sales of juvenile books have fluctuated. In 1967 they were at their high at $165 million; in 1973 they were at their low at $108.6 million.) Most books bought have been paperbacks, even adult trade books. Adult hardcover books and book clubs have registered modest gains.

The vigor of the book trade is also reflected in the number of outlets for books, described in table 1.4. The total number of bookstores of all types increased by 71 percent from 1964 to 1977. Recent growth in the number of bookshops has been fastest among general, religious, and department store bookstores. Special bookstores offer books on particular subjects—for example, the occult. While mass market paperback books are distributed like magazines through grocery stores, drug stores, and newsstands, the general

Table 1.4. Trends in the Number of Book Outlets

| | Number | | | Average Annual Percentage Change | |
	1964	1975	1977	1964–75	1975–77
Number of Book Clubs					
Total	129	195	185	3.7	-2.6
Children	25	23	17	-0.8	-15.1
Adult	104	172	168	4.6	-1.2
Total Book Outlets					
(including all types of bookstores and department stores)	9,506	11,717	16,217	1.9	16.3
Number in Selected Categories					
General bookstores	2,062	3,498	4,281	4.8	10.1
College bookstores	1,566	2,559	2,607	4.4	0.9
Religious bookstores	1,820	1,421	2,752	-2.3	33.0
Paperback bookstores (over 80 percent paperbacks)	484	598	800	2.0	14.6
Antiquarian bookstores	1,052	886	1,119	-1.6	11.7
Department stores with bookshops	882	451	1,089	-6.1	44.1
Rental bookstores	34	10	6	-11.3	-25.5
Special bookstores	304	866	1,024	95.2	8.4

Source: American Book Trade Directory (New York: R. R. Bowker, biennial).
Note: Volumes for 1979, 1975–76, and 1965–66 are used here. Book Club information is from *The Literary market Place* (New York: R. R. Bowker, annual).

bookstore has grown. Just as the smaller average readership of individual titles allows books to be tailored to smaller audiences, book buyers seem to be seeking out the broader selection of the general bookshop.

The number of adult book clubs has declined recently and unit sales by book clubs have grown little. Therefore, the number of books sold by the average book club has fallen. Book clubs are tailored to smaller, more specialized audiences. Overall, today publishers, bookstores, and book clubs offer more specialized products than in the past.

Libraries as Buyers of Books

While total public library expenditure on books increased at about the same rate as book prices from 1963 to 1971, public library book expenditures have remained constant since 1971, as indicated in table 1.5. Since book prices have increased, it is quite clear that the number of books purchased by the public library industry has been declining. While libraries usually get discount prices, the rate of discount has probably changed little. When the fact that the number of public libraries has grown is taken into account, one can realize that the average number of books purchased by each library has, on average, fallen dramatically.

Given the increase in the number of new titles published annually, libraries are buying a much smaller fraction of new books. At a time when reader interests may be more specialized and as publishers have been able to produce more specialized books, public libraries have put an even smaller fraction of new titles in their collections.

College and university libraries have fared somewhat better recently, although their expenditures have grown less than book prices. In part, they may

Table 1.5. *Library Expenditures for Book Acquisition (in millions of dollars)*

	Expenditure			Average Annual Percent Change	
	1963	1971	1977	1963–71	1971–77
All libraries	189.2	389.9	—	9.0	—
Public libraries	54.9	128.5	132.3	10.6	0.5
College and university libraries	51.8	82.4	126.3	5.8	7.1
School libraries	69.5	140.6	—	8.8	—
Special libraries	13.0	38.4	—	13.5	—

Source: The Bowker Annual of Library and Book Trade Information (New York: R. R. Bowker, 1970), p. 22, reports estimates of expenditures for 1963. The Bowker annual for 1979 reports 1977 expenditures on books.

Note: Figures for 1964 and 1975 are not available. Preliminary estimates from National Center for Educational Statistics Surveys suggest that 1974 school library expenditures on books were $165 million and 1974 public library expenditures on books were $138 million.

have shifted toward more periodicals. School library acquisitions are of about the same magnitude as those of public libraries and have grown at about the same rate until 1971. (The growth of acquisition expenditures by the special libraries tracked the increase in the number of special libraries up to 1970. More recent information is unavailable.)

Today the public library may not be serving its diverse audiences as well as it did in the past. When books were written for wider audiences, the collection of the typical branch library could serve disparate interests equally well. With more specialized books being the norm, the use of the general purpose branch public library may be declining for reasons similar to those that led to the demise of *Life* and *Look*. The increase in special purpose publications, each tailored for particular audiences, undercut those publications that tried to be all things to all people.

LIBRARY USERS

Library users are primarily book users.[6] Therefore, the public library industry should be considered in the broader context of book reading. Book readers and library users have been primarily an elite group in terms of age, education, and income. While the public library was founded on an egalitarian philosophy, a philosophy that still influences library policy, in fact the public library is not primarily an institution of the poor or even of the blue collar class.

In a national survey of adults, 55 percent reported having read one or more books in the preceding three months; 44 percent reported reading as many as one book per month. Thus, about half the adult population makes regular use of books. Book reading is more common among younger adults: 70 percent of those aged twenty-one to thirty-four have read a book in a three-month period, 57 percent of those aged thirty-five to forty-nine have done so, while only 43 percent of those aged fifty or more have done so.

The most important explanation of adult reading behavior seems to be education. Of college graduates, 79 percent had read a book in a three-month period; 59 percent of high school graduates and only 24 percent of those adults with less than a high school education had done so. Since the adults among the library's clients are primarily those who read books regularly, the population of potential library users is younger and better educated than the public at large.

An even smaller fraction of adults use public libraries. Only 30 percent of adults report having used the public library during a three-month period. Only 26 percent of the males, only 21 percent of those aged fifty years or more, and only 10 percent of those with less than a high school education report having used a library during a three-month period. Of persons with incomes less than $7,000 in 1969, 79 percent report no use of the public library. Adult users of the public library disproportionately have high incomes, are well educated, and are young.

Juveniles are the largest single client group of public libraries. Berelson reported in 1949 that 25 to 50 percent of the users of the public library were students. According to Bundy, persons aged twelve to twenty-one constituted 47 percent of users in Baltimore and Washington in 1966. More recently, juveniles accounted for 68 percent of users in a two-day survey in Youngstown and Mahoney County, Ohio. Even among adult users, 35 percent reported that they used the public library in order to assist children with homework assignments.[7] Student use of the public library is the dominant activity in most libraries. Students are not only the largest group going to the public library and borrowing books, but they are also heavy users of the reference service, which may be useful in completing school assignments. Thus, while most public libraries are usually financially independent of the schools, in fact their clientele may be shaped by the schools and the character of school libraries.

Of course, an occasional uneducated immigrant or school dropout may become self-educated by being an aggressive user of the public library. In fact, however, such users are not the norm. The public library primarily serves students and adult book readers, a group that is predominantly middle class. Just as the role that formal public education plays in reducing income inequality is open to serious challenge—to the extent that formal education attaches labels, it may increase inequality—the basis for arguing that public libraries have been important in the reduction of inequality is open to debate.[8] Supplying public library services in larger quantities is unlikely to reduce income inequality.

THE LIBRARY PRODUCTION PROCESS

The income of a library system gives a rough measure of its total activity. Changes in income of selected systems are compared in table 1.6. On average, expenditures on public libraries are less than 1 percent of all local government expenditures.[9] While income in all ten systems grew from 1964 to 1976, the rates of growth show substantial variation. Multnomah County, Oregon, grew at an annual rate of less than 3 percent, while San Diego County and Montgomery County grew at an annual rate of more than 13 percent. The great instability of public library income is even more evident in the changes that occurred from 1976 to 1978. The Boston Public Library suffered an absolute decline in income; while Multnomah County library shows a major increase. Multnomah County had low expenditure levels in the past. Many of the libraries had slow rates of growth in income at a time of substantial inflation, so the purchasing power of many library incomes fell. This financial pressure on libraries can cause sharp changes in library operations. The vari-

Table 1.6. Income of Selected Public Libraries for Selected Years
(in thousands of dollars)

	Income: Selected Years			Average Annual Percentage Change	
	1963	1975	1977	1963-75	1975-77
Central City Systems					
Boston Public Library	3,639	9,457	9,175	8.0	-1.5
New York Public Library Branches	9,119	23,864	28,000	8.0	8.0
San Diego Public Library (California)	1,653	4,637	4,851	8.6	2.3
Metropolitan Systems					
Buffalo and Erie County Public Library (New York)	3,725	9,187	10,007	7.5	4.3
Public Library of Cincinnati and Hamilton County (Ohio)	3,271	8,152	8,920	7.6	4.5
Multnomah County (Oregon)	1,801	2,546	4,159	2.9	24.5
Birmingham and Jefferson County (Alabama)	675	2,235	2,632	10.0	8.2
Suburban Systems					
Contra Costa County (California)	1,284	4,228	4,561	9.9	3.8
Montgomery County (Maryland)	990	5,167	5,365	13.8	1.9
San Diego County (California)	566	2,851	3,976	13.5	16.6

Source: American Library Directory (New York: R. R. Bowker, biennial).
Note: The 1964, 1976-77, and 1977-78 volumes used here report figures for 1963, 1975, and 1977, respectively.

ability of the finance of public libraries is in contrast with the budgetary stability hypothesized by Wildavsky for local government.[10] Incrementalism may not be the order of the day for public libraries.

The main costs of operating a library are wages, acquisitions, and building expense. The pattern of library expenditures on inputs is examined in table 1.7. Salary and book acquisition expenditures are reported as a percentage of library income. Most libraries do not include capital funds in their budgets, so income and operating expenditures are about the same. The libraries, however, may differ in their budgeting practices such that the figures reported may not be absolutely comparable.

The inflation and recent financial pressures do not seem to have twisted library expenditure patterns. Salaries seem to account for about 65 percent of library income for all three types of library systems. This was also the case in the 1960s. The sharp drop in San Diego County seems to reflect a growth in income and expenditures on nonsalary items. Book acquisition expenditures

Table 1.7.   Expenditure Patterns in Selected Libraries
(wages and acquisition as percentage of library income)

	1963	1975	1977
Central City Systems			
Boston Public Library			
Salaries	79.5	66.8	67.5
Book acquisition	9.8	8.9	11.1
New York Public Library (branches)			
Salaries	65.2	66.6	67.6
Book acquisition	14.7	13.4	11.7
San Diego Public Library (California)			
Salaries	66.5	70.9	67.7
Book acquisition	11.2	13.4	12.8
Metropolitan Systems			
Buffalo and Erie County Public Library (New York)			
Salaries	59.0	62.5	71.2
Book acquisition	11.0	8.5	9.3
Public Libraries of Cincinnati and Hamilton County (Ohio)			
Salaries	65.3	49.6	60.3
Book acquisition	14.3(a)	8.4	10.9
Multnomah County Library (Oregon)			
Salaries	65.7	64.3	63.1
Book acquisition	9.4	10.1	9.8
Birmingham and Jefferson County (Alabama)			
Salaries	58.4	51.6	52.8
Book acquisition	17.5	17.7	5.8
Suburban Systems			
Contra Costa County Library (California)			
Salaries	65.9	65.5	65.2
Book acquisition	17.1(b)	11.1	10.7
Montgomery County Department of Public Libraries (Maryland)			
Salaries	72.4	80.4	78.4
Book acquisition	20.9(a)	12.2	11.1
San Diego County Libraries (California)			
Salaries	56.9	54.7	48.0
Book acquisition	13.3	13.4	15.9

Source: American Library Directory (new York: R. R. Bowker, Biennial); volumes for 1964, 1976–77, and 1978 are used here.

Note: The full cost of capital used in library buildings is not ordinarily reflected in reported income or expenditure information. (a) includes periodicals; (b) includes periodicals and binding.

continued to account for 8 to 14 percent of income. Expenditures on serials (not reported in the table) have increased to 2.5 percent of the income at the Boston Public Library; libraries that seek to provide research facilities have shifted toward acquiring serials. Serials typically account for less than 1 percent of public library expenditures. Other library expenses, those associated with building operation and with equipment and other materials, have also been fairly stable as a proportion of library expenditure. Thus, while the price of labor, books, serials, and buildings have all increased, libraries have maintained about the same mix of inputs. With rising prices, of course, increased dollar expenditures are actually buying less.

While labor costs account for the largest proportion of library expenditures, the public library seems to be less labor intensive than average for the whole economy, and very much less labor intensive than is typical of local governments. The police, fire, and sanitation departments, and the schools are all much more labor intensive than the public library. Thus, the public library should be more resistant to the rising cost of labor without the concomitant increased productivity that may characterize other aspects of the public sector.

Innovation

Until 1970, innovation in library operations was slow. Microform materials were introduced; many libraries developed collections of music, film, and recordings that were small extensions of library services, using traditional techniques to handle new types of materials. None of these innovations changed the self-sufficiency of each library in acquiring, cataloging, and accessioning its own materials.

The innovations of the 1970s and those being discussed for the 1980s may be more fundamental. Many of the activities traditionally undertaken within each library may come to be purchased externally. Computers and telecommunications provide the basis for many of these changes. (Innovation is considered more fully in chapter 5.) This discussion is devoted to several major innovations, setting the stage for other analysis.

A national system of bibliographic control is being developed at the Library of Congress. The objective is to catalog each book placed in any library collection, identified in the same way, with the author's name, subjects, and number regardless of book location. By placing such information in machine-(that is, computer-) readable formats, the process of identifying consistent names, subjects, and numbers need only be performed once. Once the Library of Congress has done the job, all other libraries need only to search the Library of Congress file for the information they require. It is, of course, critical that the cataloging be done quickly, and that access to the Library of Congress information be rapid so that books can enter library collections quickly. A book is most valuable when it is new. Many libraries have shifted to the Library of Congress numbering system so that they can take advantage of the cataloging efforts of the Library of Congress. For many books the publisher prints the Library of Congress information in the volume.

The national bibliographic control system will also facilitate borrowing materials from remote locations. The catalog entry in any library will be the same, so book requests can be made by catalog number, a more certain label than author and title.

The Library of Congress is extending bibliographic control to all materials, including periodicals and government documents. By cooperating with similar efforts in other countries, the Library of Congress will extend the system worldwide. In the future, the Library of Congress may catalog all published material, regardless of language and format. Congressional support for this goal is weak, however.

Using computer data files to store catalog information means that the catalog can be created by machine. The Library of Congress will not enter any new materials in its card file after 1980. The new Atlanta Public Library will not contain a card file, rather its whole catalog will be created by machine. Many libraries use computer terminals and computer-based cataloging networks.

Machine-made catalogs have a number of advantages. First, new entries can be integrated into the file automatically, which creates a potential saving of labor. Second, the whole catalog can be reproduced in microform, which is inexpensive. Thus, copies of the central catalog can be shared among libraries, enhancing access to materials from remote locations. Third, author and subject headings can be updated as common usage changes; for example, all the entries under Spanish America can be moved to the Latin America entry when that name becomes more common. Fourth, the catalog might be searched by machine to create listings of materials on particular subjects. Subject entries in the catalog could include keywords that might allow more subtle searching than conventional card catalog files. The ease of such a machine-made search may reduce reference costs and enhance the quality of services libraries provide.

The development of machine-readable cataloging at the Library of Congress was made possible by grants. The funds were from the Council on Library Resources, Inc., a private agency that has been financed by Ford Foundation grants since 1956.[11] Thus, a major innovation in libraries is taking place in a government institution with private finance.

Another innovation being discussed is a National Periodicals System. This proposal is being developed by the National Commission on Libraries and Information Science, a permanent federal commission created in 1971.[12] Over half of the interlibrary loan requests are for materials in periodicals; the demands are greatest on large research facilities. Periodicals have become important in interlibrary loan requests because the prices of library subscriptions have increased very rapidly—by 200 percent from 1962 to 1974.[13] In addition, not only has the number of periodicals increased, but periodicals have become more important vehicles for the dissemination of information. Libraries have, therefore, reduced the number of periodicals they subscribe to themselves, at least in relative terms, and have relied on interlibrary loan requests for gaining access to materials they themselves cannot afford to maintain.

The National Periodicals System proposal is a plan to formalize this arrangement by creating a national center to acquire all the periodicals, perhaps

40,000 to 75,000 titles. The center would index and abstract the periodicals
and send photocopies to libraries that require particular articles. Individual
libraries might, then, need only subscribe to about a thousand more commonly used periodicals. A small group of regional centers might subscribe to
10,000 or 15,000 titles as an intermediary to the national periodical center;
such details have not been resolved. In fact, every library could make its own
decision on each periodical. The agency filling photocopy requests would
charge for copying and transmitting the document, as well as collect royalties
for the publisher of the periodical. Telefacsimile transmission is expensive;
therefore documents may be transmitted by mail. Expected improvements in
telecommunication could substantially reduce telefacsimile transmission
costs.

A third category of innovation involves computer-based information retrieval systems used for reference materials. Lockheed, Systems Development
Corporation, and others, sell on-line searches of bibliographic reference files,
often with over a million entries. Keywords specified by the user define the
sort of materials the user wants. Changes in keywords may be made as the
search progresses, to narrow the field of entries included in the custom prepared bibliography. Searches can be made from remote locations by using a
computer terminal and the telephone.

The use of on-line information retrieval is apparently growing, but is not a
completely satisfactory system. The bibliography produced by the systems
includes no indication of quality or level of material. The judgments of editors
in accepting articles for publication, and the judgments of librarians in acquiring material for their libraries, are excluded from the machine search. The
periodical repository system may suffer the same flaw. If any printed material
produced recursively can be included in the system, the reader of indexes and
abstracts will miss the winnowing function of the editors. If materials are to be
included selectively, first amendment rights may be infringed. The exclusion
of material for ideological reasons would be a powerful form of censorship
because the national periodical system would have important monopoly power
in the distribution of low circulation material.

Many of the innovations described here aim at creating a national library
network. In principle, the user of any library in the country might be able to
create a custom bibliography of all materials relevant to a particular subject by
using a computer terminal to search the indexes of the National Periodical
Center and the Library of Congress files on books. Copies of all desired
materials might then be acquired by teletransmission from whatever sources
are convenient. Thus, a personal library with a complete set of materials on a
particlar subject might be assembled on demand. Magnetic bubble storage of
information and fiber optic communications may make this fanciful network
feasible.

The implications of such a highly developed network are extreme. Benjamin Franklin's original motive in creating the public library was to share the

large fixed costs of maintaining a set of books with other book users in the vicinity. The existence of large economies of scale in maintaining a set of books for common use is still the rationale for the existence of public libraries in each locale. These fundamental cost characteristics will change if the elaborate network just described comes into existence. If every computer terminal is in effect a branch library, then the fixed costs of the branch are minimal, and branches might become as widespread as television sets. On the other hand, the supply of information into the network would entail substantial fixed costs, such that only a few national centers might supply them. The supply of information into the network might be supervised by major research libraries, the Library of Congress, or a small number of new institutions of national scope. The city library and its branches may not be necessary as access points to the network. The public library may go the way of vaudeville. The function of the library as an archive, as keeper of the historical record for the future, may not be entirely replaced, however. The public library may also continue to serve specialized users—for example, handicapped persons.

The highly developed network also raises serious questions of governance and finance. The fixed costs of putting information into the system should probably be financed through general tax revenues at the national level. Users of the system should incur the marginal costs of search and telecommunication. Alternatively, fixed costs might be financed by price discrimination. Either way, information would be sought to the point where its benefit just matches marginal access cost.

Such a centralized system raises the possibility of censorship. First Amendment rights are easier to exercise if there are many channels for the dissemination of information. There may no longer be a market test for the importance of materials of different types. Similarly, the market for books and journals may have played some function in producing new knowledge and culture. The new copyright law aims to enhance incentives for the creation of new materials, but the full-blown network might well centralize the purchase decision in a way that undercuts incentives for producing knowledge. These issues were addressed by the Commission on New Technological Uses of Copyrighted Works.

Of course, the fanciful network described here is developing slowly. Its form will be shaped by the actual technology that becomes available, and by the course of federal policy.

A PHILOSOPHICAL BASIS FOR FEDERAL POLICY

The philosophical basis for federal policy toward libraries has two edges. On the one hand, knowledge and culture are pure public goods, such that one individual's consumption need not subtract from the fund available for consumption by others, and indeed may even add to others' consumption.

Knowledge includes the stock of scientific facts, and culture includes the fund of language and shared experiences that gives substance to our social nature. Such goods will not be adequately provided if left to unregulated, decentralized markets. Libraries have played some role in creating and disseminating knowledge and culture, so there is a sound philosophical basis for government support of their activities.

On the other hand, a variety of institutions is significant in the creation and distribution of knowledge and culture. Indeed, even library services are supplied by universities, schools, and special—private—libraries. Thus, our social commitment to the creation and dissemination of knowledge and culture need not be wedded to a specific set of institutions. Technologies for the production and distribution of knowledge and culture may change, as may our collective tastes. Creative policy formulation is necessary to encourage improvements in the institutional arrangements for creating knowledge and culture.

The United States must rank as one of the most creative societies in history. Our society has been extraordinarily successful at generating new scientific insights, as well as new cultural phenomena. Moreover, the insights have been brought to bear in improving the quality of life for large numbers of people, often with little delay. In a wide number of areas, particularly chemistry, physics, medicine, and agriculture, our society is very creative.

Not all aspects of our society, however, have been shaped by creative efforts to the same degree. Even among production activities, some areas have witnessed more progress than others.[14] Housing, apparel manufacture, and railroads, for example, have had a slower rate of improvement than agriculture, medicine, chemical industry, and electronics. The uneven pattern of progress seems to be a consequence of the interests of federal programs aiding research and development and of the structure and regulation of industry. Thus, medicine, agriculture, defense, and space-related scientific advances have been rapid due to direct government support. In the chemical and electronics areas, the nature of competition and the significance of patent protection for inventions may be important. Of course government involvement with railroads and the postal service illustrates that mere government interest does not assure technological progressiveness. The point is that the rate of advance in science and culture is shaped by government action even though the advance is a stochastic process.

The lack of government support for activity in certain areas applies *a fortiori* in the development of culture. Public television has been slow to develop and its government support has been niggardly. Nor has creativity in the performing arts been sustained by substantial government action.

Thus, the philosophical idea that the production of knowledge and culture requires support may be easily recognized. However, support is not automatic. There is a tension between the mass tastes and conformity of democratic institutions and the nonconformity and uniqueness of even the successful elites necessary for the production of knowledge and culture. Support of basic science and of enduring cultural institutions requires that the public place trust in such elites. That such elites have made valuable contributions in the past has not been sufficient to guarantee continued support. And as elites become institutionalized they can become sclerotic, so automatic trust is not warranted. The effectiveness of institutions for generating knowledge and culture must therefore be continually proven.

Federal policy toward the production of science and culture needs to encourage effective activity and avoid wheel-spinning. Since the character of institutions can change over time, the pattern of federal support will shift. Yet the recognition that the institutions may change should not becloud the value of sustained government support of the production of knowledge and culture. The design of federal policy that meets these conditions, conditions probably essential for political support, is obviously difficult.

Thus, a central feature of public support of libraries would seem to be a demonstration of the effectiveness of the libraries in generating and disseminating new knowledge and culture. Thus, not only are the quantity and quality of outputs of libraries significant, but also the public libraries must be more effective than other possible institutions that may achieve similar results.

SUMMARY

The public library industry, then, exists to take advantage of scale economies in maintaining a stock of reading and related materials. The main users are students, but significant numbers of adults use the library for recreational and general reading. Nationally, circulation is five books per year per person. Public libraries are located in every major city and are available in most rural areas; over 95 percent of the population is served by a public library in one way or another. While the public libraries have suffered from budget cuts due to the fiscal crisis of local government, the libraries are less labor intensive than most of the public sector, and so their cost structure has not been twisted by the decade of inflation. Moreover, innovations that may have substantial cost saving potential seem to be at hand.

The public libraries, however, face serious difficulties. Because they acquire a smaller and smaller fraction of all appropriate materials that become available, their collections must be meeting fewer and fewer specialized needs. Thus, special libraries have grown very rapidly, meeting the needs of particularized audiences. While the consolidation of branches may be unpopular with individual neighborhoods, perhaps the greater variety allowed by the larger collections of superbranches would allow public libraries to compete more effectively. While interlibrary sharing of materials may offer some hope of allowing individual libraries to meet specialized needs, in fact such a network may enhance the position of special libraries, since the cost of access should be low. Thus, the very technologies that may improve services and lower a library's costs may change the fundamental cost structure of library operations, in a way that erodes the position of the existing branches of public libraries. Just as television decentralized audiences to the home while centralizing production in New York and California, so network library technology may put reading materials in the home while centralizing production in a few highly developed places.

A strong case can be made for federal support of the production of knowledge and culture. Leadership in these activities may not meet market tests, and public action is desirable. Copyrights and patents may not be sufficient. However, federal support has been small and sporadic. Even the Library of Congress has not received the federal support necessary to make it an aggressive leader in the development of library institutions. A more aggressive, sophisticated federal role is very important for the new technologies to meet their potential.

The public services provided by thirty-one large public library systems across the country are compared in chapter 2. Differences in services are investigated relative to differences in the cost of labor, and the size and fiscal circumstances of the systems. Differences in services are also related to the use of the library. Variations in salaries, hours of work, and fringe benefits across the systems are compared in chapter 3. A detailed examination of the value of library services relative to their costs is presented in chapter 4, using the branch services of the New York Public Library as a case study. The technical services of the public libraries, that is, the operating methods, are examined in chapter 5. Twenty innovations in technical operations are identified, and the pace of the diffusion of the innovations over all public libraries is discussed. Alternative public policies toward public libraries are considered in chapter 6.

2

Comparing
Public Services

The services public library systems provide differ substantially. This chapter compares the operation of thirty-one large public library systems across the country.[1] One concern is to discover what forces shape the library systems. For example, how are library operations different when labor costs are higher? The comparison focuses on service characteristics that are explicitly under a particular library's control, such as hours, materials, and locations. A second concern is to discover how library operations influence outcomes. For example, how is the circulation of library materials influenced by the number of hours of service or the number of branch locations? The focus here is on the user's response to library services.

In this chapter the main components of library budgets—the number of locations, the size and age of collections, the number of hours of service, and levels of staffing—are examined. Chapter 3 examines the price of labor; chapter 4 examines the operation of the New York Public Library; chapter 5 delves more deeply into issues of technical services (acquisition and cataloging of materials) and technological change.

The initial discussion of the library systems examines the libraries according to geographic type—city, metropolitan, and suburban. City libraries serve a central city alone. Suburban library systems serve suburban areas alone. Metropolitan library systems serve a central city and a substantial suburban area.[2] One question this chapter tries to answer is whether this grouping appropriately differentiates the libraries. The groupings are for exposition only, however, and do not play an important role in subsequent analysis.

MEASURING LIBRARY OPERATIONS

Central features of a large public library system include the number of locations where services are provided, the size of collections, the rate at which new materials are added, the hours of service, and the character of the staff. These features are observed in an interview survey of thirty-one large public library systems in nineteen states. The cities are identified in appendix A. An introduction to the statistical methods used in this study is presented in appendix B.

Locations

Most large public library systems operate many facilities. The total number of locations per 100 square miles of area served gives a rough indication of the average distance users must travel in order to get to a library. The average number of locations per 100 square miles among the library systems surveyed is 17.39, as indicated in table 2.1. Metropolitan and suburban library systems are significantly different from city libraries. While the central city systems average about 32 locations per 100 square miles served, the metropolitan and suburban systems average 4 and 3, respectively, per 100 square miles. The Brooklyn Public Library has an average of 84.29 locations per 100 square miles while San Antonio and San Diego County average less than 1 per 100 square miles. The great diversity in the density of branches, of course, reflects the differences in the age and density of development of the different areas, as will be seen.

A circle with a radius of 1 mile subtends an area equal to the average area served by the library facility in the average city system. Because the cities include some systems, like Houston, Dallas, and San Antonio, with relatively low branch densities, the typical older central city system has branch densities higher than the reported average for cities. The suburban systems, on average, each serve 32.79 square miles. A circle of 3.23 miles subtends such an area. The suburban group includes San Diego County and the metropolitan group includes Jacksonville, with service areas that include large amounts of undeveloped land. Thus, the effective branch densities for library users is probably somewhat higher than the average reported here. It is clear, however, that the central city systems maintain ten times as many branches per unit of area as the suburban systems. The tenfold greater branch density only reduces the average traveling distance to branches by slightly more than three times because distance and area are related by the square root.

Library service locations are differentiated. Twenty-seven of the thirty-one libraries surveyed identify one facility as a main library. Four suburban library systems eschew a main library. The New York Public Library designates four facilities as library centers. Main libraries or library centers usually offer

Table 2.1. *Library Activities and Services: Means and Standard Deviations by Geographic Type*

Variable	City	Metropolitan	Suburban	All	$F_{(2,28)}$
Locations per 100 square miles	32.11 (26.78)	4.00 (2.48)	3.05 (1.32)	17.39 (23.28)	8.74***
Bookmobiles	2.07 (1.39)	3.67 (1.22)	5.43 (7.85)	3.29 (3.93)	1.91
Volumes acquired annually per capita	0.15 (0.06)	0.11 (0.05)	0.18 (0.08)	0.15 (0.06)	2.54**
Titles acquired annually	25,667.00 (19,545.00)	13,841.00 (7,400.00)	9,926.00 (3,426.00)	18,679.00 (15,638.00)	3.54**
Serials titles	4,680.20 (2,633.57)	2,399.00 (2,065.80)	1,433.86 (1,380.31)	3,313.70 (2,612.45)	5.806***
Volumes in stock per capita	2.09 (0.90)	1.88 (0.75)	2.14 (0.78)	2.04 (0.81)	0.26
Average branch hours per week	45.33 (10.70)	48.72 (9.42)	53.43 (12.27)	48.15 (10.85)	1.38
Staff per thousand population [a]	0.47 (0.17)	0.30 (0.07)	0.49 (0.16)	0.42 (0.16)	4.29**
Percentage of public service staff in the main library [a]	41 (13)	42 (10)	8 (10)	34 (18)	23.25***
Percentage of public service staff professional [a]	39.8 (8.4)	40.6 (10.4)	32.5 (15.6)	38.3 (11.1)	1.30
Percentage of employment supported by CETA [b]	8.4 (10.3)	8.9 (10.5)	3.3 (2.4)	7.4 (9.2)	0.90
Volunteer hours as percentage of employment [c]	1.3 (2.7)	0.5 (0.9)	0.7 (0.6)	0.9 (1.9)	0.60
Number of library systems	15	9	7	31	

Source: Author's survey of library systems. Data on selected variables are reported in appendix A. The numbers in parentheses are standard deviations. The *F*-statistic tests for significant differences across the geographic groups relative to variation within groups. Statistical significance is indicated: ***0.01 level; **0.05 level. The numbers below *F* are the degrees of freedom.

Note: [a] Information not available from the Chicago Public Library; total is for thirty library systems.
[b] CETA (Comprehensive Employment and Training Act) is a federally sponsored program to provide jobs.
[c] Information available from twelve city, eight metropolitan, and seven suburban libraries. The numbers in parentheses are standard devia-

larger, more varied collections and better library service than other facilities. Some main libraries may approximate the sophistication of a college library, with subject area specialists, microfilm collections, and substantial depth of collection. The Boston Public Library operates a large research library with 3 million volumes in a noncirculating collection, a unique service for a library operating as a department of the city government. The scope of main library services will be addressed again when materials and staffing are considered.

Some library systems further differentiate their facilities by designating some branches as regional libraries. The New York Public Library, the Free Library of Philadelphia, and the Atlanta Public Library, for example, have regional libraries both to decentralize the management of the organization and to provide larger, more varied, collections in more areas of the city. In part, such regional facilities may have served as alternatives to the expansion of the main library, or as an effort to move away from overbranching, that is, as a prelude to consolidating or closing marginal neighborhood branches. (In this case, marginal means the neighborhood branch is not well utilized.) The survey did not attempt to measure the scope of regional library operations.

Some libraries operate unstaffed library stations. Small collections of a few hundred books may be kept in fire stations, nursing homes, hospitals, schools, community centers, and the like. Eighteen of the thirty-one libraries surveyed indicated maintaining one or more unstaffed stations. Dallas, Cincinnati, and Birmingham each have over 20, and Philadelphia maintains 335 stations. Library stations are not investigated here in any detail.

Public libraries also provide services by truck. Bookmobiles typically house a collection of a few thousand books and operate as mobile branch libraries. While a patron can order a book for later delivery, most select materials from those on board. Only Brooklyn and Chicago among the systems surveyed do not offer bookmobile service. Cutbacks in bookmobile service, however, seem to be a response to budget pressure; some cities that normally operate bookmobiles were not operating them at the time of the survey. Only one system operated more than five bookmobiles, and that is St. Louis County where twenty-three bookmobiles operate. St. Louis County has elected to operate fewer branches than most systems and to operate many bookmobiles. The intensity of bookmobile service also varies. San Antonio has 34 stops for its five bookmobiles; Hennepin County (Minneapolis–St. Paul) has 100 stops for its two bookmobiles. Presumably the frequency and duration of bookmobile stops also influence the amount of use of bookmobile service.

Materials

The stock of materials includes both the items in the main library and in all the branches. Materials could be disaggregated in several dimensions for analysis. The most important medium is the book. Recordings are the most important nonbook material. Prints, films, microfilm, and pamphlets play a lesser role, especially in the branches. The materials might be differentiated by audience (adult versus juvenile) and by subject (fiction versus nonfiction). Too few libraries have records that allow easy disaggregation along the different dimensions so only totals can be compared across a substantial number of systems. The systems averaged two volumes in stock per capita. There is no significant difference between the city, metropolitan, and suburban systems in the number of volumes in stock per capita.

Age is another important dimension of library materials. New materials generate much more use than old materials. The acquisition of new materials can be characterized by examining the number of volumes acquired annually per capita. While the libraries average 0.15 new volumes per capita, there is a significant difference among the three geographic types. Central city libraries acquire more than metropolitan; suburban libraries acquire more than either of the other two.

The acquisition program of a public library has a quality dimension as well. The number of new titles cataloged annually indicates the breadth and depth of collection development. (There need be no strong link between the number of volumes acquired and the number of titles acquired because most public libraries buy multiple copies of many books.) The libraries differ significantly in the number of new titles acquired annually. The city libraries average more than 25,000 titles; metropolitan, close to 14,000; and suburban, just under 10,000. These compare with the over 30,000 new titles produced in the United States each year.

The difference in the number of titles acquired reflects basic differences in the objectives of the libraries. At the one extreme is the Boston Public Library, which acquires over 90,000 titles each year. The Boston Public Library has an aggressive collections development program. It seeks to build a research quality collection in a great range of subjects. The other city libraries surveyed average just under 20,000 new titles per year, still more than double the average for the suburban libraries. With a few exceptions, the city libraries have ambitious collections development programs comparable to those of many universities. At the other extreme, the suburban libraries for the most part do not include collections development as one of their goals. Their acquisitions are aimed primarily at current use rather than at posterity. Since the suburban systems buy more volumes per capita and many fewer titles than the city libraries, we can conclude that they buy many more multiple copies. Until recently, the St. Louis County Library bought the same titles for all its locations, thus it rarely acquired a book in single copy. The contrast with the Boston Public Library is clear.

The contrast in the breadth of materials libraries acquire is also seen in the number of serials titles subscribed to. The Boston Public Library subscribes to about 11,000 serials titles. The city libraries average 4,680 serials titles, while suburban libraries average 1,434. Nine of the library systems surveyed subscribe to fewer than 1,000 titles. Of course, the suburban systems may subscribe to the same titles for each facility, while most of the titles in the research oriented main libraries will be acquired in single copy.

The objective of materials acquisition differs markedly across the public libraries. On the one hand, a library may seek to hold materials representative of the full thought and practice in a particular area, be it French literature, nuclear physics, or the federal tax system. Completeness of coverage is the target. On the other hand, a library may seek materials that will lead to the highest amount of use. Here, popular interest is the target.[3]

Some surveys compare the materials acquisitions of libraries by comparing the proportion of the library budget devoted to materials. Such a measure is inadequate for several reasons. First, higher salaries will cause personnel costs to be higher, so the fraction of the budget devoted to materials acquisition will be smaller, even though the same number of staff and the same number of materials are acquired. Second, the expenditure on materials does not indicate how many volumes are purchased, or how many titles are included in the acquisition. The measurement of number of volumes, number of titles, and number of staff gives a much clearer picture of library services as users may observe them.

Hours

The hours of service is dramatically related to library use, as found in the study of the New York Public Library in chapter 4. Branch libraries surveyed by the author are open an average of forty-eight hours per week. While there is no significant difference across the geographic types, the variance in hours in each group is substantial. The twenty-two–hour average in New York City contrasts with the seventy-two hours per week in the St. Louis County Library.

Staffing

The single most expensive item of library operation is the staff. The total professional and clerical work force is compared across library systems.[4] On average, libraries have 0.42 staff members per thousand population. However, there is significantly smaller staff per capita in the metropolitan library systems. A more detailed investigation of the sources of the differences is in the regression analysis below.

About three-fourths of the staff are engaged in activities directly related to public services. The other quarter engage in administrative and technical services. Technical services involve the acquisition and cataloging of materials. The public service staff may select materials, control circulation, and respond to user queries (the reference function).

While part of the effect of changes in staffing in public services is to change the hours of service, the nature of the public services staff may also directly influence users. The capability of the library to handle user queries, for example, may be a direct consequence of the proportion of the staff that has professional training as librarians. The libraries average 38.3 percent professional staff.[5] While there is no significant difference across the geographic types, there is some variation among the libraries. In San Antonio, Buffalo, and Nashville over half of the public service staff is professional; less than 20 percent of the public service staff is professional in St. Louis County and San Diego County.

The public service staff is allocated between a main library and branches. The city and metropolitan libraries on average have 42 percent of their public service staffs assigned to the main library. Over half of the public service staff is assigned to the main library in Boston, Dallas, Minneapolis, San Antonio, and Birmingham. Four of the seven suburban library systems have no main library; the seven suburban systems average 8 percent of their public service staff in the main library. The pattern of staff assignments confirms the differing nature of main library services indicated by the acquisitions policies of the libraries.

Part of the staff may be supported by federal Comprehensive Employment and Training Act (CETA) funds. While the CETA workers may be both clerical and professional and similar to other library employees, it may be of interest to observe the libraries' pattern of use of CETA workers. Twenty-five of the thirty-one library systems have one or more CETA employees. On average, CETA workers account for 7.4 percent of the library's work force. However, CETA workers account for over 20 percent of the work force in five of the library systems surveyed—San Antonio, Birmingham, Nashville, Brooklyn, and New York.

Libraries may use volunteers to supplement paid workers. Some libraries employ a personnel officer who coordinates and trains volunteer workers. Of twenty-seven libraries that responded to the question about volunteers, ten indicated that they use volunteers. Comparing the number of volunteer hours contributed each week to the average number of paid hours worked shows that the twenty-seven systems average about 0.9 percent volunteer effort as a percent of paid effort.

EXPLAINING LIBRARY OPERATIONS

Having measured a variety of characteristics of library operations, it is appropriate to explain the differences in activities of the libraries. Why do some have long hours of service? Why do some buy fewer titles than others?

Table 2.2. *Pearson Correlation Coefficients between Inputs (31 Library Systems)*

	Variable							Percentage of Staff		
	Locations (per 100 square miles)	Bookmobiles	Volumes Acquired (per capita)	Titles	Volumes in Stock (per capita)	Hours (per week)	Staff (per 1,000 population)	Main Library	Professional	CETA
Variable:										
Bookmobiles	−0.297*									
Acquisitions	0.062	−0.111								
Titles	0.557***	−0.112	0.092							
Stock per capita	0.046	−0.163	0.694***	0.111						
Hours per week	−0.468***	0.422***	0.145	−0.232	−0.123					
Staff per 1,000 population	0.294*	−0.210	0.783***	0.398**	0.725***	−0.112				
Percentage of staff										
Main library	0.101	−0.312**	−0.263*	0.342**	0.007	−0.212	−0.103			
Professional	0.177	−0.336**	0.041	0.124	0.165	−0.161	0.033	0.182		
CETA	0.141	−0.097	−0.357**	−0.176	−0.434***	−0.024	−0.487***	0.201	0.204	
Volunteer	−0.089	−0.073	0.469***	−0.064	0.464***	0.039	0.312*	0.087	0.131	0.057

Note: Pearson correlation coefficients are calculated with pairwise deletion of missing values. Statistical significance is indicated: ***0.01 level; **0.05 level; *0.10 level.

(Variables are as defined in table 2.1.)

Correlations Among Inputs

Because each library system is faced with a budget constraint, each must make tradeoffs among different services. For example, a library that wants to collect a large number of titles may acquire fewer volumes per capita, that is, fewer books in multiple copies. A library that operates many hours per week may have fewer locations. For these reasons, the correlations between some inputs are expected to be negative, which indicates they are substitutes. (Two factors are substitutes when more of one can compensate for less of the other.)

On the other hand, the pursuit of a particular philosophy of what public library services should be may lead a library to have higher levels of certain activities jointly. For example, a library that acquires many titles may also have a higher proportion of its public service staff in the main library. In this case, the correlations among inputs would be positive, which indicates they are complements. (Two factors are complements when more of one is necessary to make use of more of the other.)

The correlations among inputs presented in table 2.2 reveal some of both kinds of groupings. Hours of branches and the number of locations seem to be substitutes. This finding is consistent with the experience of the New York Public Library. Maintaining a large number of locations is done at the expense of fewer hours of operation at each location. The number of bookmobiles is negatively correlated both with the proportion of public service staff in the main library and the proportion that is professional. These correlations suggest that, on average, across the library systems there may be a tradeoff between bookmobile service and main library service and between bookmobile service and professional librarians. The bookmobile correlations may be influenced by the St. Louis County Library because it operates so many more bookmobiles than any other of the systems observed.

The positive correlations between acquisitions and stock, acquisitions and staff, stock and staff, and titles and staff are consistent with these activities as complements with each other. There are more titles and staff in library systems that operate more locations. Libraries that have more books in stock also seem to acquire more books, acquire a greater variety of titles, have a larger staff, and operate more locations per 100 square miles than libraries with fewer books in stock. Thus, some libraries emphasize more materials in more locations at the expense of hours while others emphasize hours of service and bookmobiles. The interactions among the different dimensions of service are, of course, complex.

DETERMINANTS OF ACTIVITIES

The variation in library activities may be associated with differences in the areas the libraries serve. For example, high labor cost may shift library activities away from labor intensive services to other services. The fiscal circumstances of the local government may shape the mix of library services through the local budget process. The characteristics of the local population may influence the character of the local public library. This section discusses the measurement of each of these factors and then examines the influence of these factors on library activities.

Labor Cost

If a library can substitute one type of service (e.g., additional materials) for another (e.g., hours of service), while being just as attractive to users, then one might expect to find different mixes of activities given different costs. That is, if a library chooses to provide as much service value as possible within a given budget, it will substitute less expensive for more expensive activities. In particular, those libraries that face higher labor costs may be expected to adjust the mix of services so as to economize on the use of labor.

Based on the libraries in the survey, the average total annual compensation for a recruit librarian, adjusted to a forty-hour work week and including fringe benefits, was $14,911 (see table 2.3). While there is no statistically significant difference across the geographic types, there is substantial variation among the libraries from a low of $10,287 in St. Louis County to a high of $26,278 in Chicago. Sources of variation in labor cost are examined in chapter 3. The range of variation in the cost of labor is sufficient to induce differences in the mix of library activities if substitution is possible and if libraries are responsive to economic incentives.

Fiscal Indicators

The fiscal circumstances of local government may influence the level of library activities through the budgetmaking process. First, those libraries that are departments of city or county governments may be more subject to tradeoffs against other government services, say schools or police, than a library that is an autonomous or semiautonomous agency. Eighteen of the thirty-one libraries surveyed are government departments. The other thirteen are at least semiautonomous. Nine of the library systems receive earmarked tax revenue, thus further insulating the library's expenditures from the exigencies of local finance.

Library activities may be influenced by the stringency of the local fiscal position in general, although the direction of the effect may be unclear. On the one hand, a locality that raises large amounts of money may have more to spend on libraries as well as on many other services. On the other hand, a city that finds it necessary to raise a large amount of revenue for other purposes may be less likely to spend a great deal on its library.

There are two main sources of funds for local government. Funds may be

Table 2.3. *Library Service Area and System Characteristics: Means and Standard Deviations by Geographic Type*

Variable	City	Metropolitan	Suburban	All	$F_{(2, 28)}$
Recruit librarian compensation [a]	$15,771.87 (3,393.54)	13,832.34 (2,349.89)	14,455.85 (2,146.16)	14,911.61 (2,921.62)	1.38
Own revenues net of library expenditures per capita [b]	$382.39 (214.06)	339.62 (97.04)	295.28 (143.22)	350.31 (171.03)	0.63
Intergovernmental revenue per capita [b]	$178.71 (176.64)	186.52 (75.71)	167.29 (47.85)	178.40 (128.83)	0.04
Percentage of libraries that are government departments [a]	53.3	55.6	71.4	58.1	0.31
Population [c] (in thousands)	1,275.78 (1,019.14)	811.46 (361.36)	619.27 (164.56)	992.73 (779.36)	2.20
Percentage of adults who are high school graduates [c]	49.51 (9.88)	54.79 (6.76)	70.74 (7.61)	55.84 (11.89)	14.58***
Population growth—1960 to 1970 [c]	3.89 (15.28)	9.83 (8.21)	52.17 (17.72)	16.52 (24.07)	28.76***
Number of library systems	15	9	7	31	

Sources: [a] Author's survey. Compensation is salary plus fringe benefits normalized to a forty-hour work week.
[b] *Census of Governments, 1972.* The Cleveland Public Library is not reflected in the 1972 Census of Governments. Survey information for 1977 was substituted.
[c] *Census of Population,* 1960, 1970.

Note: Numbers in parentheses are standard deviations. The *F*-statistic tests for significant differences across the geographic groups relative to the degree of variation within groups. Statistical significance is indicated: ***0.01 level; **0.05 level. Numbers below the *F* are degrees of freedom.

raised from local sources, principally the property tax, and funds may come from the state and federal governments. The Census of Governments reports summary financial information for 1972. In the library areas surveyed, the average own revenues per capita net of library expenditures was $350.31. Direct expenditure less revenue from local sources is taken to be intergovernmental transfers. Netting out the expenditures on libraries yields the intergovernmental figures reported in table 2.3. The library areas averaged $178.40 per capita. The per capita expenditures on libraries indicated in the Census of Governments was $6.44. It is possible that library expenditures are influenced differently by funds from local sources than from intergovernmental transfers. First, intergovernmental transfers may be subject to a variety of conditions that limit their use. State aid for education may be distributed on a matching formula that draws in local funds. In this case, expenditures on the public library may be associated with lower levels of other expenditure. On the other hand, general revenue sharing, not tied to a specific expenditure, may stimulate local expenditures on libraries more than local tax funds.

Some states provide per capita grants for public libraries. Such grants are likely to stimulate higher levels of expenditure in libraries. The census does not indicate the level of aid that goes directly to libraries.

Unfortunately, the census gives no indication of the terms that condition intergovernmental transfers, and so tied funds cannot be distinguished from untied funds. Consequently, the net direction of the association between library activities and intergovernmental transfers is unclear.

Library Users

Library services are also influenced by the character of library users. Previous studies of library use have found that use increases with income and education and declines with age.[6] In this comparison of library systems it is not possible to explore the influence of the characteristics of users. Nevertheless, the percentage of adults who are high school graduates is thought to be an important indicator of the public interest in library activities. The proportion of adults who are high school graduates varies significantly from 50 percent in the central cities, to 55 percent in the metropolitan systems, to 71 percent in the suburban areas. The variation across individual areas is even greater; it ranges from 32 percent in Brooklyn to 80 percent in Montgomery County. Adults with more education are expected to want more library services.

Library systems may respond only slowly to changes in the service area. The opening and closing of facilities is likely to be slow relative to changing use patterns both because buildings are durable and because the development of the political support necessary to make changes may take time. Therefore, the gain in population from 1960 to 1970 may be associated with differences in library activities. The suburban areas show an average of 52 percentage points of growth, while both city and metropolitan areas averaged less than 10 points. Fewer locations and smaller stocks of materials will be expected in areas of higher growth.

The total size of the area served in terms of population may also influence the mix of activities. An area with more people might be expected to have more total main library activities but fewer per capita activities because of economies of scale. That is, the more people who share the cost of a main library, the lower the cost to each. There may be other economies of scale as well, perhaps in technical services or acquisitions. Organizational diseconomies may affect the largest systems. A very large system may have a higher proportion of its budget absorbed in administration than a smaller organization. The library systems surveyed averaged 993,000 population without statistically significant differences across the geographic types. Chicago's 3,367,000 is the largest, Minneapolis's 434,000 is the smallest, in the group.

Regression Analysis of Library Operations

This section presents results of multiple regressions for each measure of library operations. Each measure is related to labor cost, the local fiscal situation, and to the characteristics of the local population. The purpose of regression analysis is to discover systematic sources of differences in library operations. An overview of regression methods is presented in appendix B.

The first measure of library operations examined is library expenditure per capita, as reported in the 1972 Census of Governments. Many studies of local government activity use expenditure per capita as the principal indicator of activity. Expenditures, however, are a poor guide to understanding operations. The expenditure regression is reported in the first column of table 2.4. Expenditures are found to be statistically significantly associated with local expenditures from own sources net of library expenditures in per capita terms. Does this mean that cities that spend more on other services also buy more library services? The regressions for the inputs themselves indicate no statistically significant relationship between own expenditures on other services and the level of library services. Thus, the use of per capita expenditures is misleading. Library expenditures per capita are found to be positively associated with labor costs. Labor costs are a component of library expenditures, so it is not surprising that a positive association is found. A negative association between expenditures and intergovernmental revenues per capita (net of library expenditures) is consistent with intergovernmental revenues being tied to other purposes. Or they may simply be directed to low spending places via distribution and project evaluation formulas. The intergovernmental revenue effect found for library expenditures does not seem to be found on most operations; it appears only for staff. Again, the examination of expenditures reveals little about operations. The examination of individual service characteristics is much more revealing.

Labor cost is associated with different operations in different ways. Hours and labor cost are negatively related. Those library systems with lower labor costs operate longer hours on average than those with higher labor costs, other things equal. No other activity (except CETA employees, to be discussed later) is negatively associated with labor cost, thus the only apparent response to high labor cost seems to be to reduce operating hours. Because the survey study is a cross section, it is, of course, inappropriate to conclude that over time libraries have been induced to cut hours because of rising labor costs. Nevertheless, the cross section evidence is consistent with such behavior. This finding tends to reinforce the evidence in the study of the New York Public Library in chapter 4: hours are more readily cut than locations or materials.

More volunteer effort relative to paid staff is found in libraries with high labor costs. Libraries may be led to put more effort into using volunteers where labor costs are high. The level of volunteer effort, however, is lower in larger library systems. Larger systems may be less effective in organizing the use of volunteers; perhaps larger systems show more bureaucratic inertia.

Labor cost is positively associated with acquisition, titles acquired, stock, and staff. High labor costs are not associated with lower levels of service in these dimensions. The strength of the positive relationship is a little surprising. While these activities differ from central city to suburban systems (as shown in table 2.1), labor costs do not differ significantly across the geographic types. Therefore, the association between labor cost and the material and staff intensive library systems reflects more than just a difference between a central city and a suburban area. Perhaps the political and organizational arrangements that lead to more materials and staff also lead to higher labor costs.

CETA employees are a smaller fraction of staff in library systems with higher labor cost. Apparently CETA employment has been concentrated in cities with lower labor costs.

Intergovernmental revenues per capita are positively associated with CETA workers. Because CETA funds may be included in the intergovernmental transfers, this association is quite understandable. Moreover, criteria similar to those used to distribute CETA funds may be used to distribute other intergovernmental transfers.

Intergovernmental transfers are negatively associated with the level of staff. This association may reflect the dominance of tied grants in intergovernmental transfers. Restrictions on grants, say for education or law enforcement, may require that local funds be directed to specific purposes, as with matching formulas. Untied aid would be expected to induce somewhat higher

Table 2.4. Results of Library Activity Regressions

Explanatory Variable	Labor Cost (thousands of dollars)	Own Expenditures Per Capita	Intergovernmental Revenues Per Capita	Department (binary)	Percentage of Adults Who Are High School Graduates	Population Growth Ratio—1960–1970	Population Served (thousands)	Constant	R^2	F	n
Expenditure (per capita)	0.963*** (2.734)	0.009** (2.176)	-0.024*** (-3.241)	-2.020 (-1.607)	-0.028 (-0.345)	0.007 (0.202)	0.002 (1.194)	-5.352	0.500	2.998**	29
Locations (per 100 square miles)	2.842 (1.626)	0.030 (1.411)	0.002 (0.045)	-2.366 (-0.351)	-0.064 (-0.152)	-0.336* (-1.800)	0.011 (1.211)	-34.182	0.600	4.710***	30
Bookmobiles	-0.758 (-1.807)	0.000 (0.000)	-0.010 (-1.085)	-2.240 (-1.495)	0.042 (0.430)	0.028 (0.644)	0.002 (1.069)	12.675	0.347	1.593	29
Volumes acquired (per 1,000 population)	12.441** (2.090)	0.011 (0.145)	0.069 (0.506)	-21.536 (-0.939)	1.902 (1.308)	-0.326 (-0.513)	-0.043 (-1.444)	-100.074	0.384	1.961	30
Titles acquired (in thousands)	3.234** (2.159)	0.015 (0.711)	-0.048 (-1.404)	0.691 (0.118)	-0.168 (-0.460)	-0.150 (-0.939)	0.003 (0.431)	-16.767	0.336	1.589	30
Volumes in stock per capita	0.271*** (4.945)	-0.397 (-0.597)	-1.068 (-0.856)	-657.425*** (-3.114)	9.992 (0.741)	-6.214 (-1.063)	-0.589*** (-2.149)	1,089.455	0.671	6.413***	30
Average weekly branch hours	-0.002** (-2.586)	0.014 (1.387)	0.027 (1.416)	-2.616 (-0.790)	-0.189 (-0.900)	0.186* (2.024)	-0.012** (-2.706)	89.559	0.540	3.694***	30

Staff (per million population)	0.046*** (3.418)	0.047 (0.287)	−0.544* (−1.756)	−72.564 (−1.386)	4.246 (1.279)	−0.881 (−0.607)	−0.023 (−0.345)	−331.450	0.487	2.983***	30
Percentage of public service staff:											
In main library	0.033 (0.297)	−0.0009 (−0.063)	−0.030 (−1.211)	6.746 (1.585)	−0.655** (−2.428)	−0.402*** (−3.413)	−0.007 (−1.344)	81.404	0.729	8.443***	30
Professional	0.062 (0.510)	0.021 (1.411)	0.004 (0.134)	0.166 (0.032)	−0.266 (−0.894)	0.060 (0.465)	−0.005 (−0.775)	0.395	0.119	0.424	30
CETA employees as percentage of total staff	−1.800** (−2.234)	−0.007 (−0.680)	0.050** (2.719)	2.827 (0.911)	−0.340* (−1.726)	0.031 (0.362)	−0.002 (−0.602)	46.110	0.464	2.726**	30
Ratio of volunteers to staff	0.328** (2.102)	−0.0001 (−0.044)	0.004 (1.069)	−0.952 (−1.275)	−0.036 (−0.759)	−0.009 (−0.454)	−0.002** (−2.645)	0.145	0.325	1.306	27

Note: Each row reports the coefficients of a regression of the dependent variable indicated at the side on the explanatory variables listed along the top. Numbers in parentheses are *t*-statistics. Two-tailed tests are applied. The statistical significance of coefficients is indicated: ***0.01 level; **0.05 level; *0.10 level. Means and standard deviations of variables are reported in tables 2.1 and 2.3. The degrees of freedom for the *F* statistics are (a) the number of variables in the regression and (b) n minus the number of variables in the regression minus one.

levels of local expenditure. Aid tied to library services would be expected to have the largest impact on libraries. The displacement effect of tied aid for purposes other than libraries must dominate the influence of untied aid and library specific aid with respect to staff. This result is a little surprising. It is unclear why this result should be found for staffing but not for other categories of library services.

Libraries that are departments of local government have less autonomy than departments that are independently chartered. Library departments may be less successful than the autonomous library in competing for local funds against the police and schools. The only statistically significant association found is with volumes in stock per capita. Fewer volumes are found in libraries operated as departments of city government than in libraries that are autonomous.

Library systems that serve areas with a higher proportion of adults who are high school graduates are little different, on average, than library systems with relatively fewer high school graduates. They have a statistically significant smaller proportion of their public service staff in a main library, and they have relatively fewer CETA employees. Suburban systems have populations with more education and are less likely to develop a main library service. One might have expected higher levels of service in areas with a population with more education because library use increases with education. That no such finding is apparent—indeed, the more highly educated populations have smaller main libraries—suggests that something other than the reading tastes of the resident population shapes the library service.

The ratio of 1970 to 1960 population is negatively associated with the number of library locations per 100 square miles. This is consistent with a substantial lag in the development of additional locations as a response to increases in population. Also, areas that show population growth will be at much lower population density than areas that have mature development. Lower densities embody automobile-oriented consumption patterns, and lower densities of library locations are desirable in such circumstances.

Libraries in areas of recent growth operate more hours per week on average than those in areas that are growing more slowly. Having fewer branches, they concentrate their energy in operating more hours. Not having inherited too many branches, they do not have to close branches in order to sustain a high level of hours of service.

The libraries in rapidly growing areas have smaller main libraries. Just as with locations, a main library takes time to develop. Therefore, it is not surprising that library systems in growing areas have smaller main libraries. On the other hand, the library systems in growing areas may have decided against providing a substantial main library service. The notion that libraries in growing areas have a different philosophy of service cannot be ruled out.

A distinction might be made here between an age effect and a vintage effect. The age effect implies that particular kinds of library service such as a main library cumulate with age. Each 25-year-old library system will have similar main libraries. The difference in main libraries may reflect the fact that the library systems are of widely differing ages; the suburban systems are much younger than the city and metropolitan systems. If the age effect is dominant, then when the suburban systems are 100 years old they will look much more like the 100-year-old city systems observed today. The weak association between population growth and the stock of materials suggests that the age effect is not very powerful.

The vintage effect implies that each library is molded at its birth by the needs that existed at that time. Libraries created in the 1920s had many neighborhood branches, a substantial demand for sophisticated main library services, and an orientation toward collecting materials for posterity. Libraries created today may reflect an orientation toward meeting the circulation requirements of current users. Whereas libraries created in the 1920s emphasized walking access, those created today emphasize automobile access. Thus longer hours, more multiple copies, and fewer locations may be appropriate. The vintage hypothesis depends on the assumption that libraries are slow to change when faced with new circumstances. An analogy might be made to grocery stores. The grocery stores of the 1950s are being transformed into larger stores more geographically dispersed in the 1970s.

If library systems are slow to change, they may reflect their vintage. It is difficult to disentangle age and vintage effects from cross section evidence alone: a cross section over time is necessary. But vintage effects may be important for locations and age effects may be important for the main library.

The size of the area served is indicated by population. Library systems serving larger populations seem to stock fewer books per capita. Perhaps there are economies of scale in the book stock. That is, perhaps certain materials are acquired in single copy for the whole system. Such materials will be spread over a larger audience in a larger system, and so the stock of materials might be smaller in per capita terms in a larger library system.

Systems serving larger populations tend to operate fewer hours than those that serve smaller populations. It is unclear why larger systems should offer fewer hours than the average system.

Overall, the differences in library services are not very well explained. Labor costs have some role especially in limiting hours of service. Libraries in growing areas have fewer locations, operate longer hours, and have smaller relative commitments to main library services than libraries in areas with smaller population growth rates. These influences do not tell the full story, however.

First, the history of each library system is probably very important. Library systems seem to be very durable; once in place they tend to stay in place. The level of bureaucratic and political inertia may be very high. It may be difficult to close or relocate branches and to change the basic features of the library services. If sophisticated main library service is developed, it may be difficult to reduce the level of such service should the demand for it change. Second, residents are not the only library users. The level of employment in central cities may be larger than the population. The demand for public library services may be influenced in important ways by the character of employment. For example, an area with a large number of financial firms and corporate headquarters may require more library services than, say, manufacturing activities. This investigation has not given sufficient attention to the history of the library systems and to the character of employment in the area.

EXPLAINING LIBRARY USE

The library activities discussed previously can be related to the use of the library systems. How do different sets of activities influence the level of use? Perhaps more hours and more books generate more use. The study of branches in New York in chapter 4 demonstrates that library use is very responsive to the hours of service, and is somewhat responsive to the acquisition of materials. In this section, use is compared across library systems.

Measuring Use

The main category of use is circulation. Circulation figures are available from most library systems and have been used as a quasi-output measure in other studies.[7] Circulation at the time of the survey is examined relative to 1970 population. On average, 4.66 books circulated per year per capita in the library systems surveyed, as reported in table 2.5. There is a statistically significant variation across the geographic types. Suburban library systems averaged over seven circulations per capita while city systems averaged under four. Pittsburgh averaged 1.75 circulation per capita while Fairfax County, Virginia, averaged over ten. The likely differential growth of the jurisdictions may exaggerate these differences somewhat.

Circulation could be disaggregated in several ways. The circulation of adult materials could be distinguished from the circulation of juvenile materials. Fiction might be distinguished from nonfiction. The circulation of books might be distinguished from nonbook materials. Too few libraries have such disaggregated information available to make analysis possible.

Circulation figures, of course, do not reflect all the dimensions of library use. In particular, the number of persons served may be as important as the number of materials used. One way of considering the number of persons who use the library system is to count the number of cardholders. Of the thirty-one systems, six either do not require cards or keep no central count of the number of cards outstanding. The renewal period varies for the cards from an annual card renewal required in San Diego, New Orleans, and Fairfax County to

Table 2.5. *Measuring Library Use: Means and Standard Deviations by Geographic Type*

Variable	City	Metropolitan	Suburban	All	$F_{(2,28)}$
Circulation per capita	3.74 (1.32) n=15	4.09 (1.36) n=9	7.34 (2.44) n=7	4.66 (2.17) n=31	12.38***
Cards per capita	0.41 (0.16) n=13	0.29 (0.08) n=8	0.41 (0.17) n=4	0.37 (0.14) n=25	2.19
Interlibrary loans received	1334.07 (1020.67) n=14	877.57 (1305.97) n=7	6393.14 (4841.61) n=7	2484.71 (3377.32) n=28	10.91***
Interlibrary loans sent	11256.07 (11878.28) n=14	10071.88 (10004.33) n=8	6198.43 (4384.19) n=7	9708.59 (9948.04) n=29	0.59
Loan period (in weeks)	3.00 (0.65) n=15	3.33 (0.71) n=9	3.14 (0.69) n=7	3.13 (0.67) n=31	0.68
Percentage allowing renewals	73.33 (45.77) n=15	55.56 (52.70) n=9	85.71 (37.80) n=7	70.97 (46.14) n=31	0.87
Average weeks wait for best seller	6.15 (6.57) n=13	4.67 (4.08) n=6	10.33 (8.39) n=3	6.32 (6.20) n=22	0.83

Source: Author's survey of libraries.

Note: Numbers in parentheses are standard deviations. The F-statistics tests for statistically significant differences across the geographic groups relative to variation within groups. Statistical significance is indicated: ***0.01 level; **0.05 level; *0.10 level. Numbers below F are degrees of freedom.

permanent cards in Houston and St. Louis County. Note that nonresidents may acquire cards in several places, and therefore the possible number of cards is not limited by the population of the area. The library systems averaged thirty-seven cards per 100 population with no statistically significant difference across the geographic types.

Library use might also be compared by observing attendance. Turnstile counts are available from only a few libraries, however, so attendance cannot be examined. Reference questions asked could also be compared across systems, and many libraries do count questions asked. Reference queries may be of many different sorts, however. It would be useful to try to identify some particular categories of questions. The survey asked how many questions were received by telephone, but too few libraries were able to sort out the number of telephone inquiries from questions from other sources. Consequently, the issue of reference questions is not examined here.

Libraries also interact with other libraries via the interlibrary loan system. The survey asked about the number of materials sent and the number received. On average, 9,708 materials were sent and 2,484 materials were received via interlibrary loan. These figures occur in the surveyed systems where circulation averaged over 3.5 million. Thus, the interlibrary flow of materials accounts for less than half of one percent of circulation. (Some libraries may require materials received via interlibrary loan to be used in the library, thus interlibrary flows may not appear in the circulation figures.) Relative to the total scope of library services, interlibrary flows seem inconsequential.

The receipt of materials through interlibrary loan varies significantly across the geographic types; city and metropolitan libraries have much smaller inflows of materials than the suburban systems. These differences may reflect the greater commitment of central city and metropolitan systems to central library services, an issue that will be explored later.

The outflow of materials does not differ significantly across the geographic types. The suburban systems on average have a rough balance of inflows and outflows. The central city and metropolitan systems are net lenders.

The library use will be conditioned by several other dimensions of the service. For example, the length of the loan period may influence the level of use of the library. The loan period varies from two to four weeks with a mean of three weeks. Nine of the thirty-one library systems do not allow material to be renewed. Because renewals count as additional circulations, libraries that disallow renewals are likely to have lower levels of circulation than those that allow renewals. Three library systems allow renewals to be made by telephone: San Antonio, St. Louis County, and Birmingham.

The quality of service may also be influenced by the length of the wait for popular materials. The survey asked the libraries to estimate how long on average one would have to wait for a bestseller. Twenty-two libraries were willing to guess at this number. The average reported wait is six weeks. The mean wait varies from one week in Milwaukee and San Francisco to over twenty weeks in San Diego and San Diego County. Of course, the actual wait will likely follow some skewed distribution with the most popular book having the longest wait. The length of the queue will vary over the life of the book, from a long queue when the book is new and heavily promoted, to a sharp dropoff when a paperback version becomes available. Nevertheless, the rough measure of waiting time may indicate a dimension of the quality of service not captured in circulation figures.

Regression Analysis of Use

Differences in use can be explored by regressing the measures of use on the library activities and the measures of public taste for library services. The central hypothesis is that use will be greater the higher the level of activity the library system provides. The more hours, books, and locations, the more use there should be.[8] Results of the regressions are reported in table 2.6.

The simple linear regression explains over 84 percent of the variation in circulation per capita across the thirty-one library systems surveyed. The most important influence is the level of education: the higher the proportion of adults who are high school graduates, the higher the level of circulation. Among library services, the most important factor seems to be the number of acquisitions. Higher levels of acquisitions are associated with higher levels of circulation. The elasticity of circulation with respect to new acquisitions, evaluated at the means, is 0.32.[9]

Libraries that allow renewals have more circulation per capita, other things equal. The coefficient indicates that on average one circulation per capita per year is a renewal. Taking into account renewal policy seems to be important in comparing circulation across library systems.

The other variables in the regression show no statistically significant associations with circulation. In particular, the average hours of service at branches is unrelated to circulation in the comparison of library systems. This result is at variance with that for the New York system. Apparently, hours are very important given the low level of hours of service found in the New York system, but are much less important in the range observed here, that is among systems averaging forty-eight hours of service in branches each week. It may also be that variance among branches within systems is important while variation across the systems is not.

The number of locations is also unrelated to circulation in the regression. The systems with large numbers of locations tend to offer fewer hours, and that effect may dominate here. The number of titles cataloged is also unrelated to circulation in the regression. Thus, there is no evidence to indicate that the large, varied, sophisticated collections of systems with larger main libraries generate more circulation than those systems with many fewer titles. The lack of association between population in the area and the per capita circulation

Table 2.6. Results of Regressions of Library use

Explanatory Variable	Circulation Per Capita	Cardholders per 100 Population	Interlibrary Loan Flows (in thousands)		Average Wait for Bestseller (in weeks)
			Received	Sent	
Locations per 100 square miles	-45.116 (-0.335)	-0.610 (-0.045)	-3.776 (-0.875)		
Weekly branch hours	0.118 (0.578)	-0.93 (-0.338)	-0.071 (-0.922)		
Volumes acquired per thousand population	0.010*** (2.924)	0.079 (1.683)	0.009 (0.715)	-0.014 (-0.424)	-0.012 (-0.549)
Titles catalogued (in thousands)	0.006 (0.412)	0.493*** (3.204)	0.0026 (0.055)	0.0001 (0.968)	0.00005 (0.677)
Loan period (in weeks)					3.489* (1.715)
Renewals allowed (binary)	0.967** (2.217)				

Card renewal period (in years)		0.874 (0.867)			
Population (in thousands)	−0.0005 (−0.155)	−0.006 (−1.633)	−0.0008 (−0.483)	−0.0008 (−0.202)	−0.00008 (−0.045)
Percentage of adults who are high school graduates	0.124*** (6.208)	0.131 (0.460)	0.035 (0.032)	0.154 (0.596)	0.286* (1.829)
Percentage of public service staff in main library			−9.274 (−1.612)	23.323 (1.411)	
Constant	−5.000	16.943	8.852	−6.049	−18.685
R^2	.846	.625	.414	.221	.393
F	18.100***	4.041***	1.921	1.246	2.069
n	31	25	27	28	22

Note: Each column reports the coefficients of a regression of the dependent variable indicated at the top of the column on the explanatory variables listed along the side. Numbers in parentheses are t-statistics. Two-tailed tests are applied. Statistical significance of the coefficients is indicated: ***0.01 level; **0.05 level; *0.10 level. The degrees of freedom for the F statistics are (a) the number of variables in the regression and (b) n minus the number of variables in the regression minus one.

tends to suggest that there may be little economy of scale in the provision of public library circulation services among these relatively large library systems.

Somewhat different factors seem to explain the number of cardholders per hundred population. In particular, many more people seem to hold cards of library systems with more titles cataloged annually. Thus, while the sophistication and variety of collections indicated by the number of titles cataloged does not seem to account for differences in circulation, they do seem to account for differences in the number of cardholders. Inclusion of a variable for the number of years between renewals of the card does not affect the relationship: the number of cardholders is apparently little affected by the renewal cycle. Thus the main effect seems to be that of titles. It would be interesting to have turnstile counts or sample surveys for the library systems indicating attendance to see whether the number of cardholders gives a clue to in-library use. One might also like to know what fraction of cardholders reside and work outside the jurisdiction of the library, as a way of examining geographic spillovers. Because holding a card is not a direct benefit, it is possible that cardholding is weakly associated with any particular library use. Nevertheless, because the cardholding patterns seem different from circulation patterns, it may be that cardholding reflects other categories of library use.

Interlibrary loan flows are not well explained by the variables at hand. One would expect that a library system with a large main library and one that is acquiring a large number of titles each year would both lend more materials and borrow fewer materials through interlibrary loan. One might further expect that some of the same factors that lead to own circulation would also lead to more interlibrary loan inflows, that is, areas with more educated adults would be expected to have more demand for interlibrary loan inflows. Finally, one might expect that larger systems would both require more inflows and be more important suppliers of interlibrary loans. These hypotheses are only weakly substantiated. Regressions of the gross flows are reported in table 2.6. The coefficients on the percentage of public service personnel who are assigned to the main library are statistically significant at the 0.10 level with a one-tailed test. Larger main libraries have somewhat lower demands for interlibrary inflows and supply greater levels of outflows. Population, titles, and volumes acquired are unrelated to interlibrary loan flows. The overall explanatory power of the relationship is low, however, and unobserved influences are probably important.

Interlibrary loan flows are never large relative to total system circulation. Users for the most part rely on materials that are locally available. Interlibrary loan becomes more important when elaborate interconnections between libraries develop. Some libraries are designated regional centers. For example, the Commonwealth of Pennsylvania has designated four libraries as resource centers, and the subject categories of the Dewey decimal system have been parceled out. A resource center library receives some state funds to support its collections development in its assigned subject areas. It then has a responsibility to respond to interlibrary loan requests in its subject areas. Library interconnections may also develop locally. The libraries in the Washington, D.C., area have daily delivery service so that interlibrary loans can be filled quickly. Some libraries have special relationships with smaller libraries in nearby jurisdictions such that all requests for interlibrary loans flow through the larger library. Interlibrary loan flows will be greater in libraries that are a part of active regional systems for the exchange of materials. The survey asked whether libraries belonged to a network; over 90 percent responded affirmatively. Yet the level of development of organizations is quite varied. Interlibrary loan operations are not free outlets either for promoting the use of large collections or for collections that are too small or thin. Interlibrary loan operations require investment in the development of institutions to make them work. Not all public libraries participate aggressively in such services.

The number of weeks a user must wait, on average, for a bestseller may be influenced on the one hand by the number of volumes acquired and on the other hand by the number of people using the system. The longer the loan period in the library system the longer each user may hold a book, and so the longer the wait, other things equal. (Some library systems have special shorter loan periods for bestsellers, but the survey inquired only about the normal loan period.)

The wait for bestsellers is only poorly explained by the regression, at least in part because the information reflects the best guess of the librarians rather than systematic data gathering. Nevertheless, some of the hypotheses are weakly confirmed as shown in the last column in table 2.6. On average, a 1-week longer loan period is associated with 3.489 weeks longer wait for bestsellers, a figure statistically significant at the 10 percent level with a one-tailed test. Second, the wait is longer in library systems with more educated adults. The pressure of demand increases the wait. Third, there seems to be no relationship between the number of volumes acquired per capita and the length of the wait. Of course, a library may meet the demand for bestsellers by renting books, so the lack of association here may not indicate a lack of response of libraries to the length of queues for popular materials.

The comparison of library use across the library systems has not done justice to the uses of main library services. While figures on circulation, cardholders, attendance, and reference questions might be revealing, especially if available in disaggregated form, an important quality dimension is overlooked. The value of a sophisticated main library service depends in important ways on the quality of the collection and the breadth and depth of study that may be done using the materials. A scholar may spend each day for weeks in a library exploring a particular theme. Simple counts will not do justice to the value of the library service to such an individual. The relevant question from the point of view of the public interest in libraries, however, is what institutions are more appropriate for meeting research library needs and how should they be financed. The results presented here suggest that the research library function may have little connection with the current circulation orientation of most public library users.

SUMMARY

Measuring library services in direct physical terms proves more revealing than relying on expenditure comparisons. The expenditure comparisons are influenced by differences in labor costs as well as by differences in the services offered. Expenditure comparisons do not reveal the differences in service mix. For example, public library systems are found to substitute hours for locations (in cross section). Library services are not provided in fixed combinations of staff, hours, materials, and location.

While the public library systems are quite varied in the combination of services they supply, a rough division seems possible along the following lines. Some libraries have many locations, buy many book titles, have larger staffs in per capita terms, and put relatively more effort into the main library. Such libraries operate for fewer hours and use fewer bookmobiles. Other libraries do the opposite. While classifying library systems geographically into city, metropolitan, and suburban systems explains some of the differences in service mix (most importantly the number of locations and the number of book titles), the geographic classification does not explain the differences in hours, stock of books, and bookmobiles.

The differences in service mix are explained in part by differences in labor costs. On average, systems with higher labor costs operate significantly fewer hours per week. The high labor cost systems also have more staff. Reductions in hours in response to higher labor costs may be seen as a temporary adjustment to financial pressure, while adjustment of locations, stocks, acquisitions, and staff may be slower and viewed as more permanent. The higher levels of materials and locations being associated with higher labor costs may indicate some historical overexpansion of expenditures.

The level of education of adults in the jurisdiction explains little of the differences in service mix, even though education is very strongly associated with differences in library use. Given the fact that adults with more education use the public library more than others, one would expect the political system to deliver significantly more library services in areas with higher levels of education. That education has little association with differences in library services suggests that the political system is not very responsive to ultimate users.

The rate of population growth of the jurisdiction is important in explaining some differences in library services. Areas that have experienced rapid growth tend to have fewer locations per 100 square miles, to have less commitment to main libraries, and to operate longer hours. To what extent these effects result from delays in the growth of library services and to what extent they reflect changing tastes and technologies in services is difficult to determine without time series evidence.

The differences in library services are associated with differences in use, but the dominant importance of hours of service found for the New York system is not found in the comparison of library systems. The important service characteristic in comparing systems seems to be volumes acquired per capita per year. This reinforced the finding that the age of the stock of materials is very important in whether one decides to use the library.

The level of cardholding, on the other hand, seems to be influenced importantly by the number of titles acquired. The greater diversity of collection as indicated by the number of titles may attract more individuals to the library. For our purposes, attendance and reference question usage information would have been more attractive usage measures.

It might be interesting to try to use the coefficients of services in the usage regressions as measures of library effectiveness. The cost of increasing each type of service might be estimated. Some method for valuing the use might be devised, and some marginal benefit cost ratios for the different services might be stated. Using the coefficient on acquisitions in the circulation regression in table 2.6 suggests that if a circulation is worth more than one-tenth the cost of acquiring an additional volume, additional acquisitions should be made. On average, the systems may be acquiring too few materials. While the coefficient of titles in the cardholder regression suggests that an additional thousand titles would attract 493 additional cardholders per 100,000 population, it is difficult to imagine what the value of an additional cardholder might be. Other important library uses are not examined, and so a complete assessment of the relative efficiency of the average library service in choosing a mix of services is impossible with this cross system evidence.

3

Labor Costs

Labor expenses dominate library budgets, although they are a smaller fraction of library expenditures than of many local government services. Labor expenditures constitute about 63 percent of total library operating budgets, on an average, a fraction that is substantially smaller than that for police or fire departments.[1]

The rates of compensation for library employees are very important in determining the character of library service. In chapter 2, a statistically significant negative association was found between librarian compensation levels and the number of hours of service in branches: libraries with high labor costs seem to economize by reducing hours. Therefore, it is appropriate to investigate the pattern of compensation levels for library employees across library systems, in order to understand the forces shaping library services.

This chapter first discusses the measurement of compensation and possible sources of variation in compensation. Then some evidence on the influence on compensation levels of collective bargaining, the cost of living, and city finances is presented.

MEASURING LABOR COMPENSATION

The central component of labor compensation is salary. Because salaries differ with skill, experience, and responsibility, it is necessary to compare salaries for comparable positions. Three benchmark positions are used for comparison purposes here: a recruit clerical worker, a recruit librarian, and a librarian with five years' experience. These three benchmark positions represent three different points on the range of skills employed in the library. The other elements of compensation are the hours in the work week and the value of fringe benefits on average relative to base salary.

The job descriptions for the three benchmark positions may differ somewhat from library to library but some effort is made to identify uniform characteristics across systems. Usually, a recruit librarian is called a librarian I. Most libraries require a Master of Library Science degree from a school of librarianship accredited by the American Library Association.[2] Because for any opening for a librarian, there are likely to be thirty or forty applicants, any public library can hire master's degree holders in library science.[3] Of course, those systems that pay more will be able to select from better quality applicants than those paying less, other things equal, because not all recruit librarians are the same. Because of an overproduction of trained librarians, some master's degree librarians may hold positions in libraries not requiring advanced training, that is, clerical positions. They may be given some preference when positions for librarians become vacant.

The mean salary for a recruit librarian was $11,636, with no statistically significant difference across the geographic types, as indicated in table 3.1. This compares with the average of $10,929 for new librarians employed in public libraries reported in the *Library Journal* survey for 1977.[4] The large urban public libraries surveyed pay somewhat more than the average public library. Among surveyed libraries, the annual salary for a recruit librarian varied from $8,820 in San Antonio to $13,906 in Hennepin County, Minnesota.

The second benchmark position is that of a librarian with five years' experience and who received normal promotions. Usually, this is taken to be the third salary step for a librarian II position, although salary schedules vary in design. The mean salary observed for librarians with five years' experience was $14,209. The annual salaries ranged from a low of $10,180 in Nashville to a high of $18,635 in Minneapolis. Experience seems to be important in librarian compensation.

The third benchmark position is that of the recruit clerical worker, usually called a clerk I position. The average salary for the recruit clerical worker was $6,909 across the thirty-one library systems interviewed in 1978. The annual salaries range from under $5,500 in Nashville and Pittsburgh to over $9,100 in Philadelphia and Contra Costa County, California. There is no statistically significant difference across the geographic groupings of the libraries, as indicated in table 3.1.

The cost of employing an additional worker in a public library system includes the provision of fringe benefits. The interview asked for the value of fringe benefits relative to base salary. The response is an average, or the figure that applies to a recruit librarian. Fringe benefits may not be in the same ratio to salary for all employees. Fringe benefits average 20.76 percent of base salary across the thirty systems reporting this information. The figure varies

Table 3.1. Averages of Labor Variables by Geographic Type (standard deviations in parentheses)

	City	Metropolitan	Suburban	All	$F_{(2,28)}$
Recruit librarian salary	$11,684	$11,412	$11,821	$11,636	0.225
	($1,190)	($1,132)	($1,586)	($1,237)	
Librarian salary after 5 years	$14,835	$13,315	$14,414	$14,299	1.506
	($2,215)	($1,887)	($2,026)	($2,121)	
Recruit clerical salary	$7,085	$6,589	$6,941	$6,909	0.584
	($1,186)	($881)	($1,121)	($1,077)	
Fringe benefits as a percentage of salary[a]	22.42	18.04	20.94	20.76	1.305
	(5.99)	(8.03)	(4.22)	(6.42)	
Hours of work per week for white collar workers	38.00	39.22	39.64	38.73	2.386
	(2.15)	(1.72)	(0.94)	(1.91)	
Percentage of librarians in area employed in system[b]	10.91	17.34	3.92	11.20	13.550***
	(4.97)	(6.81)	(1.72)	(6.94)	
Proportion requiring residency (binary)	0.47	0.44	0.00	0.35	2.683*
Proportion with collective bargaining (binary)	0.53	0.33	0.29	0.42	0.755
Percentage of state and local employees who are organized (state average)[c]	56.11	47.77	56.27	53.72	1.365
	(12.50)	(15.93)	(8.15)	(12.99)	

					F
Cost of Living Index[d]	102.50	95.67	102.29	100.32	2.342
	(0.62)	(5.74)	(3.73)	(8.00)	
Monthly teacher earnings	1,073.47	1,015.00	1,127.71	1,068.74	0.865
	(212.33)	(118.87)	(112.33)	(170.35)	
Percentage area white collar employed female	30.60	31.90	31.13	31.10	1.831
	(1.54)	(2.08)	(0.89)	(1.65)	
Intergovernmental revenues per capita net of the library[c]	178.71	186.52	167.29	178.40	0.041
	(176.64)	(75.71)	(47.85)	(128.83)	
Own expenditures per capita net of the library expenditures[c]	382.39	339.62	295.28	350.31	0.628
	(214.06)	(97.04)	(143.22)	(171.03)	
Number of library systems	15	9	7	31	

Source: The author's survey. Data for selected variables are reported in appendix A.

[a] Not available from Chicago.

[b] Denominator is from the 1970 *Census of Population.*

[c] 1972 *Census of Governments*; data are for Standard Metropolitan Statistical Areas.

Note: The F-statistic tests for significant differences across the geographic groups relative to variation within groups. Statistical significance is indicated: ***0.01 level; **0.05 level; *0.10 level. Numbers below *F* are the degrees of freedom.

from 8.5 percent in Atlanta to 32 percent in Brooklyn. Of the systems surveyed, 80 percent participate in social security; Atlanta was not among them.

The number of hours of work per week also is important to understanding compensation levels. If compensation levels are to be compared across systems, differences in hours of work must be accounted for. In some systems the work week differs between white and blue collar workers; white collar hours are examined here. The mean hours worked per week was 38.73 for the systems interviewed. There seems to be some weak tendency for the central city systems to have shorter work weeks than the metropolitan and suburban systems. Twenty of the thirty-one systems have 40-hour weeks; Boston, Buffalo, Brooklyn, New York, and New Orleans have 35-hour weeks; another six have 37.5- or 38-hour weeks.

LABOR MARKET ISSUES

The comparison of the important features of employee compensation across the large public library systems reveals substantial variation in the elements of compensation. While the range of variation is not as great as that found for fire fighters, it is important enough to induce changes in the operation of libraries.[5] Therefore, we are interested in learning more about the sources of variation in compensation.

Six labor market issue areas seem important in examining patterns of compensation of library employees. Each is mentioned briefly here, and discussed in more detail below. First, the terms of employment may condition compensation, as for example, when residency in a jurisdiction is required. Second, professionalism may play a role, as for example in the responsibilities given to master's level librarians. Third, the sex ratio of employment may be of significance. The *Library Journal* survey shows that female recruit librarians, on average, earn somewhat less than males.[6] Fourth, the nature of the local labor market may have some influence. If compensation levels are high in jobs of comparable skill in the metropolitan area, the library may have to pay more to attract workers. Fifth, the nature of local government finances may have a bearing on compensation patterns of library employees. Cities that spend a lot on other services may have less to spend on libraries and so may pay less to library employees. Sixth, employees may participate in collective bargaining, and the determinants of compensation levels may differ with collective bargaining.

Terms of Employment

Just under half of the city and metropolitan library systems studied require that their employees live in the jurisdiction. None of the suburban systems have such requirements. To the extent that employees would rather live elsewhere than in the jurisdiction and labor markets are competitive, the library system would be expected to have to pay more in order to induce such workers to accept employment. Because there are many applicants for most library positions, the library may use the residency requirement as a partial screening criterion. The residency requirement may therefore have little association with salary.

There may be other terms of employment that influence compensation. If pensions are funded and vested they may be more valuable. Workers may view their jobs differently if they have civil service protection. The value of vacation, sick leave, and holidays may not be reflected in the value of fringe benefits, and so may influence compensation levels. Of these items, only the residency requirement is examined in this study.

Professionalism

The successful operation of a library takes skill. As with many professions, library workers historically gained their skill through experience in operating libraries. Then formal education became a prerequisite for employment and substituted to some degree for job experience.[7] In most libraries at the present time, a master's in library science degree is a prerequisite to employment as a librarian. Since formal education in librarianship and experience in libraries are both important to libraries, we would expect compensation levels to be higher for librarians with both more education and experience. Examining salaries for recruit librarians and for librarians with five years' experience should control for the main differences in entrance qualifications and experience.

The skill requirements of library work, however, may play another role. Experience in a library setting may be important in promoting a career in library work. Experience in a more sophisticated library operation may be more valuable careerwise than experience in a routine library position. Therefore, librarians might accept somewhat lower compensation in an entry level position in library systems that offer more professional development and promotion opportunities than another, just as assistant professors are paid less at prestigious universities. It is possible, for example, for a subject area specialist in the main library in a large system to move into an important position in an academic library, or vice versa. The strong career potential of otherwise similar entry positions in the public libraries would be expected to be associated with lower salaries for recruits.

On the other hand, many library systems may not make the most of the skills of master's degree librarians. A system with a large proportion of professionals may have professionals performing tasks that are performed just as well by nonprofessionals in other systems. For example, master's degree librarians mount microfilm reels for patrons in one library system. They may also perform routine clerical chores in some systems. Thus, the specific duties of jobs with similar descriptions and education-experience prerequisites may differ across systems. The recruit professional librarians in systems with a higher proportion of professionals seem likely to have less responsibility, and to perform more tasks for which their education is not required, than recruits in a system with a smaller proportion of professionals. If compensation reflects actual job requirements, lower compensation for recruit librarians might be found in systems with a higher proportion of professional employees.

Some library systems have designated some positions for paraprofessionals, persons with librarianship training short of the master's degree. Presumably, systems with more paraprofessionals employ fewer professionals. The professionals concentrate on tasks that require their more specialized skills. Systems with more paraprofessionals would be expected to pay recruit librarians more than systems with more professionals. This study does not examine paraprofessionals separately.

Professionalism suggests that compensation will be lower at the recruit level, but higher for librarians with more experience, in libraries with more professionals. Entry positions that offer better on-the-job-training experiences and opportunity for career advancement should receive lower pay for that reason. Systems that use persons in professional positions for tasks that do not require professional training might be paid less, reflecting lower productivity. At the senior ranks, higher compensation would be expected where supervision of more professionals is found and more sophisticated library skills are required. The role of professionalism in determining compensation levels may be difficult to distinguish because causality may also run the other way. High rates of compensation might induce a library to substitute nonprofessional for professional job positions—for example, paraprofessionals. The proportion of employees working in public services who are professionals is taken as a rough indication of the professional orientation of the library.

Sex Ratio of Employment

There are many more female librarians than males. In recent years, males have constituted about 22 percent of the graduates of library schools. Historically, female-dominated occupations have had lower compensation levels than male-dominated occupations with similar skill requirements. It is difficult to distinguish the extent to which this pattern is due to discrimination from the extent to which it may be due to other causes. The purpose of this study, however, is not to compare the compensation of librarians with that of other occupations, but rather to examine differences in the rate of compensation of librarians in different public library systems.

While salary levels of those who work in public libraries are somewhat lower than those for academic, school, or other libraries on average, the sex ratio of recruits is about the same—about 22 percent male.[8] Public libraries as a group do not seem to have exhibited any particular tilt with respect to sex in recruitment of new librarians. On the other hand, many fewer than half of the directors of the libraries interviewed were female; thus perhaps promotion prospects differ by sex across the libraries. It is still possible that individual public libraries recruit only female librarians in order to pay less. The causality may run the other way as well, however: libraries paying less may find that they hire a greater proportion of females because female job alternatives also pay less. This particular issue is not addressed because the determination of sex ratio and of salary levels is likely to be simultaneous.

There is some evidence that the earnings of males are lower in metropolitan areas where female job opportunities are better. Apparently, households maximize family welfare jointly, and so one spouse may accept lower earnings if job prospects for the other partner are better.[9] Salary levels may, therefore, be lower in a female-dominated occupation like librarianship in metropolitan areas where there are more female jobs, especially in white-collar occupations. Expected total family income will be higher because of the greater likelihood of better jobs for the female. While other jobs for females are not perfect substitute positions for librarians, many persons with library training do hold nonlibrarian jobs. Consequently, the nature of alternative white-collar job opportunities for females may influence the salary levels for librarians in public libraries. The proportion of white-collar employees in the metropolitan area who are female is used to indicate the extent of female job opportunities in the area. The average, 31.1 percent, varies somewhat by geographic type as indicated in table 3.1.

Local Labor Market

Although librarians have specialized training and skills, the salary levels may be influenced by local labor market conditions. The cost of living varies across metropolitan areas such that libraries have to pay more in areas where living costs are higher. The Bureau of Labor Statistics prepares an index of the cost of living for each of thirty-nine metropolitan areas across the country and is available for the areas studied here.

Compensation levels in occupations with similar skill levels may also influence salary determination. On the one hand, in a competitive labor market, the compensation in comparable occupations may reflect labor market conditions and opportunities for library employees. In a collective bargaining environment, levels of compensation in comparable occupations may serve a pattern-setting role. Public library salaries may be linked to salaries elsewhere in local government. In fact, the salary scale and fringe benefit level may be determined entirely outside the library for both clerical and professional employees. Librarian salaries, in particular, may be linked to the salary scale of similar positions in the local school system. In the school system, the librarian salary may be simply the same as that of a teacher with the same education and experience. This seems to be the case in Nashville, and may be the situation in many areas. Unfortunately, the interview survey did not explore this issue in detail. Nevertheless, the average monthly earnings of teachers as reported in the 1972 Census of Governments can be used as a rough indication of compensation levels in metropolitan school systems. Salary levels for master's degree school librarians would be preferred, but these are not readily available.

Public librarians, unlike school librarians, have shifts and specific hours of work per week. No information is available about the hours of work per week in school systems. The average hours worked per week by draftsmen in each metropolitan area indicates local labor market conditions with respect to hours. If local markets have patterns in the hours of work, the draftsmen hours should reflect them.

The metropolitan area might be viewed as the relevant labor market for librarians. If the public library system employed a substantial proportion of the librarians working in the metropolitan area, it might have some monopsony power in hiring. If the library recognized that it would have to raise the earnings of all present workers in order to hire an additional worker, it would have monopsony power. With monopsony power, the library might choose to keep salary levels below what might be required to fill vacancies.

Comparing the employment of professional librarians in the surveyed systems with the number of librarians found in the metropolitan area in the 1970 Census of Population reveals that the systems on average employ about 11 percent of the librarians living in the metropolitan area. The metropolitan systems average over 17 percent. The highest figure, which is close to 26 percent, is that for Indianapolis. Even 26 percent seems too small a proportion of the librarians to give the public library significant monopsony power, and so, this hypothesis is not explored further. Fairfax County, Virginia, employs only about 2 percent of the librarians living in the Washington, D.C., metropolitan area. If school librarians were included, however, the potential for monopsony effects would be greater.

Perhaps the most important advantage for a public library's professional employees is other librarian positions. In the Washington, D.C., area, the federal salary scale for librarians may have a substantial impact on compensation levels of librarians in that metropolitan area, either through competition in the market place or as a pattern setter in collective bargaining.

Local Fiscal Circumstances

The local government's fiscal circumstances may influence the salary levels of public library employees, but the relationship may be complex. On the one hand, higher levels of expenditures on other services might indicate a greater willingness to support local government by taxpayers. Some cities may be "big spenders"; i.e., they buy more of all services and pay public employees higher salaries. Perhaps the nature of the local political system encourages expansion of activities.

On the other hand, higher levels of spending on other services may reduce the funds available for the library. If all the services feed from the same public trough, more for police, education, and streets may mean less for the library. The nature of the local political process and the interaction among agencies competing for local tax dollars are too difficult to characterize to make any detailed investigation possible. Per capita expenditures from local sources on services other than libraries are related to library labor compensation to make a small step in understanding the relationship of libraries to the local fiscal scene. Own expenditures averaged $350 per capita in the 1972 Census of Governments in the areas surveyed.

In addition to raising funds locally, local governments receive funds from senior levels of government. Such intergovernmental transfers may influence salary levels in public libraries. Higher levels of intergovernmental transfers might allow public library employees to be paid higher salaries along with other public employees. Many intergovernmental transfers are tied to particular functions, and may impose a variety of restrictions on their use. For example, state aid to education may require matching local funds. A high level of such aid may induce a larger share of local funds to go to education than would otherwise be the case. In this environment, a high level of intergovernmental transfers—matching aid to education—may cause library expenditures to be lower than otherwise. Some intergovernmental transfers may be tied to library expenditures. Some states have per capita grants to localities for the operation of public libraries. Such funds might cause library expenditures to be higher and allow libraries to pay higher salaries. The Census of Governments does not provide detailed information about the restrictions on intergovernmental aid, and so detailed hypotheses about the role of intergovernmental transfers cannot be explored very easily. Nevertheless, per capita intergovernmental transfers are related to salaries. Intergovernmental transfers averaged $178 per capita.

Other features of local government might also have some impact on salaries. Libraries that are autonomous may have more flexibility in salary determination than libraries that are departments of city government, but not necessarily. Libraries with earmarked taxes may have less interaction with the rest of local government, and so may be immune from losses at the expense of other agencies, but not necessarily. If the earmarked funds do not provide the full cost of the library, the main shape of the library's expenditures may come from the effort to seek incremental dollars from the local general budget. The characterization of the local fiscal scene used here is quite primitive.

Collective Bargaining

The librarians in thirteen of the thirty-one libraries surveyed are covered by collective bargaining agreements. Blue-collar workers may be covered by separate collective bargaining agreements, and somewhat more systems may bargain with blue-collar workers than with white-collar workers. Collective bargaining may allow workers to induce employers to pay higher levels of compensation than would otherwise be the case.

The public library is frequently part of a citywide bargaining unit covering both clerical and professional employees. The library employees may have no direct contact with library management in salary negotiations when a citywide labor contract is formed. Jobs in the library may be linked to other city positions via job classification systems. The existence of collective bargaining may forge those links. The salary levels in the library may then largely be given to the library by the city. Civil service rules may have something of the same effect even without collective bargaining.

The compensation of local government employees in a particular city may be affected by the vigor of union activity among state and local government employees statewide. Public employee union activity often works through state legislatures to create laws that enhance prospects for local government employee union activity, and that create statewide retirement systems and other fringe benefits. In addition, local government employee union activity elsewhere in a state may have a pattern-setting effect for cities without collective bargaining. These hypotheses are tested by examining the relationship between the proportion of state and local government employees in the state who are covered by collective bargaining and the compensation of librarians. The average of the states with library systems studied is 53.7 percent as indicated in table 3.1.

There have been few instances of job actions by library employees. In general, the library employees seem less militant than police, fire fighters, and teachers. The closing of the public libraries due to a strike poses less threat to public health and safety than strikes by sanitation workers or fire fighters. This fact may help explain both the lower profile of library union activity and the formation of citywide bargaining units. The threat of a citywide strike by white-collar workers is more significant than the threat of a library strike.

LABOR MARKET FINDINGS

Some of the relationships among labor market variables are examined by means of simple correlation coefficients, as in table 3.2. The correlations among the three salaries are significantly positive. Libraries that pay high salaries in one position, tend to be paying higher salaries across all categories.

Hours of work and the fringe benefit rate show only a weak association with salaries, but hours and fringe benefits are associated. All of the elements of compensation show a significant correlation with the cost of living except the salary of librarians with five years' experience. Average earnings of teachers in the metropolitan area, and the presence of collective bargaining, show expected strong correlations with library compensation. The residency requirement shows little correlation with library compensation levels. The percentage of white-collar employment in the metropolitan area that is female shows some negative association with professional salaries.

Simple correlations are difficult to interpret because the correlations may result from a variety of factors. For example, since collective bargaining tends to be found in cities with high costs of living, the simple correlation between salaries and cost of living may reflect, in part, the influence of collective bargaining. It is more revealing to try to control all the separate influences at once in order to isolate the effect of each, given the others. Therefore, the five elements of compensation are related to explanatory variables in multiple regressions in table 3.3.

Some of the hypotheses previously discussed are examined in the regressions. The residency requirement shows no statistically significant relationship with professional salaries, but does show the expected relationships with hours of work, fringe benefits, and clerical salary. Perhaps these elements of compensation, along with the residency requirement, are determined citywide rather than reflecting simply the circumstances of the library.

Professionalism was predicted to be associated with lower salaries for recruits and higher salaries for experienced librarians. The proportion of public service employees who were professional librarians, included in the regressions, showed no statistically significant relationship with any of the elements of compensation and did not change either the coefficients of the other variables or the overall explanatory power of the regressions very much. There seems to be no support here for any impact of professionalism on compensation. The percent professional variable is excluded from the reported regressions for two reasons. First, the percent professional may be viewed as an endogenous variable. That is, the level of compensation of library employees may influence the proportion of employees who are professional as well as the other way around; thus the direction of effect may be unclear. Second, the sample size for the analysis is relatively small, and the inclusion of a questionable variable reduces the number of degrees of freedom.

The proportion of white-collar workers in the metropolitan area who are female shows a statistically significant negative association with all three salary categories, as expected. Apparently, public libraries may pay less when white-collar job opportunities for females in a metropolitan area are better. Note that the expected earnings of females may be greater in such cities because of the greater likelihood of finding a white-collar job. This is consis-

Table 3.2. *Correlations among Selected Labor Cost Variables*

	Variable								
Variable	Recruit Librarian Salary	5-Year Librarian Salary	Recruit Clerical Salary	Weekly Hours of Work	Fringe Benefit as Percentage of Salary	Cost of Living	Compensation in Teaching	Collective Bargaining	Residence Required
5-year librarian salary	0.7211***								
Recruit clerical salary	0.3694***	0.4715***							
Weekly hours of work	0.0851	-0.0479	-0.2327						
Fringe benefit as a percentage of salary	0.2007	0.0913	0.2837*	-0.4490***					
Cost of living	0.3358**	0.1625	0.5873***	-0.5373***	0.6220***				
Compensation in teaching	0.4899***	0.4622***	0.5667***	-0.3375**	0.3696***	0.7133***			
Collective bargaining (binary)	0.3017*	0.3585**	0.6349***	-0.2929*	0.3474**	0.5551***	0.6812***		
Residence required (binary)	-0.1282	0.0109	0.1505	-0.2142	0.2843*	-0.0133	-0.0013	0.0529	
Percentage area white collar employment female	-0.3480*	-0.2681*	-0.1615	0.0712	0.0023	-0.1899	-0.1192	0.1020	0.3698**

Note: Statistical significance is indicated: ***0.01 level; **0.05 level; *0.10 level. Variables are as defined in Table 3.1. All correlations are based on thirty-one library systems except those involving fringe benefits. Chicago did not report a fringe benefit rate, so only thirty library systems are included in those correlations.

Table 3.3. Labor Cost Regressions (30 Library Systems)

Explanatory Variable	Expected Signs of Coefficients of Salary and Fringe Benefit Regressions	Salaries			Fringe Benefits as Percentage of Salaries	Hours of Work per Week
		Recruit Librarian	Librarian Five Years Experience	Recruit Clerical		
Cost of living	+	−5.317 (−0.095)	10.116 (0.130)	85.366** (2.285)	0.086 (0.440)	−0.085* (−1.379)
Percentage of area white collar employment female	−	−222.976* (−1.342)	−369.378* (−1.601)	−160.137* (−1.459)	−0.054 (−0.095)	0.143 (0.654)
Monthly teacher earnings, 1972	+	3.012 (1.150)	2.039 (0.560)	−0.897 (−0.519)	0.005 (0.512)	
Hours of work by draftsmen	+					1.310* (2.054)
Collective bargaining (binary)	+	215.032 (0.274)	2344.165** (2.157)	1561.074*** (3.021)	−4.992 (−1.838)	−0.232 (−0.292)
Percentage of government employees in state who are organized	+	7.894 (0.276)	−0.550 (−0.560)	−33.429 (−1.764)	0.338*** (3.395)	0.018 (0.473)
Residency required (binary)	+	−62.442 (−0.114)	236.359 (0.315)	513.320** (1.440)	3.994** (2.131)	−1.387** (−1.973)
Own expenditures per capita	+/−	−0.603 (−0.348)	−4.246* (−1.766)	−0.883 (−0.773)	0.007 (1.176)	0.002 (1.238)
Intergovernmental revenues per capita	+/−	−0.969 (−0.416)	−6.166* (−1.904)	−0.496 (−0.322)	0.005 (0.558)	0.001 (0.190)
Constant		15772.660	24069.830	5645.513	−11.869	−10.555
R^2		0.338	0.554	0.624	0.697	0.530
$F_{(8,21)}$		1.342	3.262**	4.361***	6.037***	2.957**

Note: Each column reports the coefficients of a regression of the dependent variable indicated at the top on the explanatory variables listed along the side. Numbers in parentheses are t-statistics. One- or two-tailed tests applied as indicated by expected signs. Opposite sign expected in regression of hours. The statistical significance of the coefficients is indicated: ***0.01 level; **0.05 level; *0.10 level.

tent with the rate of earnings in each white-collar job being somewhat lower. On average, the annual recruit librarian salary is $223 lower for each additional percentage point of female white-collar job opportunities.

Conditions in the local labor market are indicated by the cost of living index and by the monthly earnings of teachers. When other factors are accounted for, the cost of living index is found to be associated with the salaries paid recruit clerical workers and with hours of work. The $85.37 salary increment for each point of the price index is somewhat less than a one percentage point increase in salary for the average recruit clerical worker.

The monthly teacher earnings show no association with compensation levels in the public libraries. This nonfinding probably reflects the weakness of the measure of teacher earnings. If the specific salary paid a comparable position in the relevant school system were known, a strong association might be found. Similarly, if the fringe benefit rate of school employees were known, a link to the fringe benefits paid library employees might be found. Such detailed information is difficult to find. On the other hand, the link between hours worked at the library and hours worked by draftsmen in the area suggests that the terms of employment at the library are influenced by local larbor market conditions.

The fiscal circumstances of the local government show no association with compensation levels except for the salary of librarians with five years' experience. Higher levels of both own expenditure and of intergovernmental aid per capita are associated with lower salaries for experienced librarians. There is no evidence that "big spender" cities spend more on libraries as well as on other services, and spend more on salaries as well as in buying more service. Rather, the cities that spend more per capita on other services seem to pay somewhat lower salaries to experienced librarians. This evidence is consistent with increases in spending on other services crowding the library budget. In chapter 2, however, per capita library expenditures in 1972 were found to be positively associated with expenditures on other activities. (See table 2.3.) The evidence on interfunction competition is not overwhelming.

Intergovernmental transfers per capita also show a negative association with salaries for experienced librarians, just as they did with per capita library expenditures. This result is consistent with restrictions on intergovernmental aid on balance drawing funds away from library budgets and salaries. Obviously more detailed information about intergovernmental transfers and the limits on their use are necessary to test this hypothesis conclusively.

Libraries with collective bargaining pay statistically significantly higher salaries to recruit clerical workers and to experienced librarians. No association is found with recruit librarian salaries and with hours of work. Surprisingly, the coefficient on collective bargaining in the fringe benefit regression has a negative sign. The impact of collective bargaining on clerical workers may reflect the importance of citywide bargaining for clerical workers. The differential importance of collective bargaining for experienced librarians relative to recruits may reflect the fact that employees with more seniority may carry more influence in bargaining than new workers who have no voice in bargaining.

The $2,344.17 estimated collective bargaining differential for experienced librarians amounts to 16.4 percent of the average salary of librarians with five years' experience. The $1,561.07 differential for recruit clerical workers is about 22.6 percent of their average salary. If the $215.03 coefficient for a recruit librarian were accepted as correct, even though it is not statistically significantly different from zero, it might be compared with the mean salary for recruit librarians. It is about 1.8 percent of average recruit salary. Thus, collective bargaining seems to have yielded significant gains in salary for certain categories of library employees.

While local collective bargaining seems strongly associated with higher salaries, the more important is collective bargaining in the public sector statewide, the higher are fringe benefits. In fact, a state with 10 percent more government employees covered by collective bargaining seems to have higher public library fringe benefits by about 3.38 percentage points. This finding is consistent both with increased political effectiveness by public employees at the state level and with a pattern-setting effect of union gains in one area influencing the fringe benefits elsewhere in the state. Further exploration of these hypotheses is beyond the scope of the present study.

Overall, the explanatory power of the regressions is substantial. Only the regression for the recruit librarian salaries is not statistically significant overall. Factors other than those measured must be important in determining the salaries of recruits. Perhaps the salaries paid recruit librarians elsewhere in the metropolitan area are especially important for this entry level position. More important may be the long queue for recruit librarian positions.

SUMMARY

Compensation levels of library employees vary across library systems in ways that conform to expectations. Differences in labor market conditions and cost of living differences across areas are important. The fiscal circumstances of local government, while not observed in much detail, do bear some relationship to compensation levels. Collective bargaining is associated with higher salaries for both clerical workers and experienced librarians. These forces are important in shaping library costs and in inducing changes in library operations. The prices public libraries pay for labor services, however, may be largely given to the library by a city civil service system or collective bargaining agreement. The library itself may have little influence on these prices.

4

Efficiency in Public Services

The era of fiscal austerity and Proposition 13 have increased the interest in determining the efficient level of local government services. Of all the public services, public libraries are more vulnerable to cutbacks because the closing of libraries does not immediately threaten public health or safety. Cutbacks in fire, police, and sanitation services, in contrast, do threaten public health and safety immediately.

Public library budgets are subject to wide swings. For example, the Buffalo-Erie County Public Library suffered a 27 percent budget cutback in 1977; 11 percent of the budget was restored in 1978. Such erratic budget changes tend to destroy the morale of library employees, disrupt orderly management, and disturb public habits of library use. Because library use and public sentiment toward libraries are not subject to such severe short-term swings, it would seem that decisionmakers do not examine any data before making changes. Budget officers may be experimenting to discover what effect different budget levels have on library operations.

Budget decisions often are made with little rationale. If specific requests were based on solid evidence, then formal evaluation methods might produce a more stable budget. Formal methods involve aggregation, abstraction, and wrestling with difficult problems of assigning values; formal methods do not replace informed judgment. However, a formal approach to budget evaluation can pinpoint the area in which judgment must be applied and thus help avoid the destructive pattern of budget instability that characterizes many public libraries.

Formal analysis can also provide insight into the efficient mixture of library expenditures. Changing the mixture may produce more benefits per dollar of expenditure. Rather than choosing between spending more and spending less, public library managers can use formal budget evaluations to guide them to spend more wisely.

STUDYING EFFICIENCY IN LIBRARIES

Efficiency is used here to mean deriving as much benefit as possible from expenditures, or, more commonly, "getting the most for your money." Benefits are consumer valuations of services; expenditures include the full social costs of activities. In competitive private markets, prices convey information about social costs. Consumers judge the level of service that makes them best off (e.g., if the price of a service is higher than they want to pay, they decide they are better off without the service). Producers use sales revenues as signals of how much to produce. However, when goods are provided collectively, as with public libraries, other means must be used to determine the efficient level of activity.

The decision rule for a pattern of expenditure that will make consumers best off is simply stated: the additional benefit from one dollar of expenditure should be just one dollar. If the additional benefit were greater than that, the total benefit net of costs would increase with the additional expenditure. That expenditure would thus be justified. If the additional benefit were less than one dollar, then reducing expenditures by that amount would reduce costs more than benefits. By cutting back, benefits net of costs would be increased. Of course, in order to operate the enterprise at all, total benefits must exceed total costs. But in most situations, the problem of choosing the most efficient level of operation—the level that makes consumers best off—is the problem of identifying the level of service at which the extra benefit of additional expenditure matches the cost.

The linkage between library expenditures and consumer benefits must be carefully defined and measured. First, how do expenditures generate services (the cost function)? Second, how much use is generated by the services (the production function)? Third, how do consumers value the different kinds of use (the valuation problem)? A review of previous efforts to evaluate library operations is contained in appendix C.

In the analysis that follows, cross-sectional evidence from the branch libraries of the New York Public Library is used to determine the efficient number of branches, books, and hours of service. The New York Public Library has been chosen because its large number of branches facilitates a statistical analysis. Analysis of the efficient size of the central library services requires a different methodology because the central facilities in library systems are unique within each system. Analysis of central facilities is not attempted here.

HOW MANY BRANCHES TO OPERATE?

The first priority in judging the efficiency of an urban library system is determining the efficient number of branches. The evaluation paradigm is straightforward: the benefits and costs of each branch are measured and compared. Each branch is considered in turn as the marginal branch. The actual use of each branch is valued from the consumer's point of view. Because the estimates of costs and benefits are approximations, choices are made so as to give low estimates of costs and high estimates of benefits within the range of plausible values.

The New York Public Library, a private, nonprofit research library, operates branch libraries under contract from the City of New York in three boroughs: Manhattan, the Bronx, and Staten Island (Richmond County). Because users of research libraries generally stay at the library, the services of research libraries are not close substitutes for the traditional public library services of the branches, and so they are ignored here. The branch libraries of New York offer services for handicapped persons throughout and beyond the city. Because the service to handicapped persons is also not a close substitute for the traditional library services, it too is excluded from the analysis.

The branches are classified as centers, regional libraries, and neighborhood libraries. The centers are the largest facilities; there is one in each borough, plus one for the whole system. The centers have an average book stock of over 120,000 volumes. The thirteen regional libraries have an average stock of 33,000 volumes. There are fifty-nine neighborhood libraries in the system; each has a permanent average book stock of 24,000 volumes and a staff. Two former neighborhood libraries that are operated at a marginal level, without a permanent book stock or staff, are not included in this analysis.

In all, the branch libraries operate seventy-six regular, general-purpose facilities with permanent book stocks and staff. They serve an area of 122 square miles that had a population of 3.3 million in 1970. Summary information for an average branch of each type and totals for all seventy-six facilities are reported in table 4.1. The three types of branches seem to differ in terms other than the size of the book stock. The centers have larger staffs and operate more hours than the regional libraries, and the regional libraries operate with larger staffs and are open more hours than the neighborhood facilities. The libraries also differ with respect to the proportion of professional staff: the larger units have more professional staff than the smaller

Table 4.1. *Branches of the New York Public Library*

Variable	Average for Type of Library			
	Neighborhood	Regional	Center	System
Stock	23,947	33,535	121,166	2,333,282
Additions	2,685	3,743	19,288	284,213
Professional staff	2.18	3.42	20.50	255
Other staff	3.89	5.46	23.88	396
Hours of service (annual)	1,002	1,389	2,733	88,082
Square feet	9,442	16,335	50,698	972,257
Adult circulation	54,357	84,724	456,364	6,133,933
Juvenile circulation	22,470	33,073	44,079	1,931,960
Adult reference	14,222	24,316	425,123	2,855,697
Juvenile reference	7,749	9,969	29,017	702,840
Total use [a]	112,856	173,638	1,046,163	13,100,480
Cost [b]	$200,108	$337,920	$2,041,436	$24,365,108
Use/Stock	4.55	5.10	10.255	4.94
Circulation/Stock	3.21	3.51	4.13	3.46
Cost/Use	2.45	2.59	1.72	2.43
Percent juvenile				
Circulation	29	28	09	24
Additions as percentage of stock	11	11	16	12
Professionals as percentage of staff	34	39	44	39
Number of locations	59	13	4	76

Source: The New York Public Library, 1976–77 flows, 1977 stocks.

[a]This includes reference questions plus 1.183 times circulation. The 1.183 factor is to take into account in-library use. It is an average figure from a survey of library users in a sample of fifteen neighborhood branches in the New York Public Library.

[b]Cost is based on the operating budget for each library. Reported budget figures anticipated for 1976–77 are adjusted for part-time staff shifts among branches as reported in library documents. In addition, Comprehensive Employment and Training Act employees are added in at $9,000 each. Operating costs are inflated by 20 percent to reflect the administrative overhead costs of the system. Rent payments actually paid are excluded from costs, but five dollars per square foot is included for each facility, reflecting an approximation to the annual lease value of space. Actual rentals varied from under three dollars to over nine dollars per square foot for the small number of facilities actually rented.

ones. Note, however, that the regional branches are much more like neighborhood branches than like centers.

The usage patterns of the three types of branches also differ. The amount of use per volume in stock is much larger for the library centers than for the regional libraries and somewhat larger for the regional than for the neighborhood libraries. This is true whether use is defined simply as circulation or as the sum of reference questions and then weighted for in-library use circulation. Consequently, the cost per use is lowest at the centers; it is somewhat lower at the neighborhood than at the regional facilities. The greater intensity of use probably reflects the fact that the larger facilities operate longer hours, have larger and more varied collections, add more new books to their stocks, and have a more professional staff. On the other hand, the neighborhood libraries circulate a larger share of juvenile materials than the library centers. Surprisingly, however, juvenile materials are about as important at regional libraries as at neighborhood locations. The proximity of the neighborhood branches does not seem to dominate the regional facilities with respect to juvenile use. Note that with seventy-six locations serving 122 square miles, the average branch serves 1.6 square miles. A circle with a radius of 0.71 miles subtends such an area.

Costs of Branches

The first step in defining efficiency is to analyze costs. We use 1976–77 budgeted costs of the branch library system of the New York Public Library. The operating costs for each facility include staff costs with fringe benefits and supplies; the budget for the acquisition of new materials inflated by 34 percent to account for system processing costs; and plant security and maintenance costs. The operating costs are modified in several ways to reflect actual social costs. First, the staff work part-time in other branches. An approximate net value for such reassignments is used to adjust the budget figures. Also, employees supported by Comprehensive Employment and Training Act funds are added in at $9,000 each. Second, operating costs for each facility do not include the administrative overhead costs for borough and system offices: 20 percent is added to approximate such costs. Third, the budget includes rent expenditure for fifteen facilities that are rented. In order to make the cost figures used in this study reflect the full social opportunity cost of the system, an annual lease value is assumed for each facility. Therefore, a $5 per square foot lease charge is included in the total costs. For this reason, the social cost figures used here exceed the budget for the library system by about $4 million. These cost figures are an attempt to estimate the full social costs of each facility, including the local budget, federal support, and the value of facilities owned by the library.

The costs of each facility can be related to the level of operation. The operations are summarized in three variables: annual hours of service, the total stock of materials (both book and nonbook), and the number of gross additions of stock during the year. The possibility that high levels of use raise costs, given hours and books, is ignored. The analysis reported in table 4.2 indicates that the marginal cost of an additional hour of service annually is approximately $2,317, that is, $44.56 for a single hour.[1] Maintaining an additional item in stock for a year is estimated to cost $3.93.[2] The acquisition of a new item has an estimated marginal cost of $7.31, including average processing costs.[3] While over half of the variation in costs across neighborhood branches is accounted for by the three operations variables, it is a little disappointing that more of the cost differences are not explained. In part, this weakness may stem from the fact that the budget and actual operations may not be for exactly the same time period, and that expenditures may be somewhat different from budgets.

Benefits of Branches

The second step in the evaluation of branch activities is the evaluation of library use. The New York Public Library records library use in more detail than many other libraries. Circulation of books and other materials outside each branch is recorded separately for adult and juvenile materials. In addition, the library tries to count the reference questions asked during several sample periods each year. Thus, the total number of reference questions asked can be estimated. The only major category of use that the library does not routinely monitor is attendance; thus, the in-library use of materials is not systematically known. The library has surveyed users of twenty-seven facilities in the system. Among users at fifteen neighborhood branches, 15.5 percent indicate they planned to use library materials in the library itself. If total materials used is defined as circulation times 1.183, then 15.5 percent of the materials are used in the library itself and 84.5 percent are used outside the library. In-library use for the sample libraries varied substantially from 5 to 31 percent of circulation; sample figures for attendance at every branch would improve the figure for library use. In this study, total use is the sum of reference questions, plus 1.183 times observed circulation.

The critical problem in making a judgment about efficiency is the valuation of use. We want to know what library use is worth to consumers. The prices of goods and services purchased in ordinary markets carry important information about the valuation consumers place on their purchases. If markets work appropriately, the prices will provide just the information a planner would want before deciding just how much of a service to supply. When charges are not made for a particular service, alternative methods must be used to decide what value consumers place on the services they consume. One way to establish such a value for library service is to identify the consumer's next best

Table 4.2.   *Results of Regression of Costs*
of 59 Neighborhood Branches
(dependent variable is 1976–77 budgeted costs adjusted
for staff reassignments and CETA employees)

Explanatory Variable	Coefficients
Constant	41,427.2**
	(1.76)
Hours	2,317.12*
	(1.64)
Stock	3.93***
	(4.30)
Additions in stock	7.41***
	(2.80)
R^2	0.53
$F_{3,55}$	20.63

Note: Numbers in parentheses are t-statistics. Statistical significance is indicated as follows: *0.10 level; **0.05 level; ***0.01 level all with one-tailed tests. The operating costs excluding rents of each branch are inflated by 20 percent to take into account system administration; five dollars per square foot of space added to this to take into account the social opportunity cost of the space. Numbers below F are degrees of freedom.

alternative and determine its cost to the consumer. The cost of the next best alternative is an approximation of the value of the service actually used.

The next best alternative to an individual branch library is the closest branch library. If a single branch were closed, its users would either discontinue their library use (perhaps buying more books or doing less reading) or visit the next most convenient branch library. For the user who would visit another library, the value of having a library nearby is simply the differential in travel time and cost of visiting a more distant library over visiting one nearby. As a rough average, the additional travel time and cost will be about the same as the cost of travel from the nearest library to the next nearest. For the user who would no longer use the library if the nearest branch were to close, the value of library service must be less than the cost of visiting the next nearest library. At a maximum, the value of the nearest library branch is the cost (time and money) of traveling to the next nearest library. Whether or not library use continues at the next nearest facility, the cost of travel to the next nearest facility is an upper bound estimate of the value of the services of the nearest branch.

The method of valuing library use by looking at the cost of the next best alternative defines a value for an individual branch considered by itself. It does not reveal the value of the full library system. If a single branch closes, some users will be diverted to other branches, and so the use of other facilities will change. In addition, the next nearest branch for some facilities may change when one facility is closed. Thus, the proposed method for valuing the library services is appropriate for valuing branches on an individual basis.

The value of a particular branch is then assumed to be the cost of traveling between that location and the next nearest facility. To calculate the travel time, two uses are assumed to occur on each round trip: straight-line distances are measured and it is assumed travel occurs at the rate of five miles per hour. Travel time is assumed to be valued at four dollars per hour. This implies a valuation of each library use of eighty cents for each mile from a particular branch to the next nearest branch. In addition, another fifty-cent transit fare is assumed for both ways of the round trip to the next nearest branch. For regional branches, the distance to the library centers is used. For the three borough centers, the Mid-Manhattan Library Center is assumed to be the alternative. No effort is made to value the services of the Mid-Manhattan Center.

According to this method of valuation, branches that are used more frequently and those located farther from other branch libraries provide more benefits than branches that are used less frequently and those located near other branches.

The valuation technique obviously does not give any clues as to the relative value of juvenile versus adult circulation, or of circulation versus reference versus in-library use. In order to account for the possibility that different uses will be valued differently, a second benefit calculation is made. Adult circulation is treated as described above in the base case when all use is valued the same, whereas juvenile circulation is assumed to be worth 50 percent more than adult, in light of the greater difficulty juveniles may have traveling to another library. Reference questions are valued at half the adult circulation rate because many questions can be answered by telephone. In-library use is treated as 15.5 percent of circulation, just as in table 4.1.

The estimated benefits and costs of the branches of the New York Public Library are reported in table 4.3. Of the fifty-nine neighborhood branches, twelve are estimated to have benefits greater than costs while forty-seven have benefits less than costs. Of the twelve with positive net benefits, six are in Staten Island, five are in the Bronx, and only one is in Manhattan. Of the forty-seven neighborhood branches with negative net benefits, twenty-six have benefits that are $100,000 less than costs. Of these twenty-six branches, twenty-two are within one mile of the next nearest branch, including seven that are within a half mile of the next nearest branch. Thus, the close proximity of branches seems to be important in explaining the low level of benefits of many branches. A second factor, of course, is low levels of use.

Among the thirteen regional libraries, five show negative net benefits according to our extimates. Of these five, the Francis X. Martin Regional Library and the Grand Concourse Regional Library show a net negative difference between benefits and costs of more than $100,000. Martin Regional

Table 4.3. Costs and Benefits of Libraries

Neighborhood Libraries	Use	Benefits	Costs	Benefits minus Costs	Weighted Benefits minus Costs
Allerton	149,213	$ 172,974	$ 284,216	$ -111,242	$ -117,008
Baychester	320,393	444,526	361,976	82,550	89,938
Castle Hill	49,140	57,277	169,584	-112,307	-105,454
City Island	35,865	95,229	79,164	16,066	19,218
Clason's Point	105,979	133,603	252,800	-119,197	-107,885
Eastchester	74,739	89,483	127,316	-37,833	-37,842
Edenwald	112,016	183,249	196,890	-13,641	-3,138
High Bridge	78,991	84,559	199,228	-114,668	-105,291
Jerome Park	81,070	81,646	181,914	-100,268	-90,487
Kingsbridge	154,784	148,035	286,039	-138,004	-133,877
Melrose	66,452	87,986	199,903	-111,917	-98,110
Morrisania	56,223	74,442	231,827	-157,384	-151,526
Mosholu	184,716	245,041	231,476	13,565	12,814
Mott Haven	58,022	86,019	264,710	-178,691	-171,683
Parkchester	204,027	224,919	215,810	9,109	17,216
Pelham Bay	189,608	275,159	220,646	54,513	29,988
Riverdale	124,375	199,684	243,474	-43,790	-41,521
Sedgwick	33,838	32,999	86,198	-53,199	-46,494
Soundview	102,355	120,210	213,086	-92,876	-90,997
Spuyten Duyvil	162,451	155,368	217,758	-62,390	-55,963
Throgs Neck	111,748	204,912	214,446	-9,534	15,674
Tremont	34,213	36,622	174,123	-137,501	-132,230
Van Cortlandt	80,717	98,482	119,283	-20,801	-18,776
Van Nest	146,242	175,463	206,396	-30,933	-27,793

Wakefield	94,744	115,597	264,969	−149,372	−154,721
West Farms	40,603	53,761	240,609	−186,848	−189,956
Woodlawn Height	58,995	71,980	104,186	−32,206	−29,996
Woodstock	33,950	29,876	244,044	−214,168	−213,702
Aguilar	65,278	70,500	225,230	−154,730	−149,257
Cathedral	87,942	68,159	112,950	−44,791	−49,648
Chatham Square	260,821	203,441	275,499	−72,058	−46,496
Columbia	73,503	69,092	80,618	−11,525	−15,444
Columbus	42,130	50,556	163,982	−113,426	−114,233
Epiphany	263,446	222,348	282,484	−60,136	−61,833
58th Street	201,013	160,810	211,180	−50,370	−60,863
George Bruce	59,521	64,283	240,382	−176,099	−172,076
Hamilton Fish Park	68,141	61,327	200,422	−139,095	−137,866
Hamilton Grange	101,474	101,474	243,243	−141,768	−137,171
Harlem	27,598	23,403	151,338	−127,935	−128,995
Hudson Park	60,161	51,016	194,551	−143,534	−140,659
Kips Bay	175,492	143,903	229,370	−85,467	−84,808
Macomb's Bridge	18,514	16,293	35,579	−19,286	−17,163
Muhlenberg	119,197	125,395	204,631	−79,236	−87,120
115th Street	26,836	24,689	170,450	−145,761	−143,394
125th Street	27,511	23,439	209,441	−186,001	−186,611
Ottendorfer	91,007	75,062	176,954	−101,891	−103,650
Riverside	322,040	305,938	262,354	43,584	24,584
Seward Park	167,016	130,272	337,560	−207,288	−201,171
67th Street	102,051	97,969	211,648	−113,679	−115,784
Washington Heights	59,419	52,289	204,761	−152,472	−148,119
Webster	68,236	58,683	127,117	−68,434	−68,568
Yorkville	334,593	287,750	314,101	−26,351	−34,039
Dongan Hills	142,321	319,704	187,044	132,660	152,803
Great Kills	230,284	785,416	214,049	571,367	618,979

(continued)

Table 4.3. (continued)

Neighborhood Libraries	Use	Benefits	Costs	Benefits minus Costs	Weighted Benefits minus Costs
Port Richmond	127,721	205,123	192,477	12,646	8,980
Stapleton	64,964	108,116	126,786	−18,670	−14,898
Todt Hill	153,014	349,068	152,388	196,680	241,868
Tottenville	47,455	348,321	89,545	258,776	291,905
West New Brighton	124,362	199,725	146,193	53,532	50,612
Regional Libraries					
Bloomingdale	342,940	$ 857,349	$ 408,709	$ 448,640	$ 428,426
Countee Cullen	64,893	246,937	411,437	−164,500	−187,589
Fort Washington	142,199	810,533	325,543	484,990	460,702
Inwood	233,386	1,563,684	336,096	1,227,588	1,229,419
Jefferson Market	368,156	662,680	515,837	146,843	122,489
96th Street	132,648	298,511	286,223	12,288	25,631
St. Agnes	153,770	276,785	302,374	−25,588	−26,244
Tompkins Square	70,189	133,358	233,121	−99,763	−78,121
Francis Martin	116,793	147,253	363,278	−216,025	−200,464
Grand Concourse	87,464	160,165	326,584	−166,419	−152,629
Hunt's Point	101,933	319,091	285,383	33,708	42,787
Westchester Square	92,100	282,489	280,086	2,403	6,338
New Dorp	350,735	2,319,062	318,288	2,000,774	2,147,089
Library Centers					
Donnel	1,431,242	$1,395,747	$2,360,029	$−964,282	$−1,176,669
Mid-Manhattan	1,938,887	NA	NA	NA	NA
Fordham	460,163	3,543,255	678,892	2,864,363	2,480,005
St. George	354,359	2,809,644	478,950	2,330,694	1,874,776

Note: Use is the sum of reference questions plus 1.183 times circulation.

and Grand Concourse are about a mile apart; Martin Regional is within a mile of the Fordham Library Center. These facts may explain the low level of benefits indicated for these regional branches.

The Fordham and St. Georges Library Center show benefits that are substantially greater than costs. The valuation method does not allow an estimate of the benefit of the Mid-Manhattan Library, the largest library in the branch system. The Donnell Library Center shows negative net benefits, in part because it is within a mile of the Mid-Manhattan. The Donnell Library Center may have specialized collections for young adults, however, and so the Mid-Manhattan may not be a close substitute. The value method is more reliable in evaluating the neighborhood and regional facilities.

When use of juvenile materials is weighted 50 percent more than the use of adult materials, and reference questions are weighted at half the value of use of adult materials, the net benefit picture does not change much. Only the Throgs Neck Branch moves from negative net benefits to positive net benefits. The number of branches with net benefits less than negative 100,000 drops from twenty-six to twenty-four.

The estimates of benefits and costs presented here indicate that the New York Public Library operates many more branches than is efficient. Consumers of library services in New York City would probably be better off with fewer branches. The savings realized could be used either to lower taxes or increase other aspects of library services. Because the number of branches has grown since 1960 (as of this survey, an additional branch is planned), one might conclude that efficiency has not been the criterion for the design of this library system. Library systems in other older cities may also be overbranched (e.g., Chicago, Philadelphia, and San Francisco).

The analysis presented here could be improved in several ways. First, the estimates of use would be more accurate if attendance information were available for each location, even if only for sample periods. Second, the valuation of service might be improved with more detailed information about user travel time and costs.

HOW MANY HOURS TO OPERATE AND HOW MANY BOOKS TO KEEP IN STOCK?

The preceding analysis did not take into consideration the hours of operation, books in stock, and books added during the year. Because these characteristics of public library service are also very important budget items, it is appropriate to try to determine whether they are provided at efficient levels. Of the three steps in an efficiency calculation, the main emphasis here will be on determining how use varies with differences in service—namely, the quasi-production function.

Explaining Patterns of Use

Three characteristics of library service are related to use: the size of the stock, the number of additions to it during the last year, and the number of hours the facility is open. The size of the stock of materials in the library probably indicates the variety of materials available. Presumably, the larger the stock, the more likely that a user will find material of particular interest. Information from the branch libraries of the New York Public Library makes it possible to disaggregate the stock into adult and juvenile categories and book and nonbook (mostly recordings) categories. However, paperback stock volumes are not recorded for each facility. Therefore, the book stock figures understate stock by the amount of paperbacks on hand. Further disaggregation might be useful (for example, separating fiction and nonfiction), but only if use information were similarly broken down.

The number of materials added during the most recent year indicates how current the material is. Recently published materials (for example, bestsellers) are more in demand than older materials. Also, the library with a high volume of additions can respond to changes in users' tastes more quickly than the branch with a low volume of new materials, and should therefore be characterized by a higher rate of use. Additions are disaggregated in the same way as stock. No information about the addition of paperback books by branch is available.

Finally, the more hours the facility is open, the more accessible the materials are and the less planning a user must do in order to arrive when the library is open. The number of available hours per week is calculated by dividing the total number of hours of service for the year by fifty-two.

In addition to the three service characteristics just cited, one might also consider the proportion of staff that is professional. A predominantly professional staff may be better able to respond to reference questions than a non-professional staff, and may also play a role in improving the selection and presentation of materials. Libraries also sponsor programs, such as story hours, films, book talks, and the like. If these are viewed as promotional activity for the library, more programs might generate more library use. However, the proportion of professional staff and the number of programs offered appear to be secondary indicators of library use when compared with stock, additions, and hours; preliminary statistical investigations confirm this. Also, because only fifty-nine neighborhood libraries are available for observation, the cross-branch statistical study has limited power to make fine distinctions in many dimensions. Therefore, these two secondary characteristics have not been taken into account in this analysis.

Library use can be disaggregated in several ways. The characteristics of service may influence different types of use differently. The most commonly observed indicator of use is circulation outside the library. Cross-system studies must control for differences in circulation caused by differences in the length of the loan period and in renewal policy; renewals typically are counted as additional circulations. By using branches within one system, such variation does not arise. Circulation statistics are disaggregated into adult and juvenile, book and nonbook categories, as is the information on book stocks. The circulation figures, however, include the circulation of paperback materials, since library records do not distinguish between hard cover and paperback circulation. It is unfortunate that paperbacks are excluded from the stock figures but included in the circulation figures.

Circulation is only one component of library use; another is reference questions. During sample periods, the New York Public Library records the number of reference questions asked at each branch by adults and juveniles. Reference questions might be further disaggregated according to the skill and effort required to answer them. Such distinctions demand precise definitions and increase the cost of gathering the information. It is unusual for a library to keep detailed records of reference questions; this study benefits by the quality of information available from the New York Public Library.

The third major component of library use is how often materials and facilities are used in the library. For example, Newhouse and Alexander found that a substantial number of visitors to the Beverly Hills Public Library did not use any library materials, but simply used the facility as a study hall.[4] Thus, an important category of library use is not reflected in data on circulation and reference questions. The simplest approach to monitoring in-library use would be to collect attendance information at each location. Sample surveys might provide more detailed data on rates of use of materials in the library. Because the New York Public Library does not maintain branch attendance records, we are unable to explore how service characteristics affect in-library use.

In all, twelve measures of use are related to service characteristics: total circulation (book plus nonbook), book circulation, record circulation, and reference questions are each examined for adults, juveniles, and all users (adult plus juvenile). In terms of adult users, the stock and additions of adult materials are used as service characteristics; in regard to juvenile users, the stock and additions of juvenile materials are used. In examining the use of books, the stock and additions of books are used as service characteristics; for records, the stock and additions of records are used. Thus, each use is related to the most relevant feature of the service.

In addition to the service characteristics specific to each branch, the location of each library relative to others may influence use. Forty-one of the fifty-nine neighborhood branches are located within one mile of another library facility. In a survey at fifteen neighborhood branches, about one-sixth of neighborhood branch users indicated they live within ten blocks of the library they use. Library users do not seem to be clustered near the library. Therefore, it seems appropriate here to take explicitly into account the spatial relationship among branches. Hours of service is used as the most important service feature of competing branches. For each branch, the number of hours of service at every other branch is divided by the square of the distance between branches and summed. In the case of a branch located near other libraries offering many hours of service, the library interaction variable will be large. Where other libraries are distant and offer few hours of service, the library interaction variable will be small. A significant negative coefficient on the library interaction variable will indicate that the proximity of a competing branch tends to reduce library use at particular locations.

Library use is also determined by the tastes of people who live in the vicinity of the library. Berelson, for example, cites several studies indicating that library use tends to increase with income and decline with age.[5] Feldstein emphasizes the findings that use increases with education.[6] Because income and education are closely related, it is difficult to distinguish the two effects; however, income is used here. Age distribution is measured in terms of the percent of total population enrolled in school below the college level.

In addition, access to libraries may be influenced by the density of population in an area. Transit service, for example, may be better in a high-density area. People choosing to live in high-density areas may have tastes different from those of individuals living in low-density areas, even controlling for income and age distribution. The use figures are not deflated by population, so one would expect greater use in higher density areas. Other neighborhood population factors that may influence library use include ethnicity, sex, occupation, and length of employment. However, these characteristics are thought to be of secondary importance compared with population density, income, and school enrollment; preliminary statistical investigation confirms their secondary role. Because the neighborhood characteristic variables may reflect a constellation of neighborhood attributes, it is difficult to predict the signs of the coefficients of these variables; thus, two-tailed tests are applied.

Attribute Variables

Information about the three neighborhood attribute variables are available for 1970 by census tract. With over 700 tracts in the three boroughs, there is no obvious way to match tracts to libraries; the New York Public Library has approached the problem by defining catchment areas for each branch using census tracts. Several catchment areas are defined for planned branches or for branches that have been scaled down to station status. Some catchment areas, comprised of several tracts, are quite large, while others are small. Moreover, the assignment of tracts to branches ultimately involves some arbitrary decisions. Obviously, the residents of one tract may use several different branches, depending on their location in the tract and their preferences. Consequently, the catchment area notion is ignored here.

Indeed, the tract attributes are each divided by the square of the distance to each branch and summed over all tracts. Each borough is treated separately in this manner. By squaring distance, the attributes of nearby tracts are heavily weighted, while the value of attributes of distant tracts drops rapidly toward zero. Distance could be raised to some power other than two. (A study of individual library users might yield a more precise parameter value. But such an exercise is beyond the scope of the present study.) Because the tract attributes are entered in the estimated relationships as distance-weighted indices, the absolute value of their coefficients has no direct meaning.

The Simultaneity of Service and Use

The use relationship defined thus far purports to describe how users respond to library services. But the managers of the library may design the service in light of patterns of use. Thus, the correlation between circulation and book stock may reflect the fact that library managers provide large book stocks where use is known to be great. Since the evaluation of efficiency requires recognizing how user behavior responds to different services, it is necessary to distinguish user response functions from the choices made by library managers. Therefore, stock, additions, hours, and the spatial interaction variables are treated as endogenous; that is, partially determined by use patterns. The influence of library decisions can be purged from the user response function by a two-stage estimation technique. The first stage determines estimated values for the endogenous variables, using a set of instrumental variables that may influence the library manager's choices but which themselves do not influence use.

Three groups of variables are used as instruments. Each reflects an influence on library decisions other than the desire to meet the demands of users.

The first group is the cost of space. The cost of buying or leasing space for a library differs substantially within the city. More branches can be efficiently provided in low-cost areas than in high-cost areas. Because no index of the cost of space for small areas in the city is readily available, land use information is used. The percent of land in residential use and the percent of land in high-density areas with residential, industrial, and commercial use are entered as instruments relating to the cost of space.[7] The land use zone characteristics are weighted by the reciprocal of the squared distance to each library and summed. Census tract data on the value of housing units and contract rents for 1970 are also used.

The second group of variables reflects the fact that library managers may be responsive to political pressures. The percentage of votes for Mayor Beame in the 1973 election is used as an indicator of the political power of an area. This is, of course, a less-than-perfect measure of political power. The percentage of registrants voting was used in preliminary investigations, but it proved no better than the Beame vote variable. Political power is a subtle, shifting attribute, and ethnic ties are often more important than geography.

Although the mayor may be less important than other political figures, it nevertheless seems appropriate to include some measure of political activity, no matter how primitive. The Beame vote variable is recorded for a random sample of 987 electoral districts, weighted by the reciprocal of the square of the distance to each library and summed.

The third group of factors influencing library decisions consists of lagged values of the variables. Branches are costly to move or expand, and book stock is likely to expand to fill the available space. Moreover, additions to stock and hours of service may tend to follow past patterns. Thus, inertia in the design of the library system is substantial; the current pattern of branches, stocks, and hours is not likely to be modified instantly to respond to each variation in use. Therefore the hours, stock, and additions in 1960 are included as predetermined variables and used as instruments to estimate use relationships. In the case of eleven neighborhood branches that were not open in 1960, zeros are entered. (Two of these branches were closed for renovation in 1960.)

Findings on Patterns of Use

Estimates for use relationships are reported in tables 4.4 through 4.7: table 4.4 covers total circulation (book and nonbook), table 4.5 covers book circulation, table 4.6, record circulation, and table 4.7, reference questions. Each relationship is estimated for the fifty-nine neighborhood libraries. The regional branches and centers are excluded because they may offer a wider assortment of services not reflected in the service attributes measured. (In fact, results with regional libraries or with centers do differ somewhat from those for neighborhood branches alone.) An ordinary least squares (OLS) estimate and a two-stage least squares (TSLS) estimate are reported for each relationship. These statistical procedures are described in appendix B. One-tailed tests are applied to the four library attributes: positive coefficients are expected for stock, additions, and hours, while a negative coefficient is expected for library interaction. Two-tailed tests are applied to the other coefficients. (See appendix B for explanations.)

The most dramatic result is the relationship between use and hours of service; the amount of use a library experiences is significantly associated with the number of hours of service. Currently, the neighborhood branches average just under twenty hours per week of service, down from thirty-nine hours in 1960. The association between use and hours holds for both adult and juvenile materials, for books and records, and for reference questions.

Moreover, the result for hours persists in the two-stage estimates, where, for the most part, the influence of the other service attributes does not remain statistically significant. If the two-stage estimates are interpreted as the more correct estimates of user response, with the influence of library decisions

Table 4.4. Results of Regression of Book and Nonbook Circulation across 59 Neighborhood Branches

Explanatory Variable	Adult		Juvenile		Total	
	OLS	TSLS	OLS	TSLS	OLS	TSLS
Stock	2.147***	−0.068	0.829***	−1.006	0.842**	−1.298
	(3.379)	(−0.019)	(2.564)	(−0.375)	(2.011)	(−0.509)
Additions	4.544***	0.983	5.134***	24.889	3.400***	13.826
	(2.405)	(0.025)	(4.394)	(1.168)	(2.838)	(0.593)
Hours	5423.610***	8155.520***	1782.500***	3063.810*	8918.250***	11356.700***
	(8.437)	(2.769)	(6.766)	(1.493)	(11.996)	(2.937)
Library interaction	−9.680*	33.184	−5.851**	9.456	−16.174**	31.251
	(−1.539)	(0.70)	(−1.816)	(0.213)	(−2.332)	(0.456)
Population density	−18.887***	−24.030	−0.504	1.133	−24.618***	−23.067
	(−3.123)	(−1.388)	(−0.180)	(0.105)	(−3.817)	(−1.010)
Percent enrolled in school	−1.612**	−2.113	0.350	0.326	−1.406*	−1.440
	(−2.161)	(−1.195)	(0.853)	(0.161)	(−1.700)	(−0.543)
Income	4.582**	6.343	−2.230**	−2.320	3.958**	3.127
	(2.487)	(1.353)	(−2.454)	(−0.493)	(2.267)	(0.607)
Constant	−82007.200***	−110978.000***	−21383.600***	−55167.300	−101481.00***	−152098.00**
	(−8.518)	(−2.002)	(−4.295)	(−0.909)	(−9.419)	(−1.717)
R^2	.870	.661	.725	−1.610	.884	.413
$F_{7,51}$	48.668***	14.207***	19.160***	−4.494	55.663***	5.131***

Note: Stock, additions, hours, and library interaction are treated as endogenous variables; percentage Beame vote, percentage dense land use, housing value, 1960 stock, 1960 hours, and 1960 additions are excluded exogenous variables. The numbers in parentheses are *t*-statistics. Statistical significance is indicated as follows: *0.10 level; **0.05 level; ***0.01 level, with one-tailed tests for additions, stock, hours, and interaction; otherwise, two-tailed tests are applied. Numbers below *F* are degrees of freedom.

Table 4.5.   Results of Regression of Book Circulation across 59 Neighborhood Branches

Explanatory Variable	Adult		Juvenile		Total	
	OLS	TSLS	OLS	TSLS	OLS	TSLS
Stock	2.238***	0.573	0.855***	−0.656	0.883**	−0.684
	(3.533)	(0.187)	(2.639)	(−0.317)	(2.090)	(−0.371)
Additions	4.978***	−7.961	5.185***	20.708	3.607***	9.847
	(2.532)	(−0.161)	(4.320)	(1.295)	(2.885)	(0.524)
Hours	5214.560***	7616.050***	1740.260***	3036.170**	7934.510***	1062.500***
	(8.300)	(2.590)	(6.799)	(1.839)	(11.893)	(3.564)
Library interaction	−9.655*	33.461	−6.227**	2.075	−16.291**	25.645
	(−1.548)	(0.721)	(−1.948)	(0.062)	(−2.373)	(0.482)
Population density	−18.116***	−24.823	−0.272	0.484	−23.656***	−23.106
	(−3.037)	(−1.232)	(−0.099)	(0.057)	(−3.733)	(−1.275)
Percent enrolled in school	−1.455*	−2.083	0.416	0.848	−1.320	−1.044
	(−1.963)	(−1.370)	(1.044)	(0.576)	(−1.640)	(−0.572)
Income	4.268**	6.320	−2.300**	−2.942	3.959**	2.690
	(2.303)	(1.284)	(−2.539)	(−0.840)	(2.315)	(0.701)
Constant	−72290.000***	−99491.700*	−20961.200***	−50065.900	−98919.200***	−140295.000*
	(−8.309)	(−1.755)	(−4.298)	(−1.033)	(−9.359)	(−1.956)
R^2	.867	.606	.717	−.708	.882	.613
$F_{7,51}$	47.609***	11.194***	18.417***	−3.021	54.683***	11.537***

Note: See footnote to table 4.4.

Table 4.6. Results of Regression of Record Circulation across 59 Neighborhood Branches

Explanatory Variable	Adult		Juvenile		Total	
	OLS	TSLS	OLS	TSLS	OLS	TSLS
Stock	3.186***	3.159*	0.887***	1.763**	2.161***	2.435*
	(6.714)	(1.507)	(3.712)	(2.257)	(5.728)	(1.646)
Additions	−1.096	−4.449	0.510	−0.849	−0.623	−4.115
	(−1.087)	(−1.052)	(1.230)	(−0.467)	(−0.855)	(−1.145)
Hours	131.389***	264.718**	60.135***	35.296	194.887***	340.415**
	(4.566)	(1.978)	(4.952)	(0.831)	(4.978)	(1.952)
Library interaction	−0.319	1.704	0.030	0.633	−0.326	1.569
	(−0.909)	(0.645)	(0.204)	(0.645)	(−0.688)	(0.426)
Population density	−0.588*	−0.744	−0.119	0.025	−0.748*	−0.816
	(−1.823)	(−0.899)	(−0.891)	(0.122)	(−1.746)	(−0.875)
Percent enrolled in school	−0.059	0.030	0.018	0.008	−0.026	0.124
	(−1.298)	(0.176)	(0.928)	(0.137)	(−0.415)	(0.492)
Income	0.111	−0.088	−0.112***	−0.085	0.007	−0.280
	(1.192)	(−0.338)	(−2.697)	(−0.807)	(0.051)	(−0.692)
Constant	−1981.520***	−4116.840*	−458.576*	−375.618	−2418.640***	−4601.030
	(−3.541)	(−1.687)	(−1.985)	(−0.464)	(−3.258)	(−1.495)
R^2	.708	.241	.665	.453	.689	.285
$F_{7,51}$	17.695***	2.319**	14.488***	6.044***	16.147***	2.905**

Note: See footnote to table 4.4.

Table 4.7. *Results of Regression of Reference Questions across 59 Neighborhood Branches*

Explanatory Variable	Adult		Juvenile		Total	
	OLS	TSLS	OLS	TSLS	OLS	TSLS
Stock	0.546**	−0.102	0.078	0.569	0.266*	0.706
	(2.342)	(−0.061)	(0.639)	(0.894)	(1.317)	(0.787)
Additions	3.365***	11.955	4.665	7.409*	3.890***	8.614
	(4.854)	(0.655)	(0.319)	(1.465)	(6.731)	(1.050)
Hours	970.761***	1142.750	316.187***	441.858	1381.290***	1040.520
	(4.115)	(0.838)	(3.102)	(0.908)	(4.189)	(0.765)
Library interaction	−1.438	−7.387	−1.783*	3.535	−3.407	−1.227
	(−0.623)	(−0.371)	(−1.430)	(0.336)	(−1.018)	(−0.051)
Population density	−0.560	0.774	0.852	1.867	−0.271	4.349
	(−0.252)	(0.097)	(0.786)	(0.726)	(−0.087)	(0.542)
Percent enrolled in school	−0.146	−0.332	−0.177	−0.561	−0.458	−0.871
	(−0.534)	(−0.405)	(−1.118)	(−1.172)	(−1.148)	(−0.934)
Income	−0.599	−0.081	−0.453	0.432	−0.518	−0.220
	(−0.886)	(−0.037)	(−1.253)	(0.387)	(−0.615)	(−0.121)
Constant	−15255.70***	−21588.60	−2778.110	−15247.700	−17974.600***	−35545.400
	(−4.318)	(−0.841)	(−1.442)	(−1.058)	(−3.458)	(−1.141)
R^2	.716	−.177	.762	.151	.702	.197
$F_{7,51}$	18.363***	−1.093	23.292***	1.298	17.159***	1.787

Note: See footnote to table 4.4.

purged by the first stage, then consumers seem much more responsive to changes in hours than to other attributes of service.

Stock and additions also have statistically significant coefficients. Additions seem to be more important in relation to book circulation, while the quantity in stock is a more important variable in record use. Thus, it seems that books become obsolete faster than records. Perhaps best sellers are more important to public library patrons than are the largest selling records. The number of additions also appears to be important for reference questions, since timeliness of materials is related to use.

Stock and additions do not appear to be significantly associated with use in the two-stage estimates, except for record circulation. In terms of book circulation and adult reference questions, the stock of materials and additions to stock do not appear to be significant factors in use decisions. This lack of significance may be due to the weakness of the instruments in explaining library decisions; two-stage estimates are not as reliable as ordinary least squares.

The library interaction variable has a statistically significant negative coefficient for several OLS estimates—total circulation, book circulation, and juvenile reference questions. The statistical significance of these coefficients reinforces the finding that the existence of nearby branches tends to reduce the use of a neighborhood library.

The three neighborhood characteristic variables yield some surprising results. First, population density shows a statistically significant negative relationship with book and record use by adults and no significant positive coefficient. Thus, the notion that library use will be greater in higher density areas because of easier access does not seem to hold. Rather, the tastes of people living in high- and low-density areas differ: those living in low-density areas appear to have a stronger preference for library services than those living in high-density areas, with income held constant.

Income has the expected positive coefficient for adult book use, but a surprising negative coefficient for juvenile book use. Since juvenile books are relatively inexpensive, perhaps higher-income households buy more juvenile books than low-income households and rely on the library to obtain the more expensive adult books.

The percentage of population enrolled in school has an unexpected negative coefficient for adult book use and no other significant coefficients. Because school enrollment is closely related to the number of young persons living in an area, and because library use is generally thought to decline with age, a positive sign would be expected. The negative coefficient indicates that adult book use is greater where there are fewer children.

The overall statistical power of the relationship is significant in all cases except the two-state results for juvenile book use and for reference questions. The library service characteristics are strongly associated with library use in expected ways. The neighborhood characteristics also help explain library use, but in somewhat surprising ways. The two-stage results, while generally weaker than the ordinary least squares, emphasize the importance of hours of service as a determinant of patterns of use.

Efficient Operations

Using these careful estimates of relationships between library service characteristics and use, it is now possible to determine service efficiency in terms of hours, stock, and additions. The marginal costs of each activity were reported in table 4.2. The marginal benefits of an additional unit of each activity are calculated in table 4.8. The coefficients of the regressions in tables 4.4 and 4.7 are estimates of how use will respond to an increment in a particular library activity, other things equal. By weighting circulation by 1.183 to take into account in-library use and adding reference questions, one arrives at an estimate of the total increase in library use associated with one more unit of activity. Marginal use figures are reported in column (b) of table 4.8. Thus, an additional hour of service is associated with 11,392 more uses of the library using the ordinary least squares results. Using the two-stage results, an additional hour of service is associated with 14,475 more uses of the library. Because the coefficients are subject to statistical error, it is appropriate to report a 90 percent confidence interval for the associated difference in use. The 90 percent confidence intervals are reported in column (c).

By dividing the marginal cost of an activity, say an additional hour of service, by the expected increase in use that results, one can estimate the marginal cost of increasing library use in different ways, as reported in columns (d) and (e) of table 4.8. The ordinary least squares estimates indicate that an additional hour of library use could be generated for each $0.19 spent to expand hours. Spending $3.12 to increase the size of the book stock at a branch will be expected to increase library use by one unit, while spending an additional $0.94 for new materials would expand library use by the same amount.

An efficiently designed library system would expand each activity as long as the marginal benefit of an extra unit of the activity—for example, an extra hour of service—exceeds the cost of providing the extra unit. If the cost of an extra unit of the activity exceeds the benefit derived, then consumers would be better off with the savings in tax dollars or expenditure on a more productive item, and that activity should be cut back. As an activity is expanded, we expect that less benefit will be derived from each additional unit. As an activity is reduced, we expect each additional unit cut back to have a larger impact on benefits. Thus, the estimates of marginal benefits presented here reflect the marginal values of current levels of library activities. The marginal benefits will differ at different levels of activity.

The assumption that the marginal benefit of additional uses is the same

Table 4.8. Marginal Benefits and Costs of Hours, Stock, and Additions

| | | | | | Marginal Cost per Use | | Marginal Benefit | |
Activity	Marginal Cost	Estimation Method for Use	Point Estimate of Use per Activity	90 Percent Confidence of Use	Point Estimate	90 Percent Confidence	Point Estimate	90 Percent Confidence
	(a)		(b)	(c)	(d)	(e)	(f)	(g)
Hours per week	$2,317	OLS	11,392	10,360	$0.19	$ 0.22	$15,750	$13,675
		TSLS	14,475	7,488	0.16	0.31	18,819	9,884
Volumes in stock	3.93	OLS	1.26	0.36	3.12	11.07	1.66	0.47
		TSLS	0	0	—	—	—	—
Additions to stock	7.41	OLS	7.91	5.32	0.94	1.39	10.44	7.02
		TSLS	24.97	0	0.30	—	32.96	—

Note: Marginal costs are as reported in table 4.2. The estimates of use involve multiplying the respective coefficient in table 4.1 times 1.183 to reflect in-library use and adding the respective coefficient from table 4.7. The marginal cost of increasing library use is found by dividing column (a) by columns (b) and (c), respectively. The value of a use is taken as $1.32, the average benefit per use for the fifty-nine neighborhood branches in table 4.3.

whether the uses result from an extra branch, extra hours, or extra books is too strong. As hours change, the marginal benefit of uses due to a branch or extra materials will change. Perhaps a detailed analysis of individual library users would allow the estimation of a more complete demand relationship. Such a relationship could be used to identify the value of intramarginal uses. Such a detailed study is beyond the scope of the present work. The constant marginal benefit assumption used here is a simplification.

The average benefit of library use at the fifty-nine neighborhood libraries presented in table 4.3 is $1.32, although there is substantial variation among the branches. The marginal benefit of an additional unit of activity can be compared with the marginal cost of the activity either by comparing the marginal cost per use of columns (d) and (e) with the value of benefits, $1.32, or by multiplying the estimated changes in use, columns (b) and (c), and comparing the results with the marginal cost of the activity, column (a).

The marginal benefit of an additional hour of service each week substantially exceeds the assumed marginal cost. Using either the ordinary least squares or two-stage estimates, the point estimates or the 90 percent confidence intervals, the marginal gains from additonal hours substantially exceed the marginal cost. Our analysis shows that the average of twenty hours per week of available use offered at the fifty-nine neighborhood branches of the New York Public Library is not efficient. Expanded hours of service would generate a substantial increase in library use, worth more to consumers than the costs of the expanded service.

The marginal cost of maintaining more volumes in stock is less than the marginal benefits derived. Thus, on average the neighborhood branches of the New York Public Library seem to be too large to be efficient. Because the biggest impact of stock on use seems to be made by recordings, it may be that maintaining a larger stock of recordings is justified.

The evidence on the relative value of acquisitions and the size of stock presented here may be a little simplistic. When a branch is fully stocked, the acquisition of a new item must involve the discarding of old material. Real effort is required to weed out the least valuable materials. Even simple weeding rules, like "discard all material over ten years old unless it has been used in the last year," require substantial effort to implement. Deacquisition involves not only identifying the material and discarding it, but also deleting catalog entries. While the estimated marginal cost of an acquisition in table 4.2 presumably includes the cost of weeding out old material to make way for new, the study has not accounted for the quality of the weeding effort. A more detailed analysis would be necessary to consider how much effort should be put into weeding. The message here is simply that the size of the stock is less important than the quality of the stock, including its timeliness.

Acquiring new material seems to have benefits that exceed costs, at least for the point estimates. Thus, while the evidence is not as clear as for hours, there does seem to be a case for acquiring new materials. New materials seem to generate use worth more than their cost.

FOR EFFICIENCY, FEWER BRANCHES OPERATE FOR MORE HOURS

Overall, then, there seem to be too many branches operating too few hours, buying somewhat too few new materials, but maintaining a stock of materials that may be somewhat too large. The evidence for the number of branches and the number of hours of service is quite clear, the evidence on stocks and new materials is less clear. Because the current mix of library activities favors extra branches rather than more hours of service, it is not possible to say whether the current budget is at the right level or not. The important finding is that an efficient library design would have fewer branches and operate more hours per week.

The influence of a hypothetical reallocation of the budget to operate fewer branches for more hours can be estimated using the information presented thus far. The first step is to close branches. For the sake of this exercise, suppose that the seven branches whose benefits were at least $175,000 less than their costs were closed. None of the seven is located geographically next to another.[8] The closings would save $1.9 million annually, including the rental value of the space. With the branches closed, some of the library use would shift to the remaining branches. For the sake of this exercise, let's assume that all the use shifts to nearby branches. In addition, some of the branches that are closed may be physically located closest to some remaining branches. The best alternative for these remaining branches will now be a more distant branch. Consequently, the value of library services at the next nearest branches will be greater.

The second step of this exercise is to assume that the cost saving from closing the seven branches is used to increase the hours of service at the remaining sixty-nine facilities in the system. At $2,317 per hour, the $1.9 million made available by closing the seven branches will buy 11.9 hours each week for each remaining facility in the system. If each hour added 14,475 uses as suggested by the two-stage point estimates, the use of each branch would be expected to increase by more than 172,000.

The costs and benefits of each branch if seven neighborhood branches were closed and the funds reallocated to increase hours at the remaining branches are reported in table 4.9. Of the remaining fifty-three neighborhood branches, only four have negative net benefits following the branch closings and expansion of hours. The assumption that the hours would be expanded the same way at every facility is perhaps too simple. The assumption that each additional hour will have the same impact on increasing use as the estimate of the first hour may be too strong. Nevertheless, the change in the efficiency of the operation—in the quality of service, given the budget—is striking. Of course, the changes will make people in areas where branches are closed travel farther to get library services, and so they can be expected to oppose the shift. On the other hand, perhaps a branch system with fewer branches should change the locations of its current branches. The relocation of branches is not examined here.

Table 4.9.   Estimated Use, Benefits, and Cost of System with Seven Branches Closed

Neighborhood Libraries	Use	Benefit	Cost	Benefit minus Cost
Allerton	321,227	$ 372,379	$ 311,753	$ 60,626
Baychester	492,407	683,185	389,513	293,672
Castle Hill	221,154	257,774	197,121	60,653
City Island	207,879	551,963	106,701	445,262
Clason's Point	277,993	350,453	280,337	70,116
Eastchester	246,753	295,431	154,853	140,578
Edenwald	284,030	464,650	224,427	240,223
High Bridge	251,005	268,700	226,765	41,935
Jerome Park	405,962	408,848	209,451	199,397
Kingsbridge	326,798	312,547	313,576	−1,028
Melrose	304,976	403,803	227,440	176,363
Morrisania	236,726	313,436	259,364	54,072
Mosholu	356,730	473,232	259,013	214,219
Mott Haven	0	0	0	0
Parkchester	376,041	414,547	243,347	171,200
Pelham Bay	361,622	524,785	248,183	276,602
Riverdale	296,389	475,851	271,011	204,840
Sedgwick	358,730	349,833	113,735	236,098
Soundview	274,369	322,232	240,623	81,609
Spuyten Duyvil	334,465	319,882	245,295	74,587
Throgs Neck	283,762	520,333	241,983	278,350
Tremont	359,106	384,387	201,660	182,727
Van Cortlandt	252,731	308,355	146,820	161,536
Van Nest	318,256	381,846	233,933	147,913
Wakefield	266,758	325,471	292,506	32,965
West Farms	0	0	0	0
Woodlawn Height	231,009	281,853	131,723	150,130
Woodstock	0	0	0	0
Aguilar	246,461	266,178	252,767	13,411
Cathedral	259,956	201,476	140,487	60,989
Chatham Square	474,589	593,236	303,036	290,200
Columbia	265,355	249,434	108,155	141,279
Columbus	214,144	256,972	191,519	65,454
Epiphany	435,460	367,528	310,021	57,507
58th Street	373,027	298,421	238,717	59,704
George Bruce	0	0	0	0
Hamilton Fish Park	281,909	253,718	227,959	25,759
Hamilton Grange	293,326	293,326	270,780	22,546

A POLICY RECOMMENDATION

The results of the analysis of library use may be difficult to convert into policy. The political process shapes library expenditure patterns, and efficiency considerations may not dominate the political scene. First, the political process recognizes the history of the institution and the possibility of seemingly irreversible changes. Second, equity consideration may play some role. Third, federal policy may have some impact on local choices. Fourth, the political process simply may be imperfect.

Table 4.9. (continued)

Neighborhood Libraries	Use	Benefit	Cost	Benefit minus Cost
Harlem	208,772	198,333	178,875	19,458
Hudson Park	232,175	196,885	222,088	−25,203
Kips Bay	347,506	284,955	256,907	28,048
Macomb's Bridge	190,528	190,528	63,116	127,412
Muhlenberg	291,211	306,354	232,168	74,186
115th Street	198,850	182,942	197,987	−15,045
125th Street	0	0	0	0
Ottendorfer	263,021	216,940	204,491	12,449
Riverside	494,054	469,351	289,891	179,460
Seward Park	0	0	0	0
67th Street	274,065	263,102	239,185	23,917
Washington Heights	231,433	203,661	232,298	−28,637
Webster	240,250	206,615	154,654	51,961
Yorkville	506,607	435,682	341,638	94,044
Dongan Hills	314,335	706,109	214,581	491,528
Great Kills	402,298	1,372,093	241,586	1,130,507
Port Richmond	299,735	481,381	220,014	261,367
Stapleton	236,978	394,388	154,323	240,065
Todt Hill	325,028	741,480	179,925	561,555
Tottenville	219,469	1,610,902	117,082	1,493,820
West New Brighton	296,376	475,980	173,730	302,250
Bloomingdale	514,954	1,287,384	436,246	851,138
Countee Cullen	259,929	987,730	438,974	548,756
Fort Washington	314,213	1,791,012	353,080	1,437,932
Inwood	405,400	2,716,178	363,633	2,352,545
Jefferson Market	540,170	972,305	543,374	428,931
96th Street	304,662	685,611	313,760	371,851
St. Agnes	325,784	586,411	329,911	256,500
Tompkins Square	242,203	460,185	260,658	199,527
Francis Martin	0	0	0	0
Grand Concourse	435,715	797,881	354,121	443,760
Hunt's Point	290,922	910,702	312,920	597,782
Westchester Square	264,114	810,090	307,623	502,467
New Dorp	522,749	3,456,419	345,825	3,110,594
Donnel	1,603,256	1,563,495	2,387,566	−824,071
Mid-Manhattan	2,110,901	NA	NA	NA
Fordham	820,093	6,314,715	706,429	5,608,286
St. George	526,373	4,173,509	506,487	3,667,022

The current operation of the New York Public Library reflects the severe budget cutbacks of the 1970s. Instead of cutting back both hours and branches in an effort to retain an efficient mix, the hours have been cut back severely while almost all branches have been retained. Cutting back hours has been politically easier than closing branches. In January 1976, the library announced the planned closing of eight branches as a way of coping with budget cuts. The announcement of closings created a substantial political reaction that prevented the closings. Neighborhood citizen groups coalesced around the preservation of individual branches. While reduction in hours might be seen as temporary, the closing of branches may have been seen as permanent. Rather than accept the budget cuts as permanent, the political friends of the library may have viewed cutting hours as a way of preserving the option of restoring former service levels.

On the other hand, the library had been expanding the library system in the 1970s. In 1960, forty-eight of the present fifty-nine neighborhood branches were operating and two others were closed for renovation. Thus, the number of neighborhood branches has grown by more than 15 percent over the last twenty years. Of the nine new neighborhood branches, six have opened since 1970. While the opening of new branches may have been an appropriate response to the changing location of library use, it may be that older branches should have been closed at the same time.

In 1960, neighborhood branches were open an average of thirty-nine hours each week. Other urban library systems currently average in excess of forty hours per week at branch locations. In 1970, however, the neighborhood libraries in New York averaged forty-eight hours of service per week, an above average number. The substantial growth in branch library activity during the 1960s, even as library use began to decline (it peaked in 1964), did not put the library in a very good position to deal with the budget cuts in the 1970s.

Equity considerations may also play a role in shaping political support for the library. Public library services are sometimes discussed in terms of their value for poor people. At the turn of the century and again during the Great Depression, the public library provided recreation without charge and offered access to learning for adults eager to better themselves. Evidence of the distributional consequences of library activities is not overwhelming, however.

If the net effect of the local government's library expenditures is to improve the relative position of poor people, then the beneficiaries of the services must have lower incomes on average than people who bear the burden of the taxes used to pay for the services. The question of the incidence of the taxes used to pay for the library is not simple. Currently, over a quarter of the employees of the branch libraries of the New York Public Library are paid with federal Comprehensive Employment and Training Act (CETA) funds. Presumably, general revenue-sharing funds also have an impact. Federal revenue sources are moderately progressive. The share of library revenues accounted for by local tax sources may be less than 50 percent. The most important local tax is the property tax. Recent literature on the property tax indicates that it may be capitalized into land values or borne by the owners of capital. Therefore, the property tax is likely, except for administrative deviation, to be somewhat progressive. Those individuals earning higher incomes pay relatively more in taxes supporting local services than those earning lower incomes.

The beneficiaries of the service also seem to be disproportionately higher income earners. In particular, we find that adult use of the library is greater in areas with higher-income residents, whereas the use of juvenile materials seems greater in lower-income areas. Use as reflected by reference questions appears to be unrelated to income. Because the use of juvenile materials accounts for less than 30 percent of total use, the aggregate effect seems to be that higher-income households use the library more than lower-income households. This finding generally conforms to those of other studies, although the other studies do not differentiate between adult and juvenile use. Because the income variable is a distance-weighted index of census tract information, the coefficients cannot be used to calculate income elasticities of use.

If both the sources of finance and the use of the library are disproportionately represented among higher-income groups, it is possible that local expenditure on public library services is distributionally neutral. However, since neither the distribution of those who finance libraries nor the distribution of those who benefit from library services is very carefully observed, no firm conclusion about distributional consequences can be made.

Note, however, that just because the beneficiaries tend to have higher incomes or the services are distributionally neutral, does not mean that the services should not be performed in the public sector. Even though not all citizens use the library, it may still have characteristics that make it substantially public in character, justifying its support by general taxes. That library users gain by library expenditure relative to nonusers does not in itself prove an inequity in the fiscal system. Nonusers may value the option of using the library, and so the apparent inequity may overstate the underlying welfare effect. Moreover, the important equity result is the net effect of the full fiscal system. Nonusers may gain disproportionately from other government services. The important equity result is that for the full fiscal system; there is no reason why each service matched with its source of finance should be distributionally neutral or progressive. Finally, the net benefit of services may be capitalized into land values.

Since in-library use has not been observed, we do not know the distributional gains from such use. Is in-library use greater among lower-income groups? A better understanding of the distributional consequences of library activity requires more information on in-library use, particularly attendance data by branch.

Suppose that we accept the view that library services are distributionally advantageous. Suppose, too, that library services are used effectively by poor people, especially children, and that library use improves school performance and literacy levels, and is an important vehicle for social advancement by low-income urban families. (Note that each of these claims is unproven and indeed difficult to prove; the important issue is the effectiveness of libraries relative to other expenditures.) How would public library services best be provided to low-income households? The very substantial response of use of all kinds to the number of hours of service suggests that even low-income households respond to the number of hours. The high density of branches in low-income areas of the city, on the other hand, does not appear to have generated very high levels of use. It seems likely that the results of this study may also apply to library use by low-income persons; that is, low-income library users, like the average user, might be better served by longer hours in fewer larger branches. Low-income families may also value their time at lower rates than high-income families. Thus, it is not obvious why library services should be characterized by more branches and fewer hours of service in consideration of equity.

The combination of more branches and fewer hours of service may also be explained by the political environment that shapes the library system. Perhaps public library service is quite local relative to the size of the city. The benefits of service in a particular location may be concentrated in a small area, while the costs of providing the branch service are widely diffused. Neighborhood demands for services may be made with little concern for costs; in effect, there may be a free rider problem among neighborhoods, with weak central control. This hypothesis represents a substantial simplification of a complex historical process that deserves more careful study. The point is that distributional impact across neighborhoods may play some political role.

Federal policy may have some impact on library decisions. As already noted, over 25 percent of library employees are federally-financed CETA workers. President Carter has proposed new restrictions on CETA funds that would prevent professional librarians from being paid with CETA funds. The central fact is that a substantial part of library operations is contingent on the availability of federal CETA funds. In the present setting, funding cuts produce cuts in hours.

Federal grants also support the construction of a new branch. While public works projects may be an appropriate response to high levels of unemployment in the city, the further expansion of library branches in a system already overburdened with too many branches is of questionable value. The operating costs of the new facility may force further reductions in hours in other facilities. Six new branches in the Queens Borough Public Library, a separate system, remain unopened for lack of operating funds.

Finally, one must question whether the political constraints on the library that have prevented a more rational response to budget cuts can be changed. Presumably library users who live near branches that would be closed would be made worse off by the closing. At least those who have flexible enough schedules to be able to use the facility when it happens to be open may be worse off. Is this the dominant force in shaping the library services? Or is the tactic of preserving locations at the cost of low levels of operation throughout the system one that will yield more funds for libraries over some longer term? Perhaps better information about library operations will improve the political outcome.

This chapter is an effort to understand efficiency in public libraries. The effort might be improved in several ways. The library use relationships might be estimated with different functional forms. They might also be explored over time in an effort to discover why use began to fall perhaps a decade before services were cut. The lack of annual demographic information may hamper this inquiry. Finally, a study of individual users might refine the estimated relationships presented here.

5

Technical Systems
and Innovations

Most libraries divide their operations into two parts: public services and technical services. Public services deal directly with users, while technical services deal with preparing and maintaining materials for use. The specific functions of technical services may not be divided in exactly the same way in every library, but technical services in general involve selecting, ordering, cataloging, and processing materials for use in the library system. On average, the large public library systems assign about 13 percent of their staffs to technical services. This chapter is devoted to technical systems in public libraries. These systems include selection, cataloging, and circulation control.

Technical services are concerned with the flow of newly acquired materials into the library. The main difference between a warehouse stacked with books and a library is the character of technical services applied. Technical services give order to the materials so that they can be matched to users as directly as possible. In the selection of materials, the emphasis is put on getting materials that will be used. Cataloging systems give a shelf number to each item so that the materials will be shelved near related material. The catalog itself refers to the shelf number in a variety of ways so that a user can find materials based on titles, authors, or subjects. Technical services may put labels, covers, bindings, or antitheft devices on materials before placing them on shelves. Older materials may also get preservative treatment, but that is a secondary function of most technical service operations.

This chapter defines and discusses possible criteria for evaluating them in a general way. The main emphasis is on the pattern of use of particular techniques. How rapidly are particular innovations diffused over all public libraries? What features of the public library systems are associated with early adoption of innovations?

Several other activities, though not normally performed by technical service divisions of libraries, are technical in character. These activities are important areas for innovation and also are discussed in this chapter. These activities include the control of circulation records, antitheft activities, microfilm materials, and photocopying services.

THE QUALITY OF TECHNICAL SERVICES

Selection

METHOD.   A first problem of technical services is materials selection. In some libraries, book selection is performed by individual unit librarians, say a branch librarian or a subject specialist in a central library. Selection aids may include *Publishers' Weekly*, a periodical that lists new titles with brief descriptions, and other book review media. Single copies of new titles may be received by libraries on approval from publishers under an arrangement called the Greenaway Plan. Under this regime, the books themselves may be examined before acquisition decisions are made by the individual library units. Of thirty-one large public library systems surveyed, 81 percent currently use the Greenaway Plan, as indicated in table 5.1. Some libraries that formerly used the Greenaway Plan have abandoned it. Book selection in many cases is now centralized. For example, in the St. Louis County Library the same books are ordered for each branch, with selection a central responsibility. A substantial effort is made to order books requested by users of the library.

Some libraries use an approval plan in which a detailed profile of a particular library's reading needs is prepared and given to a jobber, who ships books that fit the profile even though no individual titles have been ordered. For example, in terms of fiction a library might specify 10 percent science fiction, 20 percent mystery, 10 percent romance novels, 20 percent westerns, and so on. Similar specification may be made for each subject area. A variety of language and quality stipulations may also be made. The bookjobber makes a detailed classification of each new title that is announced by the publishers, and sends books that match the library's profile within the constraints of the library's budget. The library is free to reject books received under the approval plan and it can order books outside the plan. Five of the thirty-one large public libraries use some form of approval plan as indicated in table 5.1. Approval plans may be more widespread among academic libraries than among public libraries.

The Brooklyn Public Library works closely with a bookjobber to select books. The jobber, Bookazine, prepares a list of new titles with descriptions

Table 5.1. *Selection and Cataloging Activities: Means and Standard Deviations by Geographic Type*

Selection	City	Metropolitan	Suburban	All	F or Chi-square
Greenaway plan (binary)	13 of 15	8 of 9	4 of 7	25 of 31	3.217
	86.7%	88.9%	57.1%	80.6%	(2)
Approval plan (binary)	1 of 15	1 of 9	3 of 7	5 of 31	4.857*
	6.7%	11.1%	42.9%	16.1%	(2)
Acquisition lag (weeks)	13.23	11.00	7.60	11.46	0.421
	(9.58)	(17.01)	(4.04)	(11.51)	(2,23)
	13	8	5	26	
Computer-based ordering (binary)	5 of 15	3 of 9	4 of 7	12 of 31	1.295
	33.3%	33.3%	57.1%	38.7%	(2)
Cataloging					
LC-MARC based computer-produced catalog (binary) [a]	6 of 15	1 of 9	5 of 7	12 of 31	6.049**
	40.0%	11.1%	71.4%	38.7%	(2)
Network Cataloging Information used (binary) [b]	11 of 15	5 of 9	0 of 7	16 of 31	3.724
	73.3%	55.5%	0.0%	51.6%	(2)
Cataloging lag (days)	77.83	38.33	19.17	51.63	2.319
	(82.32)	(29.37)	(20.62)	(61.93)	(2,26)
	12	9	6	27	
Libraries surveyed	15	9	7	31	

Source: The author's survey.

Note: For binary variables, the number of libraries that use the technique of those responding is indicated with the percentage given underneath. The chi-square statistic is reported to test for significant variation across the geographic types. Degrees of freedom are in parentheses below the statistic.

For continuous variables (the two time-lag variables) the mean is reported with the standard deviation in parentheses. If not all libraries responded, the number responding is indicated below the standard deviation. An *F*-statistic from an analysis of variation is reported to test for differences in means across the geographic types. Degrees of freedom are in parentheses below the statistic.

Statistical significance is indicated: ***0.01 level; **0.05 level; *0.10 level.

[a] LC-MARC stands for Library of Congress, Machine-Readable Cataloging.

[b] The Ohio College Library Center (OCLC) is used to catalog information in most cases. The San Francisco Public Library uses Stanford University's BALLOTS system and the San Antonio Public Library uses TRINCO. BALLOTS and TRINCO are similar to OCLC.

several weeks before publication date. Unit librarians in the Brooklyn system select books from the list. The jobber orders the books and makes them available before publication date. This arrangement allows the bookjobber to order materials before actual publication on the basis of the library's orders. The library gets faster service, while retaining control of materials selection.

ERRORS.　The quality of book selection may reflect errors in acquisition, the timing of acquisition, and the cost of selection. Two kinds of errors can occur in book selection. The library can fail to buy material that would have been used—a type I error or false negative. Alternatively, the library can buy materials that are little or never used—a type II error or false positive. A highly successful book selection system would buy only materials that are most used and avoid buying books that are little used. One might want to assign different values to different uses, for example, reflecting the intensity of use or the value of use to the user as Newhouse and Alexander propose.[1] Because selections must be made before use occurs, selections are made on the basis of expected use. Consequently, both type I and type II errors will occur. Alternative selection methods, however, might be evaluated ex post facto in light of the actual type I and type II errors observed. A circulation control system that tracked use by title might indicate how many new titles had not been used within the first year of acquisition, an indicator of a type II error. An accounting of requests for materials not acquired might indicate the degree of a type I error. (Of course, most users will be unaware of materials the library did not acquire.) Current library record keeping does not measure these errors nor would such record keeping be justified for this purpose alone. More sophisticated control systems may generate such information as a by-product. Alternatively, sample studies might be made at moderate cost for the purpose of comparing alternative selection systems.

SPEED.　A second dimension of the quality of technical services is the speed with which materials become available in the library. New materials are in high demand in public libraries; new acquisitions are more important in generating use than the size of the stock of materials. The average length of time a book spends on the bestseller list is six months.[2] The half-life of a new book—the length of time in which half of all readers who will ever read the book have read it—is about one year for fiction, and somewhat longer for nonfiction. Books become obsolete. Some books have advertising campaigns keyed to their publication date. Others have ties to movies or television. Interest in such materials falls rapidly after an initial boom. Demand for books at the library may fall when a paperback edition becomes available. The value of materials falls with age, especially after the publication date. Therefore, a library that succeeds in making materials available to users quickly will be more valuable than a library that selects, orders, catalogs, and processes new materials six months after the publication date.

For the twenty-six large public libraries willing to estimate the length of time from publication date until a book is available on the shelf the mean lag was, on average, eleven weeks. Thirteen central city libraries averaged thirteen weeks; five suburban systems averaged eight weeks. The estimated lags ranged from fifty-two weeks in Birmingham to zero in Brooklyn. These estimates reflect the best guess of the librarians and not necessarily systematic data gathering. There are important differences in the acquisition lag across public libraries, and differences in selection techniques may play a role.

The public libraries may have automated ordering systems that perform the accounting functions of keeping track of orders and payment. Such systems may lower costs and increase the accuracy of order record keeping. Thirty-nine percent of the thirty-one libraries surveyed had automated ordering systems in 1978, as reported in table 5.1.

Cataloging and Processing

Once materials enter the library's door they must be made accessible to users. The first step is assigning each item a place on a shelf, and the second step is creating references to the item by title, author, and subject so that users can easily find materials they are interested in. The first step is accomplished by assigning each item a unique catalog number that indicates where the item will be located on the shelf. The second step is accomplished by inserting a suitable reference to title, author, and subject for the new material in a master list of materials called a catalog. The physical catalog may be a printed book (dictionary catalog), a card file, or microfilm. The new book or other material will be processed by labeling the spine, inserting a mark of ownership, and perhaps attaching a pocket and card for circulation control purposes.

CATALOGING SYSTEMS. The quality of the shelf arrangement will influence the ease with which users locate materials of interest. Grouping books on similar subjects together facilitates browsing for those materials. The basic choice in shelf arrangement is between the Dewey decimal system and the Library of Congress (LC) system. Most public libraries use the Dewey system.

In the Dewey decimal system, each digit is an appropriate aggregation of each subsequent digit: a one-digit code gives a gross indication of subject matter; a two-digit code is somewhat more specific; and so on, up to a full six-digit number. For a relatively small, general collection of materials, the Dewey shelf order will put like materials together very successfully.

For a large research collection of materials, the Library of Congress method may be preferred. When a new topic develops, the Library of Congress may introduce a new label that is not in sequence with previous labels; thus, certain new books may not be placed near other related materials. Users of research libraries will welcome the narrower definitions of subjects and be less concerned with proximity of materials whose subjects are not closely related. That is, the hierarchical nature of the Dewey system may be less important, and the better definition of individual subjects may be more important, in a large research library. The LC system fractures a small or moderate-sized general collection because it is not especially hierarchical. Thus, the Dewey system is used in all the thirty-one large public library systems surveyed except the Boston Public Library. The Dewey arrangement serves public libraries well, whereas the LC system serves research libraries well.

The maintenance of a physical catalog once required that each book be examined by a skilled cataloger for the purpose of identifying the subject. Searching in various bibliographic references may have been required to identify the author in more detail than that given on the title page, so that authors with similar names were not confused.

In the first decade of this country, the Library of Congress began selling copies of its catalog cards.[3] This reduced the time an individual cataloguer in one library would have to spend preparing the book for use. Now, a library orders cards of books it has purchased and inserts them in its card catalog. Both Dewey and LC numbers are printed on the card. In this way, a library can rely on the author, subject, and numbering designations of the Library of Congress. Cards are also prepared by bookjobbers. A library can buy books from some bookjobbers with catalog cards and labeling already prepared according to local specifications.

In 1968, the Library of Congress began Machine-Readable Cataloging (MARC) in a form usable by other libraries.[4] The information available on cards is entered into computer readable form in a standard format. For about $2,000 per year, a library can subscribe to the LC-MARC service and receive biweekly tapes reporting the latest LC cataloging. (A Dewey decimal number is included.) For less than $200 per year a library can receive biweekly microfilm copies of the LC cataloging from private firms. Because the microfiche comes automatically as soon as LC information is available, cataloging information is available locally much faster than if cards were ordered. Seven of the thirty-one libraries depend on the microfiche as the basic source of cataloging information, as reported in table 5.2. Two of the seven create computer-based catalogs locally.

Once a computer readable cataloging information base for local holdings is available, a library can have a computer-generated catalog at low marginal cost. While computer-based cataloging can produce dictionary catalogs, computer output microfiche (COM) cost less. The computer can sort new entries into a catalog much faster and more accurately than new cards can be entered into a card file by hand. Periodically, the computer file is used to produce a new physical catalog that reflects holdings as of a particular date. Computer output microfiche catalogs (COMCAT) can be produced in multiple copies at

Table 5.2.   *Cataloging and Circulation Control Methods of 31 Library Systems*

Library System	Network	Jobber	Fiche	Circulation Control Method
City				
Boston	OCLC			Computer
Brooklyn			Manual	Microfilm
Chicago	OCLC	Brodart		Manual
Cleveland	OCLC			Microfilm
Dallas	OCLC			Computer
Denver		Auto		Microfilm
Houston	OCLC	Brodart		Computer
Milwaukee	OCLC			Computer
Minneapolis	OCLC	Blackwell		Computer
New Orleans	OCLC			Microfilm
New York		Own-NYPL		Microfilm
Philadelphia	OCLC			Microfilm
San Antonio	TRINCO	Baker		Microfilm
San Diego			Manual	Microfilm
San Francisco	BALLOTS			Manual
Metropolitan				
Atlanta	OCLC	Bid 1978		Computer
Birmingham		Baker		Microfilm
Buffalo	OCLC			Microfilm
Cincinnati	OCLC			Computer
Indianapolis			Manual	Microfilm
Jacksonville	OCLC			Microfilm
Nashville			Manual	Manual
Pittsburgh	OCLC			Computer
Sacramento		Bid 1978	Manual	Microfilm
Suburban (counties)				
Contra Costa		Auto		Microfilm
Fairfax		Auto		Microfilm
Hennepin		Own-NYPL		Microfilm
Montgomery		Bid 1978	Computer	Microfilm
Prince Georges			Computer	Computer
St. Louis		Brodart		Microfilm
San Diego		Auto		Microfilm

Source: Author's survey.

Note: OCLC = Ohio College Library Center; Auto = Autographics; NYPL = New York Public Library; Baker = Baker and Taylor. Not all computer circulation control systems are systemwide. Microfilm and manual methods may also be in use in these systems.

very low cost; consequently, copies of a system catalog could be available in each branch as well as outside the system. The cost of updating catalogs must be balanced against the value of having public access to current information about holdings. Many libraries produce revised catalogs each quarter.

Ways to use the computer as an aid in cataloging have been in development for about the last thirty years. In the early 1950s, computer cards were used to sort cataloging information. Computer cards are limited to eighty characters of information, not enough to hold even the full catalog number, author's name, and title. Thus, such systems were not completely useful because full catalog information files were not maintained. The Milwaukee Public Library was a pioneer in using such a card based file; however, it does not make complete use of the computer for cataloging.

In the 1960s, more sophisticated systems developed. These systems were capable of handling more complete cataloging information files. One such system, the Ohio College Library Center (OCLC), began batch processing Library of Congress cataloging data files in 1968. Currently, OCLC makes cataloging information available via computer terminals and telephone lines. Library participants can search OCLC files for cataloging information and purchase catalog cards, which are published on demand. Participating libraries can enter original cataloging information for materials not located in the OCLC files. In this way, original cataloging from a variety of sources can be shared. Stanford University developed a similar system called BALLOTS. Sixteen of the thirty-one libraries use such networks as sources of cataloging information, as indicated in table 5.2.

Individual libraries developed improved systems internally. More complete cataloging information is maintained in computer managed data files, such that a variety of formats of catalogs can be produced. The usefulness of some of the systems is limited. The Dallas Public Library, for example, maintains a master bibliographic data base. The base is in a format that does not allow sorting by subject, however, so the data base cannot produce a catalog that can be publicly used. The card catalog must continue to be maintained.[5] The data base is used to produce spine labels and book pockets.

More recently the Prince Georges County Public Library in Maryland developed an internal computer produced cataloging capability. The local catalog data base, however, is not compatible with Library of Congress MARC formats, so that the catalog information must be manually entered into the Prince Georges system rather than simply being copied from LC-MARC tapes. The Prince Georges system is remarkable because it was developed in 1972 after the availability of the LC-MARC system tapes. Montgomery County has a similar system but developed it in 1963 before MARC was promulgated.

In 1969 the New York Public Library froze their card catalog and began producing dictionary catalogs of new acquisitions using locally developed computer software. The format of the computer-based catalog information files, however, is compatible with the LC-MARC tapes. Thus, the New York Public system can locate Library of Congress cataloging information by searching computer tapes and copy the information for locally acquired material into computer files representing the local collection. The computer file of catalog information of locally owned materials is flexible enough to allow production of a full catalog description of each item complete with author, title, and subject references. The computer programs developed at the New

York Public Library were transported to Hennepin County in Minnesota and are used there. The Bibliothèque Nationale, housed in the Pompidou Center in Paris, also uses the New York Public Library's computer programs.

The nature of the costs of operating a computer-generated cataloging capability, however, militates against a library that develops and implements in-house systems. The cost of maintaining the capability of searching LC-MARC tapes for cataloging information and then generating a computer file of locally held materials is substantial. The marginal cost of processing an additional hundred titles, given that several hundred are already being processed, is quite small. The fixed costs of the computer based catalog operation can be spread over many libraries by private contractors who produce the catalogs for many libraries.

The catalog contractor receives a list of titles ordered or received by its client library. Personnel at the client library may search LC-MARC microfiche and locate an LC-MARC number for each new book. If the microfiche do not contain the material, the cataloging information may be produced locally. The catalog jobber then searches the LC-MARC tapes and copies the full LC cataloging information for each item the library has acquired. The jobber then produces a computer output microform catalog that reflects the holdings of the local library. Perhaps ten firms offer catalog jobber services including Autographics, Brodart, Blackwell NA, and Baker and Taylor. (A comparative review of their services is available.)[6]

Twelve of the thirty-one large public library systems surveyed currently have computer-generated catalogs whose cataloging information is copied directly from LC-MARC tapes; three more libraries were looking for contractors in 1978, as indicated in table 5.2. Except for the New York Public Library and Hennepin County library system, all fifteen of the surveyed systems who get their catalog information from LC-MARC tapes use catalog jobbers. Computer produced catalogs are also generated in Prince Georges and Montgomery Counties in Maryland, but catalog information is manually introduced into these systems rather than being copied from LC-MARC tapes. Partial bibliographic data files are manipulated on computers in Dallas, Milwaukee, and elsewhere, but these files do not contain enough information from which to produce a computer based catalog.

The computer-generated catalog using LC-MARC tapes as the basic source of information appears to be the "climax technology." That is, other cataloging techniques are likely to be replaced by the catalog jobbers using LC-MARC tapes as sources. While more sophisticated uses of computers that integrate circulation control and the catalog function are conceivable, these uses are likely to be built on the LC-MARC produced local catalog rather than replacing it. As computer costs fall, on-line access to the local catalog may become feasible. The use of catalog cards for new materials is declining, and cataloging services that are linked to cards seem likely to be replaced. OCLC and BALLOTS are basically card-oriented services and their value may decline.

> The online network systems are primarily designed to support the production of current cataloging materials, not the conversion to machine readable form of cataloging already in existence. The charges and system features of these systems are oriented toward the production of catalog cards and other printed products.[7]

The conversion of existing manual catalogs to machine based catalogs is costly and may never take place in the largest libraries. Manual catalogs can simply be frozen, and the machine based catalog begun with materials acquired after a particular date. The cost of converting a manual catalog to a machine catalog may run between $1.06 and $3.28 (in 1978 prices) per title depending on the number of characters of information included in the machine based catalog.[8]

The success of catalogs produced by jobbers using LC-MARC depends in part on the breadth of coverage of Library of Congress cataloging and in part on the speed with which LC cataloging information becomes available. For most standard materials acquired by public libraries, Library of Congress cataloging is available in a timely manner. Prepublication cataloging is often published in books under the Library of Congress's Cataloging in Publication program. The Cataloging in Publication information may change somewhat after the book is actually published—titles, author's names, and even subjects may have been misspecified. Therefore, most libraries insist on ultimate LC-MARC cataloging for their catalogs. Libraries that acquire fewer than 10,000 titles annually typically find a very high proportion of the titles, say over 85 percent, available on LC-MARC at the time material is to be cataloged.[9] The main deficiencies are in foreign materials—the Boston Public Library delays cataloging such materials until LC information is available— government documents, and music, both recordings and sheet music. The delay in foreign materials may continue, but the Library of Congress has undertaken ambitious programs to catalog both government documents and music.[10] If successful, the scope of LC-MARC information may cover the acquisitions of a very high proportion of most public libraries.

CATALOGING QUALITY.   The success of the catalog might be measured by the length of time users take to locate materials and by the success rate in finding materials, given that the materials are, in fact, referenced in the catalog.[11] The quality of the catalog is apparently substantially influenced by how consistently materials are treated as their references are entered into the catalog. While cataloging librarians' skill in applying standard rules may be important in maintaining consistency, another procedure may also be important.

Cataloging systems may maintain authority files. Authority files are independent lists of names of people and subjects to be used in cataloging. Considerable effort may be put into maintaining the veracity of the authority file. New materials to be cataloged may, then, be checked against the authority files to assure consistency in names and subjects. In this way, materials on Zimbabwe can be kept together and referenced together whether called Zimbabwe, Rhodesia, or something else. Materials by or about Muhammad Ali can be referenced together whether he is referred to as Muhammad Ali or Cassius Clay. The quality of the catalog will reflect the effort put into maintaining consistency.

The creation of local computer-based catalogs from LC-MARC tapes may be enhanced if authority files for the local catalogs are maintained. The software developed by the New York Public Library included automated authority file checks from the late 1960s. As of the late 1970s, the Library of Congress is automating its authority files. An important difference among catalog jobbers may be the extent of local authority file checks included in the service. Among the jobbers, Autographics and Library Interface Systems include both subject and name authority file maintenance. Brodart and Blackwell include only subject authority file checks. A major complaint with the service of OCLC and similar cooperative catalog information services is the lack of any authority files.[12]

The quality of the cataloging operation may also be indicated by the length of time required to catalog an item. The length of time between delivery of an item to the library and its availability (after processing) was estimated by twenty-seven libraries. On average, fifty-two days elapsed from delivery to shelving, as indicated in table 5.1. The suburban libraries, however, average just nineteen days compared with the seventy-eight days required on average in city libraries. The substantial variance in the cataloging lag in each group, however, means that the differences in means are not statistically significant across the geographic types. The cataloging lag may be shorter for libraries using catalog jobbers, because the request for cataloging can be made when the book is ordered, a possibility that is examined later in this chapter. Thus, the cataloging may be available at the time the book is delivered. The cataloging lag will then be just the time required to process the book (e.g., entering labels).

MANAGING THE CATALOG JOBBER   A central difficulty with the use of a catalog jobber is the problem of hiring, monitoring, and replacing the contractor. Many public library systems are required to accept the lowest bid for a contract and to rebid contracts every three years. It is difficult to include all the dimensions of service quality in the contract. The library will be concerned with the speed of receipt of the catalog, with the error rate in cataloging materials, and with the skill of authority file maintenance and checking. Because contract termination for cause will invite heavy legal expenses and possible chaos if catalog materials cannot be retrieved in usable form from the jobber, libraries will be understandably reluctant to terminate contracts before they expire. Therefore, it may be appropriate for the contracts to include penalties for slow delivery, for high error rates, and for inadequate authority file maintenance.

When the contract is rebid, a different jobber may win the contract. The transition from one jobber to another may be difficult and expensive. One jobber's computer files may not be compatible with another's. The library may want to specify formats for the catalog and authority files so that they can be easily transported to other jobbers. Perhaps a transition period of a few months should be included in the contracts so that the old and new jobbers can be brought together. When contracts are rebid, a locality may want to allow the library board to choose among the three lowest bidders both so that the contractor need not be changed unless the gains are significant, and so that a contractor can be dismissed for poor performance even if it is the lowest bidder. The library must manage contracts carefully if contracting services are to yield high quality services over a long period of time.

Serials

Technical service operations will also handle serials. Serials include periodicals (annual or more frequent regular appearance) as well as other serials (items published in sequence, not necessarily with regular periodicity). Libraries typically maintain subscriptions to serial publications. The library must keep track of subscriptions, payments, and receipt of materials, as well as alert publishers when materials are not received and when subscriptions are canceled. Many libraries use computer based systems to keep track of serials. This study has not examined the use of computer serials control systems in public libraries.

Alternative Materials

The public library can avoid cataloging and processing costs in two ways: by buying paperback books and by renting books. For popular titles in substantial demand, all of the thirty-one large public library systems surveyed except the Boston Public Library buy substantial numbers of paperback books. About 28 percent of the books purchased by the branch libraries of the New York Public Library are paperbacks. The library systems averaged 40,000 paperback volumes, as indicated in table 5.3. Paperbacks are usually shelved in wire racks and are not cataloged. Since many paperback titles have a short reign of popularity, multiple copies will not be retained by the library. Thus, the library can lower costs by buying paperbacks, even though it assumes the books will have disintegrated or been lost within two years. Paperbacks are less expensive than hardbacks, and paperbacks are handled in a way that avoids the expense of cataloging. Many paperback books are shipped directly to branches from jobbers.

Twenty of the thirty-one large public library systems surveyed rent books, as indicated in table 5.3. Josten's and McNaughton's are the two principal firms that rent books to libraries. The libraries can contract for the maintenance of a rental collection of a particular number of volumes in a location, say 480. Each month, 120 new volumes may be received. The library can either select titles it wants, or it can specify a profile of interests, say 40 percent bestsellers in multiple copies, 20 percent mysteries, 10 percent science fiction, and so on. In the latter case, the rental firm will track the bestseller lists and monitor new titles and ship rental volumes according to the profile of the branch. The rental volumes will be shipped directly to the branch already jacketed, processed, labeled, and ready for use. The branch library returns rental books it no longer wants, even those in the current shipment if they are not suitable. The cost for a 480-volume rental collection with 120 new volumes replaced each month is about $200 per month (in 1978).[13] Lower cost plans that include used books are also available. A certain fraction of the used books may be retained by the library, and others may be purchased at low cost. The books returned to the rental company may be rented to other libraries as used books or may be sold in secondhand book markets.

The Fairfax County Public Library uses a book buyback service of the Ingram Book Company in Nashville. Ingram agrees to buy back books within a specified period of time. The main difference between the rental and buyback services seems to be that the cost of lost books is absorbed by the rental firms while their cost is born by the library with the buyback service.

The rental-buyback services allow a library to acquire multiple copies of popular books while incurring relatively low processing-cataloging costs and with a regular procedure for weeding out unneeded books. In this way, handling books acquired for popular use can be kept separate from more permanent acquisitions. The expense of processing and cataloging materials with short useful lives is reduced by using the preprocessed books of the rental firm.

Libraries can also make microform materials available to users. While microform materials are more difficult to use because they require a device to project the film, the cost per page of materials is much lower than the cost of the printed page. Therefore, more microform pages than book pages can be bought with the same funds. Microforms also require less storage space. The use of microform materials in public libraries is limited, however, to large facilities. All the systems surveyed have microform readers in the system, although not in each library in the system. Among thirty public systems reporting this information, however, only Houston has microform readers in all its branches, and only Fairfax, Montgomery, and Prince Georges Counties have microform readers in over half of their branches. Microforms must be

Table 5.3. *Alternative Materials and Circulation Control Activities:*
Means and Standard Deviations by Geographic Type

Materials	City	Metro	Suburb	All	F or Chi-square
Volumes of paperbacks acquired annually	51,269.25 (45,079.97) 12	14,751.00 (17,152.73) 4	35,971.57 (15,714.37) 7	40,262.43 (36,246.97) 23	1.693 (2,20)
Rental book uses (binary)	10 of 15 66.7%	8 of 9 88.9%	2 of 7 28.6%	20 of 31 64.5%	6.316** (2)
Percent of branches with microform readers	21.17 (32.56)	26.36 (29.44)	40.26 (28.98)	26.99 (30.86)	0.910 (2,28)
Percent of branches with photoduplication services	91.49 (9.04)	69.21 (28.52)	85.73 (21.18)	83.46 (21.18)	3.647** (2,28)
Circulation Control					
Manual system used (binary)	2 of 15 13.3%	1 of 9 11.1%	0 of 7 0.0%	3 of 31 9.7%	0.912 (2)
Microfilm system used but not the computer (binary)	8 of 15 53.3%	5 of 9 55.5%	6 of 7 85.7%	19 of 31 61.3%	2.285 (2)
Computer-based system used in part or all (binary)	5 of 15 33.3%	3 of 9 33.3%	1 of 7 14.3%	9 of 31 29.0%	0.954 (2)
Antitheft Systems					
Guards and parcel checks (binary)	12 of 15 80.0%	5 of 9 55.6%	0 of 7 0.0%	17 of 31 54.8%	12.336*** (2)
Electronic security checks (binary)	10 of 15 66.5%	5 of 9 55.6%	2 of 7 28.6%	17 of 31 54.8%	2.799 (2)
Either guards or electronic security (binary)	15 of 15 100.0%	7 of 9 77.8%	2 of 7 28.6%	24 of 31 77.4%	13.930*** (2)

Source: Author's survey of library systems.

Note: For binary variables, the number using the technique of those responding is indicated with the percentage given underneath. The chi-square statistic is reported to test for significant variation across the geographic types. Degrees of freedom are reported in parentheses below the statistic.

For continuous variables, the mean is reported with standard deviation in parentheses. If not all libraries responded, the number responding is indicated below the standard deviation. An *F*-statistic from an analysis of variation is reported to test for differences in means across the geographic types. Degrees of freedom are reported in parentheses below the statistic. Statistical significance is indicated: ***0.01 level; **0.05; *0.10 level.

used in the library, are inconvenient, are more difficult to read than print, and so their use seems to be limited to materials that are not widely used. Thus, it is not surprising that microforms are only used in less than a third of the branches of public libraries.

Many public libraries offer photoduplication services to patrons. Seven of thirty systems reporting this information have photoduplication services available in every branch, as indicated in table 5.3. All but three have photoduplication services available in more than half of the branches. The New York Public Library does not have the service in a few older branches that have direct current wiring (duplication machines require alternatiing current). While changes in the copyright law may discourage the use of photoduplication to some extent, such services are widely accepted in the public libraries. Because the use of the machines is paid for by patrons—coin-operated machines are common—the equipment may generate some revenue for the library. The availability of photoduplication services may reduce the theft and vandalism of materials.

Circulation Control

Circulation control systems note materials that are charged out of the library, check those that are returned, and send notices to borrowers who have materials that are overdue. Some circulation control systems may be able to inform a patron when an item is already borrowed and establish a queue of future borrowers for material currently on loan. The system may also identify materials that are lost. Some circulation control systems generate summary information on the circulation of materials; for example, the number of materials circulated, by type of material.

The conventional circulation control system was a manual system. The borrower filled out a card, the card was filed and recalled when the material was returned. Three of the thirty-one library systems surveyed continue to use the manual system of circulation control. The specific systems are indicated in table 5.2. Summaries by geographic type are given in table 5.3.

Beginning sometime in the early 1950s some libraries began substituting microfilm records for the manual card system. In microfilm circulation control a picture is taken of the borrower's card and the book card, together with a unique transaction number. Recording on film can be done more quickly than recording on paper; microfilm systems apparently speed up the time it takes to check out materials, and possibly reduce the clerical staff needed for circulation control. When the book is returned, the card with the transaction number at charge-in is matched to the charge-out transaction numbers. Card sorters or computers may be used for this matching procedure. Those books for which no charge-in number is matched to the charge-out are considered overdue. The microfilm record is searched for the overdue transaction numbers. But overdue notices are produced manually from the information available on the microfilm. Nineteen of the thirty-one library systems report using the microfilm circulation control system.

Nine of the thirty-one systems use more computer intensive circulation control systems. At charge-out, a computer readable book card and borrower's card are read by machine, which creates a computer manipulable record of the charge-out. When the material is returned, the information is again entered in computer readable form. The computer can match returns with charge-outs, identify overdue materials, and print overdue notices using information in a computer file on borrowers. In this respect, the computer based circulation control can duplicate the microfilm systems output with substantially less labor effort.

The capability of the computer-based systems exceeds that of the manual and microfilm systems, however. First, the computer can check the borrower's card against a list of borrowers with overdue materials. Such a credit check can be used to deny library privileges to persons who seldom return materials. Second, the computer can check the book against a list of requests. A renewal, for example, can be made with the assurance that no one else is waiting for the item. Requests anywhere in the system can be honored by materials available anywhere else in the system. The sophisticated handling of requests is given as an important advantage of computer-based circulation control. While computer-based circulation control systems can be handled with batch processing in large central computer facilities, on-line systems using microcomputers seem likely to dominate. The on-line system gives the rapid credit check and updates the ''on-loan'' file immediately. Batch systems may be updated, say overnight. As the costs of small computers fall, the on-line circulation control systems are likely to become important.

Third, a computer may be the base for a self-charge system which would reduce the size of the clerical staff. A self-charge system might operate like the twenty-four hour mechanical teller now common in banks. A borrower's card is magnetically coded and read by machine. A secret code number must be keyed in to verify the user's identity. A book card, or perhaps the book jacket, is inserted into the device and a charge-out is recorded. Perhaps an optical code similar to that now used in grocery checkouts might be used. Perhaps the charge-out device will also deactivate the antitheft strip. The charge-out can be denied if the borrower's card is not valid, or if the book is reserved. Self-charge-out via a computer terminal device has not appeared at this time, but seems to be a logical extension of new circulation control technology.

Computer-based circulation control can produce very sophisticated information about circulation as a byproduct. The books can be characterized in substantial detail by subject, level, language, and age. Monitoring requests might also be detailed by subject, level, and language. Such information might be used to evaluate acquisitions policies, for example the acquisition of multiple copies, the use of rental materials, the length of the loan period, and type I and type II errors in book selection. While I doubt that any library currently uses its circulation system in this way, it may be that as such systems develop, their value as management tools will increase.

The quality of the circulation control systems might be evaluated by considering the shrinkage rate for library materials. Shrinkage can occur if charged out materials are not returned and if materials are "borrowed" without being charged out. Twenty library systems were willing to speculate about the proportion of charged out materials that were not returned. The nonreturn rate varied from less than 0.1 percent to 8 percent, with a mean of 2.4 percent. The theft of materials not charged out can be detected by taking inventory of the stock. Inventories are expensive, however, and thus are rarely undertaken. Of fifteen libraries that had undertaken an inventory, the mean latest year of an inventory was 1968, ten years before the interview. While full inventories are not undertaken frequently enough to give a consistent guide to solving the theft problem, sample inventories might be undertaken more often in order to evaluate the circulation control and antitheft systems.

Antitheft Systems

An effective circulation control system can discourage patrons from charging out materials they do not intend to return. Unless measures are taken to discourage theft, these patrons may steal the materials they want. The conventional method of theft control is to have guards checking parcels at the exits of the libraries. Seventeen of the thirty-one large library sytems reported having guards check parcels somewhere in their systems. Most have such checks only in a few locations. The use of guards and parcel checks is concentrated among central city and metropolitan systems; it is not found in any of the suburban systems surveyed.

In the last few years electronic systems have become available to discourage theft. A magnetic strip is placed in each book or other material. If the material is taken through the exit check, a tattletale sounds off. Some systems are designed to have the material passed around the check at exit. Others are demagnetized at checkout and are remagnetized when they are returned. The electronic antitheft systems are relatively inexpensive. The tattletale leases for less than $1,000 a year. The magnetic strips can be inserted in the books for $0.25 to $0.30 by bookjobbers; in-house processing costs may be less. The strips cost less than $0.10 per item. Theft detection strips need not be put in the entire collection. Insertion in new materials will capture the most valuable materials. Reference books, rare books, and other especially valuable materials might be retrofitted.

Electronic security devices are in use in seventeen of the thirty-one library systems, including ten that have guards and parcel checks somewhere in the system. Seven use the electronic system but do not use the guards. Seven have guards but no electronic system, and seven have no antitheft system.

The low cost of the electronic systems should make an antitheft system appropriate for libraries that previously had no antitheft system. And the electronic systems should replace the guards and parcel checks in most situations, except where guards are required for personal security reasons whether they search parcels or not. Guards and parcel checks are both several times more expensive and a greater inconvenience to patrons than the electronic systems. The effectiveness of antitheft efforts might be judged by taking sample inventories to measure the stock shrinkage rate. One librarian commented that employee theft may be significant. Neither guards nor electronic systems seem likely to affect employee theft. Only 8 percent of public libraries used electronic antitheft devices in the early 1970s, according to Bingham.[14] Bingham did not consider parcel checks.

Reference Activities

While reference services are the purview of the public service division of most libraries, several technical arrangements are available to support reference activities. A variety of large bibliographic reference files have been entered into computer storage. The computer can be used to search for key words to select items for a bibliography. *Chemical Abstracts*, for example, can be searched in this way. A variety of vendors, including Lockheed, Bibliographic Retrieval Services, and Systems Dynamics Corporation, provide this service via telephone lines and computer terminals. The user need pay only for the connect time (a monthly minimum may be required), say twenty-five dollars per hour, and two cents or five cents per citation printed out. The service is most useful to scholars who do scientific and medical research. Ten of the thirty-one library systems offer access to such computer bibliographic search services. (See table 5.4.) Most of the participating public libraries are central city systems.

Some public libraries have developed their own computer-based information retrieval systems. The New York Public Library has an index of community service information, a file of agencies indexed by the problems and persons they are prepared to help. The Public Library of Nashville indexes the local newspapers because a high proportion of their reference inquiries concern the local newspapers. Six of the thirty-one library systems maintain some form of local index on a computer. (See table 5.4.)

Reference services may require information not available in the local library. Twenty-six of the thirty-one systems have teletypes that are used to request materials via interlibrary loan. Eleven have wide-area telephone ser-

Table 5.4. Use of Technically Based Reference Activities by Geographic Type

	City	Metropolitan	Suburban	All	Chi-square
Reference Service					
Computer-based bibliographic reference	7 of 15 46.7%	2 of 9 22.2%	1 of 7 14.3%	10 of 31 32.3%	2.875 (2)
Computer-based index—locally operated	4 of 15 26.7%	2 of 9 22.2%	0 of 7 0.0%	6 of 31 19.4%	2.241 (2)
Wide-area telephone service	3 of 15 20.0%	4 of 9 44.4%	4 of 7 57.1%	11 of 31 35.5%	3.321 (2)
Teletype for interlibrary loan	13 of 15 86.7%	6 of 9 66.7%	7 of 7 100.0%	26 of 31 83.9%	3.402 (2)
Electronic Accounting					
Payroll	15 of 15 100.0%	9 of 9 100.0%	7 of 7 100.0%	31 of 31 100.0%	—
Personnel records	7 of 15 46.7%	6 of 9 66.7%	6 of 7 85.7%	19 of 31 61.3%	3.222 (2)
Budget system	9 of 15 60.0%	6 of 9 66.7%	5 of 7 71.4%	20 of 31 64.5%	0.298 (2)

Source: Author's survey.

Note: The number of libraries that use the technique relative to those responding is indicated with the percentage given below it. The chi-square statistic is reported to test for significant variation across the geographic types. Degrees of freedom are reported in parentheses below the statistic.

vice (WATS) for use in interlibrary loan. Only four libraries—Denver, Cleveland, Indianapolis, and Atlanta—do not have teletype or WATS lines to facilitate interlibrary loan.

Electronic Accounting Functions

Data processing is used in the public libraries for routine accounting functions. Payrolls may be prepared, personnel records may be maintained, and budget records may be processed by computers. These activities may be moved to computers on a citywide basis. That is, the city or county government may introduce computer-based payrolls for all employees, including those in the library. Thus, the decision to adopt computer based accounting systems may be made outside the library. The use of these activities is considered here so that the possible interaction between library specific data processing activities and citywide data processing activities can be considered. Autonomous library systems, however, may act alone in adopting electronic accounting functions. The payrolls of all the public library systems surveyed are prepared electronically, as indicated in table 5.4, sometimes by contractors. Personnel and budget records are handled electronically in over 60 percent of the library systems.

RATES OF DIFFUSION OF INNOVATIONS

The descriptions of technical services presented in the preceding sections indicate that substantial technological change is occurring in the public libraries. Innovations have appeared in a wide variety of areas of library activities; some are related to the use of computers while others are not. It may be appropriate to examine the pace of technological change. How rapidly do innovations spread from the time a first library begins a new practice until all similar libraries are using the practice? Are there easily recognizable characteristics of early adopters that might indicate the motivation for technological change? Answers to these questions may suggest policies that might promote useful technological change.

Diffusion Paths

When a library evaluates a new practice, it has limited evidence on which to decide whether the benefits of the new practice will justify the costs. Until the library has experience with the practice itself, it will not be able to determine the benefits and costs of the practice. A library that picks up every possible new practice will incur substantial costs in discovering practices that are worthwhile because many practices will fail. A library that always delays the adoption of innovations will incur the costs of maintaining expensive antiquated systems when new practices that save money and enhance output are available. The optimal innovation strategy involves some balance between adopting untried practices quickly when they work, and avoiding costly failures. Because the adoption decision must be made on limited evidence, this balance may not be easily struck.

From an industry point of view, some libraries must be willing to experiment with new practices. Once a few libraries have found a new practice successful, other libraries can more confidently mimic the new practice. The pattern of the diffusion of innovations from early to later adopters generally traces a sigmoidal curve.[15] That is, a cumulative percentage of libraries that have adopted the innovation will grow slowly at first during a trial period. If the innovation is successful, the pace of diffusion will accelerate. Once most have adopted the innovation the pace will decelerate again.

The patterns of diffusion of twenty innovations across the thirty-one large public library systems surveyed are described in table 5.5. The year of first use indicated by any of the surveyed systems is reported in the first column. The proportion of systems that currently use the practice is reported in the second column. Only three of the twenty innovations began before 1950, thus only recent innovations are considered. Only three of the innovations are currently used in all the surveyed library systems, suggesting that on average over thirty years are required from first use by a system until a practice becomes universally adopted. This conclusion may be unwarranted, however, for several reasons.

The diffusion rates are explored further by noting the year when half of the systems were using the technique, reported in the third column of table 5.5.[16] The number of years from first use to 50 percent use is reported in column 4 of table 5.5, with linear extrapolations in parentheses for practices that have not yet reached 50 percent use. (The linear extrapolations will overstate the time to 50 percent adoption if the diffusion path is sigmoidal.) Of the twenty innovations, nine took more than fifteen years to reach 50 percent adoption. But of these nine, four have been abandoned by some library systems. Thus, it seems the average time it takes for an innovation to become universally adopted is somewhat less than thirty years (assuming symmetry between the first 50 percent and the second 50 percent of adoption). Overall, the pace of diffusion of innovations in libraries is faster than in urban fire departments and compares favorably with the pace elsewhere in the economy.[17]

The process of the diffusion of innovations may be slowed by the complex interaction among innovations. In particular, we observe new innovations becoming available to replace older innovations before the older innovations are fully diffused. Thus, a latecomer may leapfrog certain technologies and move directly to the most recent technology. For example, a library currently using a manual cataloging system could now move directly to using a catalog contractor to prepare computer based catalogs. Such a library may never make use of intermediate computer based bibliographic files such as those in Milwaukee and Dallas. Moreover, such a library might never make use of the cataloging networks, such as OCLC. For another example, a library using a manual circulation control system might move directly to a computer-based circulation control system without ever using the microfilm systems. Security is a third area where the electronic systems are being adopted by libraries that never used guards and parcel checks.

Technologies may have finite lives defined by the introduction of subsequent techniques. Innovations might therefore be classified according to the likelihood of their obsolescence. An innovation that seems likely to become obsolete might be termed an intermediate technology. An innovation that seems likely to persist for a long period of time might be called a climax technology. The extent of diffusion of a particular innovation is likely to be influenced by the likelihood that the technology will become obsolete. A climax technology is likely to be diffused more widely than an intermediate technology. The fact that only three of the twenty innovations studied have reached universal application among surveyed libraries reflects the fact that many of the innovations studied are intermediate technologies. Newer technologies dominate the intermediate technologies for many libraries.

The pattern of diffusion will also be influenced by the extent of local development required to make a technique useful in an individual library system. Modular innovations that can be introduced immediately into a library with little modification of existing programs and procedures will be expected to be adopted more quickly than innovations that require the development of new procedures and substantial adaptation to local circumstances.

For example, a coin-operated photoduplication service can be plugged in where alternating current is available. The service can be provided incurring only a minimum of local development expense. The introduction of this service has little impact on other library operations. A cataloging network like OCLC is another example of a service that can be introduced without making major changes in existing practices. The local card catalog remains intact, and control of the cataloging function is retained in-house. In contrast, the use of an approval plan relocates the responsibility for selection and may change the activities of most of the professional library staff. Use of a catalog jobber to produce a computer output microfiche catalog replaces the card catalog and may cause a potentially significant reduction in the cataloging staff (at least compared to manual cataloging). Much of the control of the catalog passes to the jobber. This may explain why the use of the catalog network has diffused much more rapidly than the use of the LC-MARC computer generated catalog even though the LC-MARC catalog may be a climax technology.

The pace of diffusion may also reflect differences in the services public libraries seek to provide. A system with no central library that concentrates its resources on the current demands of readers may be more interested in using

Table 5.5. Summary of Diffusion Patterns

Area of Innovation	Year of First Use in Surveyed Libraries	Percentage of Systems Currently Using Innovation	Year When 50 Percent Were Using Innovation	Years from Introduction to 50 Percent Use (a)	Number of Libraries Using but No Year Given (b)
Acquisitions					
Greenaway plan	1954	80.6 [c]	1963	9	5
Approval plan	1972	16.1	—	(16)	0
Computer-based ordering	1965	38.7	—	(17)	0
Cataloging					
LC-MARC based catalog	1969	38.7	—	(12)	0
Cataloging network	1973	51.6	1978	5	0
Materials					
Paperbacks	1958	96.8	1970	12	4
Rental books	1957	64.5 [c]	1974	17	3
Microform readers	1939	100.0	1949	10	13
Photoduplication	1954	100.0	1964	10	5
Circulation Control					
Microfilm	1948	61.3 [c]	1964	16	2
Computer-based	1972	29.0	—	(10)	0

Antitheft Systems					
Guards and parcel checks	1892	54.8ᶜ	1978	86	4
Electronic security devices	1969	54.8ᶜ	1978	9	1
Reference Service					
Computer-based information retrieval	1967	32.3ᶜ	—	(17)	1
Computer-based local index	1969	19.4	—	(23)	0
WATS line	1968	35.5	—	(14)	0
Teletype	1960	83.9	1969	9	3
Electronic Accounting Functions					
Payroll	1960	100.0	1968	8	3
Personnel	1960	61.3	1977	17	1
Budget	1966	64.5	1975	9	1

Source: Author's survey.

[a] Linear extrapolations are given in parentheses for innovations that have not reached 50 percent diffusion.

[b] A count of the respondents using the technique, but who could not indicate when first use occurred. These are assumed to be among the first 50 percent adopting.

[c] The technique may have been abandoned by some library systems.

approval plans to get books quickly, in purchasing paperback books to make more current materials available, and in using jobber cataloging to reduce catalog lags. Such a library may never adopt computer-based information retrieval. A system with more commitment to research support services, with a large central library, may adopt microform readers and a WATS line more quickly. They may be more reluctant to give up the decentralized management of selection, cataloging, and circulation control that computer based systems threaten.

Overall, the patterns of diffusion reported in table 5.5 reflect characteristics of the innovations—how quickly will they become obsolete and how easily are they adapted to a local library—and characteristics of the libraries—how well does the innovation meet the particular objectives of the library? Given these factors, the pace of innovation among the large public libraries seems reasonably swift.

Early Adoption

The process of innovation may be explored by looking for patterns among early adopters of innovations. One issue is whether the same libraries tend to be early adopters of a variety of innovations, or whether most libraries participate in early adoption of some innovations. A second issue is whether libraries that are among early adopters of particular innovations are different in obvious ways from later adopters.

These issues are explored by classifying each library as either an early or late adopter. For innovations that have not reached 50 percent diffusion, all current users are treated as early adopters. For innovations that have exceeded 50 percent diffusion, all systems that adopted through the year when 50 percent diffusion was reached are treated as early adopters. The number of libraries treated as early adopters is indicated in the first column of table 5.6. In some cases, a substantial number of libraries adopted the innovation in the year the fiftieth percentile of diffusion was reached, thus the number of early adopters exceeds 50 percent in several cases.

CONTINGENCY TABLES.   The interdependence of early adoption is examined to determine whether early adoption of one innovation is related to early adoption of others. Contingency tables are constructed for each pair of innovations. An individual library can be classified in four ways: adopted both innovations early; adopted neither innovation early; adopted innovation A early and B late; adopted B early and A late. The contingency tables for each pair of innovations are summarized in table 5.6. The first number is the number of libraries that adopted both innovations early; the second is the number of libraries that adopted either or both innovations early. Random distribution of the thirty-one libraries over the four cells of the contingency

Table 5.6. Comparisons of Early Adoptions of Innovations

	Number in Early Adopter Group	Greenaway	Approval	Ordering	LC-MARC	Network	Paperbacks	Rentals	Microfilm	Photoduplication	Microfilm	Circulation Computer	Guards	Electronic Theft	Information Retrieval	Local Computer Index	WATS Line	Teletype	Payroll	Personnel
Approval plan	5	4/15																		
Computer ordering	12	5/23	3/14																	
LC-MARC based catalog	12	5/23	3/14	6/18																
Cataloging network	16	7/25	1/20	6/22	4/24															
Paperbacks	22	11/27	4/23	9/24	8/26	10/28														
Rental books	17	11/22	4/18	6/23	5/24	9/24	13/26													
Microform readers	17	11/22	4/18	6/23	5/24	11/22	12/27	12/22												
Photoduplication	17	9/24	2/20	6/23	8/21	11/22	9/30*	10/24	12/22											
Microfilm circulation	16	10/21	4/17	8/20	5/23	9/23	11/27	9/24	7/26	8/25										
Computer circulation	9	4/21	2/12	5/16	3/18	8/17*	5/26	4/22	5/21	6/20	5/20									
Guards	17	10/23	2/20	5/24	5/24	12/21*	9/30*	8/26	11/23	11/23	11/22	5/21								
Electronic theft	17	7/26	2/20	7/22	5/24	11/22	12/27	9/25	9/27	8/26	9/24	7/19	10/24							
Information retrieval	10	7/19	2/13	5/17	4/18	6/20	6/26	7/20	5/22	8/19	9/17*	4/15	6/21	5/22						
Local computer index	6	3/19	0/11	3/15	3/15	4/18	1/27*	4/19	2/21	5/18	5/17	2/13	4/19	3/20	4/12					
WATS line	11	5/22	3/13	3/20	6/17	5/22	6/27	7/21	6/22	7/21	3/24	3/17	5/23	5/23	2/19	2/15				
Teletype	15	9/22	2/18	6/21	7/20	9/22	10/27	6/26	9/23	10/22	7/24	5/19	10/22	7/25	6/21	2/19	6/20			
Payroll	17	9/24	2/20	6/23	6/23	9/24	11/28	7/27	9/25	11/23	8/25	3/23	12/22	9/25	6/21	3/20	6/22	10/22		
Personnel	15	10/21	3/17	7/20	6/21	8/23	12/25	8/24	10/22	7/25	8/23	4/20	8/24	7/25	3/22	3/18	5/21	8/22	6/26	
Budget	17	11/22	3/19	8/21	6/23	8/25	14/25	9/25	9/25	9/25	10/23	5/21	10/24	8/26	4/23	2/21	6/22	8/24	9/25	12/20*
Number in early adopter group		16	5	12	12	16	22	17	17	17	16	9	17	17	10	6	11	15	17	15

Note: The first number is the number of library systems that were among the first 50 percent of libraries to adopt both innovations. The second number indicated is the number of libraries that were among the first half adopters for either innovation. The total number of systems examined is thirty-one. Statistical significance of a chi-square test of a contingency table indicates whether the early adoptions are independent. * indicates lack of independence at the 10 percent level.

table should put about eight libraries in each cell when fifteen or sixteen are treated as early adopters. In this case, the first number in each cell in table 5.6 should be close to eight and the second number should be close to twenty-four. If the adoption of one innovation is a necessary first step to adoption of another, or if circumstances that lead to the adoption of one also lead to the adoption of another, then early adopters of one innovation should be early adopters of the other. The first number indicated in each cell in table 5.6 should be large and the second number should be relatively small. Very few such circumstances are found in table 5.6. Another possibility is that adoption of one innovation precludes the adoption of another. In this case, the first number should be small and the second large. This case is not found in the table either. Therefore, the adoption of each innovation studied seems relatively independent of the adoption of the other innovations. A formal statistical test of this independence is performed by calculating a chi-square statistic for each contingency table. While the chi-square statistics are not reported, those cells of table 5.6 with statistically significant chi-square statistics are indicated by asterisks. Of 190 contingency tables calculated, only 7 have chi-square statistics suggesting interdependence at the 10 percent level. Of these, only the interaction of automated budgeting and personnel records seems consistent with some strong technical link. It does not seem to be the case that libraries that have adopted some computer based innovations have tended to be early to adopt others. Nor has early adoption of computer based accounting systems—payroll and personnel—been associated with early adoption of specific computer systems.

No small group of library systems seems likely to stand out as especially innovative; rather, most libraries seem to participate in the early use of some innovations. This pattern may be desirable. The early use of innovations may involve investment in development that can be avoided by latecomers. Early users may also incur more risk of failure than latecomers. Therefore, it may be appropriate that most library systems participate in testing innovations. The innovations are also sufficiently varied that different circumstances may apply in the adoption of each. Therefore, it is not surprising that no single group of the thirty-one library systems surveyed stands out as a trendsetter in all areas of library innovation.

DISCRIMINANT ANALYSIS. The specific characteristics of library systems that are early adopters are explored for each innovation by discriminant analysis. The explanatory variables are the same as those used in the analysis of library inputs in chapter 2 and fall into three groups. First, the cost of labor to the library, indicated by the compensation of a recruit librarian, may influence the decision to adopt an innovation. If some innovations are viewed as labor-saving, libraries with higher labor costs would be expected to adopt them before libraries with lower labor costs.

Second, the fiscal circumstances of local government may influence the innovation decision. This effect may work in two directions, however. On the one hand, the development of an innovation may require slack resources. Some of the innovations require large setup costs in order to lower continuing costs. Library systems in local areas with higher expenditures per capita and larger levels of intergovernmental revenues per capita would be expected to adopt such innovations first. On the other hand, high levels of local government expenditures may reflect high competing demands from other agencies and so may indicate that less money is available to finance change in the library. Therefore, the direction of association between local governments' own expenditures per capita and intergovernmental revenues per capita and the early adoption of innovations is ambiguous. A more detailed characterization of the local fiscal scene is very difficult. The flexibility of operations may differ for libraries that operate somewhat autnomously from local governments than for those that are departments. For example, a department may have less flexibility to incur the fixed costs of computer systems in order to save operating costs.

Third, the demographic characteristics of the area served may influence the decision to innovate. Large systems may be better able to incur the costs of developing new practices. Some new techniques may involve economies of scale such that only larger systems can use them. On the other hand, very large systems may be more bureaucratic, and managers may find innovation more difficult. The population of the area measures the size of the system.

Areas with more educated adults use the public library more intensively, and so certain innovations may be more useful in such libraries. Adults in central cities tend to have lower education levels than those in the suburbs, yet the central city systems tend to have larger central libraries and more specialized library services than the suburbs. Innovations such as microfilm readers, that meet specialized needs, would seem more likely to be adopted in central city systems before being adopted by suburbs.

Finally, the recent growth in population in the area serviced may influence the innovation decision. Rapid growth may pressure a library system so that new techniques are sought. A library system in a growing area may be less tied to traditional practices. Innovation may be easier with growth.

Standardized discriminant coefficients for each of twenty discriminant analyses are reported in table 5.7. Each is reported such that a positive sign on the coefficient indicates that the variable is associated with a higher probability of being an early adopter. The rank order of the coefficients in each analysis indicates the relative importance of each variable in discriminating early from late adopters. The chi-square statistic for each analysis makes a probability statement about the ability to discriminate.

Overall, the discriminant analysis exercise is not very successful, as represented in table 5.7. Only four of the twenty discriminant functions are statistically significant at the 5 percent level with the chi-square test: Network Cataloging, Guards, Rental Books, and Automated Budgeting. That is, given the values of the seven variables used in the exercise, one can make a statistically meaningful estimate of which libraries would adopt a particular innovation early for only four innovations. A second method for observing the ability to discriminate early from late adopters on the basis of library characteristics is to calculate what proportion of the libraries is correctly classified as early or late by the discriminant function. The value of each variable is multiplied by the discriminant coefficient and the products are summed for each library, establishing a discriminant score. If the score is greater than some critical value, the library is predicted to be an early adopter. The proportion correctly classified is reported at the end of each row in table 5.7. Since the classification is based on the same libraries from which the discriminant functions were estimated, the classification exercise is not statistically meaningful, yet the values make clear the nature of the discriminant functions. Coin flipping would tend to classify 50 percent of the libraries correctly, so a powerful discriminant function should correctly classify a much higher proportion of the libraries. Over 80 percent of the libraries are correctly classified for only five innovations: the same four indicated by the chi-square statistic and automated personnel records.

The role of individual variables in discriminating early from late adopters—other things equal—is summarized in table 5.8. The variables with the first and second largest coefficients when ranked in absolute value are reported for each innovation. No single observed factor is pushing early adoption of innovations. Each variable is positively and negatively associated with early adoption of different innovations. High labor cost seems associated with early use of the automation of several accounting and recordkeeping functions, but has played no strong role with automated cataloging or circulation innovations. Fiscal stringency, represented by lower per capita expenditures from own sources and from intergovernmental sources on local government functions other than libraries, is associated with early adoption of some innovations, including network cataloging and computer-based circulation. Yet the fiscal variables appear important for only a few of the innovations.

Libraries that are departments of city governments seem somewhat less likely to adopt approval plans and computer based circulation control systems early. This suggests that the flexibility of more autonomous library organizations may be important for early adoption of these innovations. Yet this association is found to be important for only a few innovations.

The characteristics of the area served by the library also seem important for early adoption of some innovations. Larger library systems seem more likely to have adopted LC-MARC computer-generated catalogs and automated payrolls early. Yet smaller library systems seem to have been more likely to adopt automated ordering, personnel records, and budgets early. Areas with more adults who are high school graduates seem less likely to have adopted network cataloging and more likely to have adopted LC-MARC computer-based cataloging and approval plans. Areas that grew more rapidly in the

1960s seem more likely to have adopted microfilm circulation control systems early, but less likely to have been early users of rental books, microfilm readers, photoduplication, and guards. In part, these differences may reflect differences among city, metropolitan, and suburban systems.

Overall, it is difficult to generalize about the features of library systems that are early adopters of innovations. Each innovation has its own characteristics and consequently different factors seem important for the early adoption of different innovations. The hypotheses about the role of high labor costs, fiscal stringency, and the size and growth of the area served each find modest confirmation in the evidence but none are important for more than a few innovations. Needless to say, the process of early adoption of innovations is complex.

Interaction between Inputs and Innovations

The effort to explain early use of innovations relative to the external characteristics of library systems subsumes the fact that other input choices the library makes may be important in the decision to adopt an innovation. For example, a library acquiring more materials and more titles may have a greater need for new cataloging aids. Therefore, it is appropriate to compare the inputs of libraries that have adopted an innovation and those that have not. The difficulty with such a comparison is that the choice of inputs and innovations may be simultaneous. An innovation may allow a library to acquire more titles than it previously did, just as the acquisition of a large number of titles may influence the decision to innovate, say, in cataloging. A library with high operational costs may adopt innovations and in so doing may lower its operational costs. Both effects will shape a comparison of costs between innovators and noninnovators. Thus, the comparison of input levels between library systems using an innovation and those not using an innovation is for descriptive purposes rather than an exercise to explore causes of innovation.

The mean value of the input is reported separately for the library systems that have adopted a particular innovation and for those that have not. An F-statistic indicates whether the difference between the two means is statistically significant. One input variable is binary, indicating whether the chief librarian had been promoted from within the library. A chi-square test indicates whether there is a statistically significant association between adoption and promotion from within. The statistics are reported in table 5.9. Five innovations that might be expected to have important associations with other library inputs are examined.

Do the major technical service innovations lower library expenditures? Library expenditures per capita are higher in libraries that have LC-MARC cataloging than in those that do not; the same is true for libraries that use computer-based circulation control. The higher expenditure levels, however,

Table 5.7. Standardized Discriminant Coefficients for Early Adopters

Explanatory Variables	Labor Cost	Own Net Expenditures	Intergovernmental Expenditures	Department (binary)	Population in 1970	Percent of Adults High School Graduates	Percent Growth—1960-1970	Chi-square	Percent Correctly Classified	Number in Early User Group
Greenaway plan	-0.193 (5)	-0.490 (3)	0.739 (1)	-0.558 (2)	-0.116 (7)	0.131 (6)	-0.313 (4)	4.740	64.52	16
Approval plan	-0.006 (7)	0.291 (4)	-0.231 (5)	-0.533 (2)	0.130 (6)	0.585 (1)	0.494 (3)	7.799	77.42	5
EDP ordered	0.813 (2)	0.080 (5)	0.495 (3)	0.084 (4)	-1.393 (1)	-0.007 (7)	0.074 (6)	7.333	70.97	12
MARC cataloging	0.145 (5)	0.105 (6)	-0.660 (3)	0.057 (7)	0.964 (2)	0.992 (1)	0.154 (4)	6.064	70.97	12
Network cataloging	0.338 (4)	0.256 (6)	-0.520 (2)	0.121 (7)	-0.309 (5)	-0.606 (1)	-0.397 (3)	17.632**	83.87	16
Paperbacks	0.393 (2)	-0.254 (4)	0.338 (3)	0.186 (5)	-0.085 (7)	0.760 (1)	0.139 (6)	6.398	77.42	22
Rental books	-0.674 (2)	-0.113 (6)	-0.164 (5)	0.253 (4)	-0.031 (7)	0.566 (3)	-0.985 (1)	13.226*	87.10	17
Microfilm	-0.237 (5)	0.360 (3)	0.009 (7)	0.542 (2)	0.295 (4)	0.142 (6)	-0.797 (1)	4.096	74.19	17
Photoduplication	0.349 (3)	0.209 (4)	-0.396 (2)	-0.001 (7)	0.096 (5)	0.067 (6)	-0.825 (1)	10.290	77.42	17
Microfilm circulation	0.539 (4)	-0.459 (5)	0.066 (7)	-0.395 (6)	-0.631 (3)	-1.158 (1)	0.722 (2)	4.669	61.29	16

Innovation	(1)	(2)	(3)	(4)	(5)	(6)	(7)			
Computer circulation	0.343 (4)	0.623 (3)	−0.932 (1)	−0.625 (2)	−0.252 (5)	0.026 (7)	−0.052 (6)	7.575	70.97	9
Guard	0.141 (4)	−0.060 (5)	0.010 (7)	0.050 (6)	0.102 (3)	−0.819 (1)	−0.163 (2)	16.644**	83.87	17
Electronic check	0.599 (1)	−0.482 (2)	0.120 (7)	−0.300 (3)	0.232 (5)	−0.196 (6)	−0.249 (4)	3.215	61.29	17
EDP information	−0.222 (6)	−0.562 (1)	−0.333 (4)	−0.207 (7)	0.542 (2)	−0.254 (5)	−0.466 (3)	3.291	64.52	10
EDP index	−0.118 (5)	0.012 (7)	−0.549 (2)	−0.099 (6)	−0.385 (3)	−1.027 (1)	0.230 (4)	10.499	74.19	6
WATS line	−0.446 (4)	0.537 (1)	−0.077 (7)	0.510 (2)	−0.482 (3)	0.229 (6)	−0.301 (5)	4.700	74.19	11
Teletype	0.326 (3)	0.195 (6)	0.394 (1)	−0.079 (7)	0.364 (2)	0.242 (5)	−0.296 (4)	8.242	70.97	15
Payroll EDP	−0.083 (5)	−0.054 (6)	0.603 (1)	0.302 (3)	0.580 (2)	−0.103 (4)	0.013 (7)	5.589	64.52	17
Personnel EDP	1.137 (1)	−0.176 (6)	0.254 (5)	0.057 (7)	−1.128 (2)	−0.300 (4)	0.334 (3)	11.080	80.65	15
Budget EDP	0.778 (2)	−0.451 (4)	0.572 (3)	0.063 (6)	−1.161 (1)	−0.026 (7)	0.075 (5)	15.474**	80.65	17

Note: Each row reports a separate discriminant analysis of the innovation listed at left. The first number in each cell is the standardized discriminant coefficient where a positive sign indicates a greater probability of being an early adopter if the variable is larger, other things equal. The second number, in parentheses, is the rank order of the standardized discriminant coefficient in absolute value. Statistical significance is indicated: **0.05 level; ***0.01 level.

Table 5.8.   Summary of Discriminant Functions: First or Second Rank Coefficients

	Negative	Positive
Labor costs	Rental books [a]	Paperback books Electronic security Automated personnel [a] Automated budget [a] Automated ordering
Own net expenditures per capita	Electronic security Information retrieval	WATS line
Intergovernmental expenditures per capita	Network cataloging [a] Photoduplication Computer circulation Computer index	Greenaway plan Teletype Automated payroll
Department (binary)	Greenaway plan Approval plan Computer circulation	Microfilm WATS line
Population in 1970	Automated ordering Automated personnel [a] Automated budget [a]	LC-MARC based cataloging Information retrieval Teletype Automated payroll
Percent of adults high school graduates	Network cataloging Microfilm circulation Guards [a]	Approval plan LC-MARC based cataloging Paperback books Computer index
Percent growth in population— 1960–1970	Rental books [a] Microfilm Photoduplication Guards [a]	Microfilm circulation

Note: The classifications reported here summarize the discriminant functions reported in table 5.7.

[a] These innovations were over 80 percent correctly classified by the discriminant functions.

may indicate that the library systems that adopt innovations offer higher levels of service or face higher labor costs. Perhaps the higher costs have led to adopting innovations as a way to save money. One cannot infer that the innovations have raised costs.

In a very few instances there are associations between the main library activities and the innovations. Libraries with computer-based ordering systems have fewer locations per square mile and more volumes in stock per capita than those that have not adopted that innovation. Libraries with computer-based circulation control buy more titles. There is no difference in branch hours per week or in public service staff per capita between libraries with these innovations and those without. Libraries using cataloging networks have a larger proportion of their public service staffs in the main library. Perhaps the networks are more valuable for main library services.

One might expect that the electronic innovations examined here, especially approval plans, ordering systems, LC-MARC cataloging, and computer-based circulation control, would enable a library system to be more centrally managed. Thus, technical librarianship skills might be applied in central decisions, while individual library units could be operated successfully with less professional skill. One might also expect smaller and less professional technical service staffs. Few such effects are apparent from comparing input levels between innovators and noninnovators. Those libraries with LC-MARC computer-generated catalogs have a smaller fraction of public service workers professionally trained. One would expect, however, that the strongest effect on the public service division would be in ordering, selection, and circulation control rather than in catalog preparation, a function mainly of technical services. Therefore, there is little evidence here that libraries that have adopted the innovations use less labor than other libraries. It is quite possible that the libraries that have innovated have been the largest, most labor intensive libraries and have reduced labor inputs in technical services from former levels or from levels that would otherwise be necessary to provide similar levels of service. A much more detailed study of specific library operations would be necessary to estimate what labor requirements might be in the absence of innovation in the libraries that have innovated.

The technical service staffs of the libraries are compared. The technical service staffs include selection and ordering, if personnel are assigned specifically to these functions. They include cataloging and processing. Some technical service operations are organized in ways that makes separating the subfunctions difficult; therefore, the total technical service labor force and labor costs are compared. Libraries using the cataloging networks and computer-based circulation systems are found to have larger technical service labor forces. One might expect that some of the innovations would lead to less professional staff in technical services. In particular, the use of LC-MARC computer-generated cataloging might allow a library to substitute less skilled labor for more skilled labor. On average, 19 percent of the technical service staffs of libraries that use LC-MARC computer produced catalogs are professional, while 26 percent of the technical service staffs of the other libraries are professional. This difference is only slightly statistically significant (at the 15 percent level).

The labor cost of technical services can be estimated by multiplying the number of professional workers by the salary of professional workers with five years experience (a benchmark value) and adding in fringe benefits. A similar calculation is made for clerical workers and a sum taken. While there are apparently large differences in the labor costs of technical services, only those for the cataloging networks and for computer based circulation are statistically significant, with the innovators having larger expenditures. This evidence is consistent with certain innovations being adopted by high-cost libraries. A technical service labor cost per title is derived by dividing the total labor cost estimate by the number of titles cataloged. The labor cost per title is

Table 5.9. Library Inputs and Innovation Interactions: Average of Sample with/without Innovation

	Computer-based Ordering	Approval Plan	LC-MARC Computer-generated Catalog	Cataloging Network	Computer-based Circulation Control
Number of systems with/without innovation	12/19	5/26	12/19	18/13	9/22
Library expenditure per capita	7.02/6.07 (0.468)	6.64/6.40 (0.017)	8.05/5.41 (4.031*)	6.73/6.63 (0.254)	8.44/5.62 (3.996*)
Locations per square mile	0.08/0.23 (3.208*)	0.07/0.19 (1.269)	0.19/0.16 (0.110)	0.19/0.16 (0.098)	0.14/0.19 (0.184)
Acquisitions per thousand population annual	166.82/132.35 (2.235)	132.99/148.14 (0.230)	149.04/143.57 (0.053)	151.17/138.11 (0.309)	147.98/144.76 (0.016)
Titles cataloged annually in thousands	13.84/21.73 (1.932)	11.99/19.97 (1.094)	22.33/16.38 (1.067)	22.48/13.42 (2.675)	26.30/15.56 (3.239*)
Volumes in stock per capita	2.34/1.85 (2.895*)	2.28/2.00 (0.490)	2.02/2.05 (0.013)	2.18/1.85 (1.249)	2.30/1.93 (1.329)
Hours per week in branches	48.24/48.08 (0.001)	47.54/48.26 (0.018)	47.41/48.61 (0.086)	47.87/48.52 (0.026)	46.11/48.98 (0.437)
Public service staff per thousand population	0.33/0.31 (0.251)	0.35/0.31 (0.443)	0.34/0.31 (0.593)	0.33/0.30 (0.519)	0.35/0.31 (0.682)
Percent of public service staff professional	40.72/36.69 (0.953)	38.99/38.16 (0.023)	33.87/40.87 (2.970*)	41.11/34.6 (2.657)	40.64/37.30 (0.562)
Percent of public service staff in main library	31.46/35.09 (0.282)	22.41/35.88 (2.426)	27.09/37.43 (2.384)	40.46/24.71 (6.684**)	41.34/30.34 (2.450)

Years chief librarian has been chief	5.67/8.95 (3.164*)	6.60/7.88 (0.252)	7.42/7.84 (0.048)	7.50/7.92 (0.049)	6.89/8.00 (0.287)
Chief promoted from within library (binary) (chi-square test, 1 degree of freedom)	42.1/50.0 (0.004)	42.3/60.0 (0.056)	42.1/50.0 (0.004)	38.9/53.8 (0.212)	33.3/50.0 (0.201)
Cataloging lag in days	49.54/53.06 (0.020)	33.8/55.68 (0.499)	58.5/47.59 (0.189)	62.07/38.58 (0.957)	68.13/44.68 (0.800)
Acquisition lag in weeks	15.1/9.18 (1.668)	12.5/11.27 (0.037)	16.44/8.82 (2.763)	10.93/12.18 (0.072)	9.63/12.28 (0.286)
Total technical service staff	46.17/45.60 (0.003)	34.1/48.17 (1.111)	45.39/46.08 (0.004)	54.35/34.68 (4.256**)	58.5/40.39 (2.959*)
Percent of technical service staff professional	25.13/22.91 (0.266)	17.99/24.96 (1.601)	19.34/26.38 (2.845)	25.47/21.62 (0.841)	24.25/23.61 (0.020)
Technical service labor cost (thousands of dollars)	749.070/665.52 (0.217)	493.06/740.12 (1.131)	686.28/706.27 (0.012)	847.90/504.15 (4.292**)	928.04/600.76 (3.217*)
Technical service labor cost per title	55.28/34.68 (6.292**)	42.09/43.09 (0.007)	42.30/43.28 (0.011)	44.93/40.30 (0.269)	44.09/42.42 (0.029)

Note: Numbers in parentheses are *F*-statistics except for ''Chief promoted from within library.'' Statistical significance is indicated: ***0.01 level; **0.15 level; *0.10 level. The degrees of freedom are 1 and 29.

significantly higher among libraries with ordering systems. Again, the evidence suggests that high-cost libraries have adopted innovations, but the evidence is not so strong that this association holds for all innovations.

These cost and staffing comparisons would be more meaningful if information about staffing for particular functions were available from a larger group of libraries. The use of an approval plan and an automated ordering system may have larger impacts on selecting and ordering staffs and no impact on cataloging and processing operations. The use of computer assisted cataloging may influence cataloging and processing operations but not ordering and selection. The use of computer-based circulation may influence public service operations, but not cataloging, processing, or ordering. The processing of overdue notices may be performed in different divisions in different libraries; the costs of this function might be compared for the computer-based circulation control innovators and noninnovators. Moreover, one would like to know about expenditures on data processing and contractual services in order to compare total costs. These more detailed cost comparisons are beyond the scope of the present study.

One might expect that the approval plan, ordering system, and cataloging systems would reduce both acquisition lags and cataloging lags. The comparison of mean acquisition and cataloging lags of innovators and noninnovators shows no significant differences. Again, however, the libraries with the longest lags may have innovated to reduce the lags; the present evidence does not reveal the changes in lags, if any, following the adoption of an innovation.

There may be an association between the characteristics of the chief executive of the library system and the adoption of innovations. A new chief executive, for example, may have more authority to adopt innovations. This seems to be the case for ordering systems, but not for the other innovations. A chief promoted from within the library system may feel acclimated to traditional practices in the system, while an outsider may be more interested in bringing in new techniques. Chief executives of public libraries are sometimes recruited from academic or special libraries. A national search may yield persons with varied library experiences. Note, however, that most appointments of chief executives follow a search both within and without the system; thus, promotion from within need not imply a ratification of the status quo in library operation. Moreover, librarians sometimes move among systems as assistant chief executives so that promotion from within need not imply that the new chief executive has no managerial experience in other library systems.

SUMMARY

A wide array of innovations is sweeping the public library industry. Most parts of the operation of a public library system may be changed by adopting innovations. These include areas of material selection, ordering, cataloging, and circulation control. These innovations seem to be diffused rapidly across the large public library systems surveyed. While this study has not attempted to document the cost-saving potential of these innovations, substantial benefits are presumed to exist.

The pattern of diffusion is influenced by the fact that many innovations may become obsolete before they are completely diffused. Only a few innovations may be climax technologies that will be completely diffused before becoming obsolete. Computer-based circulation control, LC-MARC-based computer generated catalogs, and electronic antitheft devices may be such climax technologies.

No single group of libraries (among the large systems surveyed) stands out as a pacesetter. Each system has been among relatively early adopters of some innovations and no system has been among early adopters of all innovations. Moreover, no particular characteristics of libraries seem especially significant in the decision to adopt innovations. Labor costs, fiscal circumstances, and system characteristics may each play some role, but the relative importance of each will change from innovation to innovation.

Two factors deserve mention as sources of technological change in public libraries. First, the development of the Machine Readable Cataloging by the Library of Congress has allowed private firms to distribute LC cataloging information at very low cost in microform. Other firms are able to use the LC-MARC tapes to prepare local catalogs. The cataloging information has public goods qualities: the cost of making the information available to additional users is very low relative to the cost of generating the information in the first place. Thus, the advance of cataloging services at the Library of Congress (with Ford Foundation support) has provided substantial benefits to public libraries.

Second, the chief executives of public libraries are professionals. They typically attend professional meetings at least once a year. They contribute to and read many periodicals on library methods. They participate in national markets and usually are offered their positions only after library boards conduct national searches. The professional characteristics of library managers probably enhance the pace and diffuse character of innovation among libraries.

6

Policy

OBJECTIVES

A variety of government actions shape the public library industry. This chapter considers the objectives of policy, efficiency and equity being the most central, discusses the potential conflict among objectives, and reviews organizational and financial aspects of policies.

Efficiency

One of the most important aspects of policy is efficiency. For libraries, efficiency requires that the mix of library activities provide as much value of service as possible given the dollars spent, and that the last dollar spent actually yield a dollar's worth of value. The number of locations, hours of service, and number of new materials acquired each year should reflect a balance between the additional use of the library from additional activities and the cost of those additional activities. The examination of the New York Public Library in chapter 4 suggests that at the present time that library system operates too many branches, each of which operates too few hours with too few new materials. A policy whose main goal is efficiency would recommend that the New York system close branches and operate more hours with more materials.

As for efficiency of materials, the comparison of library use across systems in chapter 2 suggests that on average library systems provide too few materials given their cost. For the average library, policy should tilt toward more materials relative to other library activities. The issue of how large the library budget should be is more difficult to resolve because of the difficulty of making precise statements about the value of services. The evidence from the New York Public Library suggests that their budget is not too large; that with fewer branches operating more hours with more materials, the last dollar spent in the library system would probably generate at least a dollar's worth of use. This conclusion, however, is more speculative than the finding about the appropriate mix of library activities.

Efficiency also has a dynamic dimension. Libraries should adopt innovations at an appropriate rate that would reflect the potential gains, the cost of development, and the likelihood of failure. Organizational and financial arrangements of a library should encourage it to adopt innovations. Our analysis of the pattern of innovation among the large public library systems in chapter 5 indicates that important innovations have been adopted by 50 percent of the large public libraries in less than fifteen years. While this pace of change compares favorably with other local government functions and with some private industries, policy might seek to reduce the cost of research and development and so enhance the pace of innovation. Policies should not limit a library's choice of methods of operation. As new techniques become available the most desirable mix of activities and even the optimum choice of organization may change.

Another efficiency issue concerns the stability of a library's finances. The organizational and financial structure of libraries should change as the real use of library facilities and costs change, but the libraries should not be subject to random sharp turns. Sharp downturns in financial status lead to radical changes in activities, such as not purchasing any new materials or cutting library hours. These short-run changes may cut library use much more than would a planned reduction of the same magnitude in which library activities could be adjusted together. Unexpected upturns in financial status are probably rare, but may also be difficult to assimilate.

Abrupt downturns in finance have occurred frequently in public libraries during the last several years. In 1977, the Buffalo–Erie County Public Library suffered a 27 percent cutback in its budget; 11 percent was restored in 1978. In 1979, the Free Library of Philadelphia suffered a 15 percent budget cut; the acquisitions budget alone was cut 31 percent.[1] Public libraries that operate as special districts in California suffered very serious financial cutbacks as a consequence of Proposition 13; the special districts did not receive much state aid to offset the cutbacks. The Los Angeles County Library system budget was reduced by 25 percent and no new materials were acquired during at least a seven-month period.[2]

The sharp turns in library budgets hardly reflect sharp shifts in the use, value, or cost of library services. That is, the efficient level of library services does not change so markedly from year to year. Rather the sharp turns may reflect the small size of libraries relative to total city budgets, the fact that the deterioration of library services does not pose an immediate threat to public health or safety, and the fact that political support for libraries may not coalesce until a crisis is at hand.

Whatever the cause, the financial instability of public libraries causes misallocations in library activities. Policy for libraries should be designed to stabilize the financial status of libraries so that budget changes would be planned and abrupt changes avoided. Of course, efforts to maintain stability may conflict with the desire to create incentives for innovation and organizational change. One's view of different policies may be determined in part by the relative importance given to the organizational structure and financial stability of libraries.

Equity

The simplest view of equity concerns the direct value of services to families of different income levels. If the value of public services net of taxes is proportional to income, public libraries will be distributionally neutral. If the net benefits are relatively larger for lower-income families, the direct redistributional effects are positive. Benefits might be larger for lower-income families if low-income families used library services more than higher-income families. Evidence from the New York Public Library in chapter 4 tends to suggest that this is not the case, except for children. Benefits might be larger for lower-income families if they valued the use of the library more highly than a higher-income family. For example, suppose the use of a library is more valuable for children than adults. If an adult use is worth $1 and a juvenile use is worth $10, the value of use by lower-income households might be said to exceed that of higher-income families. I suspect, however, that the value of a library use differs relatively little with income and, therefore, on balance the value of library services is somewhat greater for higher-income families because they use the library more.

That the public library system does not tend to redistribute well-being from higher- to lower-income groups need not preclude its being a function of government. The distributional effect of the whole fiscal system, not each individual component, is important for equity. The public library is such a small part of local government—typically less than 1 percent—that the distributional effect of the library can easily be offset by other parts of the fiscal system. For this reason, the direct redistributive character of public libraries need not be of overriding concern in the evaluation of policy.

A second equity perspective emphasizes equality of opportunity. The public library may provide persons from lower-income backgrounds a way to improve themselves. Andrew Carnegie had something of the sort in mind when he granted funds to build public libraries all over the United States and beyond. Our society may choose to place special emphasis on making it possible for individuals to reach their full potential. Of course, the cost effectiveness of public libraries should be compared with the cost effectiveness of other activities (e.g., schools, health services, job training). The library should be as effective on a per dollar basis.

Some library systems make special efforts to be useful in this way. Branch librarians may be recruited from ethnic groups served in the branch's neighborhood, as suggested by Levy, in order to make services more useful.[3] Some libraries provide literacy programs to teach adults how to read. Some considered the movement to stock paperback books as an effort to provide materials that lower-income persons can more easily approach. Various outreach programs also have this goal. Whatever the distribution of direct benefits of public libraries, one may value the equity consequences of the public library if it is an important vehicle for social advancement. Unfortunately, there is no hard data about how the cost effectiveness of public libraries compares with the cost effectiveness of schools or job training programs as vehicles for social advancement.

A third equity perspective puts libraries in the context of freedom of speech. Access to library materials might be viewed as a right of citizenship on a plane with freedom of the press and speech. One may suggest as a matter of equity that everyone have reasonable access to government documents that provide information for the debate of public issues. The First Amendment to the Constitution does not mention libraries, and no legal principle dictates that library services are a fundamental right of citizenship, as voting is. Yet, the archival function of libraries does play a role in giving citizens access to information that is useful in performing citizenship responsibilities like voting, petitioning the government, and running for office. Thus, a philosophic case is made for the provision of public library services as a matter of fairness. While most public libraries may perform this function to some extent, it may be that relatively centralized facilities performing archival functions are more relevant than the typical branch library function.

Conflict among Objectives

The problem of evaluating policies is more difficult when the objectives conflict. If the same mix of library activities maximizes the value of the use of the library, maximizes the usefulness to lower-income families, and is most effective in promoting social advancement and in supporting citizenship responsibilities, then the evaluation of policy is simpler than if different mixes of activities are most effective for each objective.

The problem of conflicting objectives is also simpler if separate activities are undertaken for each objective. If outreach and adult literacy efforts are the significant activities for promoting social advancement, then these activities can be evaluated with respect to this objective, while other activities are evaluated with respect to other objectives. To some extent, the social advancement objective is the target of outreach and special programs and the support of citizenship responsibilities is the target of special, central archival services.

The problem of conflicting objectives is most severe when each activity is significantly associated with several objectives. Then the library must make explicit tradeoffs among the objectives. For example, lower levels of total use may be necessary in order to have more service available to lower income families. In this case, the objectives must be reduced to a common metric. That is, the policy maker must have a sense of the relative value of an additional unit of each objective.

One possibility is to assume that a unit of library service is worth the same to each user and that libraries are not likely to be very successful as redistributive agencies. Another possibility is to assume that a unit of library service is somewhat more valuable for low-income families than for higher-income families. This reflects libraries as agencies for social advancement, as support for citizenship responsibilities, or as agents of direct redistribution. Some such ethical weights must be applied in creating policy when objectives conflict. In practice, the political process makes such judgments in deciding how to expand or contract a library system. The distribution of facilities across neighborhoods ultimately involves the most elemental political confrontations of winners and losers. That the winnings may be much larger than the losses may be less relevant to results than who wins and who loses. A possible explanation of the political reversals of some central city libraries may be the relative decline in the political power of the library-using middle class.

The following discussion of policy instruments emphasizes the goal of achieving an efficient public library service. For some policies, possible conflict with equity objectives will be identified. The reader will recognize that the success of policy proposals in the political arena will have a great deal to do with who wins and who loses.

POLICY INSTRUMENTS

A variety of policy instruments is available to all levels of governments to influence public library services. First, the federal government can provide services that have high fixed costs and very low marginal costs, such as original cataloging. It can also undertake research and development of library methods. Second, state and local governments can charter libraries in a variety of ways. Libraries can have varying degrees of autonomy, be a special purpose program or part of a general purpose government, and cover geographic areas of different sizes. Third, federal and state governments can provide grants to libraries in a variety of forms. Such intergovernmental transfers might include funds to match local expenditures, capitation grants, and funds tied to various expenditures. Fourth, libraries may adopt various internal policies that affect the efficiency and equity of services. For example, charges might be levied in a variety of ways. A library might choose to be more centralized. Fifth, the vitality of competing institutions as alternatives can be considered. Each of the five categories of policy instrument is discussed in turn.

Technical Support

A variety of technical support services can be performed once for the whole country. For example, the preparation of original cataloging information—documenting titles, names, and subjects—need be performed only once for most materials. The cost of making the cataloging information available to additional users once it is prepared is quite low. Therefore, it is appropriate that the original cataloging be performed only once and then shared with all libraries who can use it. The cost savings from avoiding duplication of the original cataloging effort are substantial. There are substantial economies of scale achieved by letting any library use the results of the single source original cataloging. Similar advantages from a national scale of operation may occur in the operation of a national periodicals library—a lending library of last resort for all periodical publications. A system of lending libraries of last resort for all materials other than periodicals also involves economies of scale of national scope. Research and development in library operating methods may also involve national economies of scale.

The federal government is the logical location for these technical support activities when national economies of scale are present. Only the federal government can require the deposit of copyrighted materials. The deposit requirement means that a designated federal agency can acquire all copyrighted published materials at the time of publication. Automatic early receipt of materials is essential in the timely preparation of original cataloging if the cataloging information is to be made available to other libraries as they acquire the books. Automatic receipt of materials is also important in the development of exhaustive collections of materials. An exhaustive collection can be more readily developed if all materials are received automatically instead of having to be sought out. A library of last resort is essentially an archive, and so the permanence of a federal institution is desirable.

The national services might be supported by user charges. Suppose different prices could be charged to different groups of users of the national services reflecting the different marginal value of the service to each. In this case of perfect price discrimination, all of the benefits of the service would be reflected in the revenues. The value of the national service could be judged quite simply in terms of its costs versus its revenues. Note that under this regime some users will pay prices well above both average and marginal costs. Others will pay only the marginal cost of their participation, given the participation of all others, and contribute nothing to the support of the fixed costs of the operation. Thus, marginal users are not discouraged from using the national system when the value to them just covers marginal costs. Inframarginal users, who receive the most value from the service, bear the fixed costs as well as the marginal costs of participation.

The support of utilities with price structures differentiated by class of user is fairly common. Identical telephone service is priced differently to households and businesses. Electricity and water rates often vary with the quantity of use. The application of price discrimination for the finance of national library services such as machine-readable original cataloging might require different prices to different groups of users. Presumably the service is more valuable to larger, more research oriented libraries and to jobbers who sell cataloging products to libraries. The service might have much less value to smaller public libraries. The success of price discrimination finance of the national library technical services depends on the ability to identify different customers, so that each bears an appropriate fee.

Price discrimination may not be successful. If the customers who should be charged high prices, reflecting the higher value of the service to them, somehow succeed in disguising themselves and are able to get the service at the lower rates, then the multitier price system will become effectively a single price system. The single price will become an average price fee for the service. Marginal users, those who value the service at less than the average cost but at more than the marginal cost of their participation, will not buy the service. They will undertake separate activities at higher cost than the marginal cost of participation in the national system, and so the cost of local libraries will be greater than necessary. The system will be smaller than is socially desirable.

If price discrimination is unsuccessful, then it may be appropriate to consider general tax support for the fixed costs of the national technical services. Each user can be charged the marginal cost of its own participation, given the participation of all others. The decision about whether a national service is worthwhile is the same as under price discrimination: is the total value of the service greater than its cost? The difficulty with tax support of fixed costs is that revenues do not indicate the full benefit of the service. Political judgment, an uncertain measuring rod, is required to determine the appropriate budget for fixed costs. Of course, if direct support to libraries is contemplated anyway, direct support of national technical services may be an appropriate vehicle.

The different national library services need not be performed by the same federal agency. While the Library of Congress receives two copies of each new copyrighted material and performs both the original cataloging function and to a lesser degree the library of last resort function, other arrangements are possible. In Britain, six copies of new materials must be deposited for copyright registration. The six copies are distributed to several institutions performing national library functions. For example, the British Library Lending Division at Boston Spa receives a copy for its lending library of last resort function. In the nineteenth century, the Smithsonian Institution performed some archival functions and received copyrighted depository materials. It would be entirely possible to designate individual federal agencies to perform particular national library services.

The Library of Congress has been criticized because its primary responsibility has been in providing library services to the Congress. The development of national library services lagged. The computer-based cataloging systems were developed within the Library of Congress but with financial support from the Ford Foundation. The development of national lending library services of last resort has been slow in part because the Library of Congress has been unable to establish such a service, yet no other agency is so well positioned to do so. The Library of Congress has not ensured the development of exhaustive national collections of materials in all fields. Only those areas of special interest to the Congress have been developed exhaustively. The National Libraries of Agriculture and of Medicine are exhaustive in their areas, but many other areas are not so well developed. Moreover, the Library of Congress has not organized itself in a way to make lending across the nation fast and inexpensive. Thus, one might argue that the Library of Congress redefine its responsibilities to include the more forceful development of national library services. Or one might argue for the development of new institutions for the provision of particular national services, say a national lending library to include an exhaustive periodicals collection. Developing exhaustive collections in all areas might be assured by designating and supporting particular libraries in particular subject areas.[4]

The technical services of central concern to public libraries are mainly the machine readable cataloging information services and secondarily, the lending library of last resort services. Both services are even more valuable to research libraries. The extension of Library of Congress cataloging to include music and government documents will enhance an already very valuable service. Improvements in lending library services, say with a national periodicals service, will be more useful to public library systems with large central library services. Federal leadership and financial support of national library services may be justified on efficiency grounds. Existing services are quite valuable and improvements will increase the value of the services. Of course, such services benefit all libraries, not just public libraries.

Organization

A second category of policy toward public library services concerns organization. The action of state or local government is necessary to charter public libraries. The charters may specify the area served, the relationship with the local general purpose government, and the source of finance. The organizational facts that define the local library system may be of substantial importance in determining the character of local library services. Changing the organizational arrangements may have varied effects on services.

SIZE OF LIBRARY SYSTEM. The first organizational issue is size. At one extreme, a separate organization might be defined for each location. For example, in New England and the Northeast, public libraries may be operated by municipal governments, most of which are small. Many such town library systems operate a single facility. At the other extreme, a library system might encompass a whole state, as in Hawaii. Intermediate arrangements are represented by county library systems serving many municipalities with a number of locations, as for example in Cincinnati–Hamilton County.

The choice of size of organization hinges on three issues—economies of scale, sensitivity to differences in demand, and spillovers. If a larger organization can operate comparable facilities at lower cost than a group of smaller organizations, then the larger organizational form may yield more library services for given expenditure. This might be the case if ordering, cataloging, and processing can be automated on a larger scale. On the other hand, large size may cause organizational diseconomies such that the larger organization will be more expensive than a group of smaller organizations providing the same service. A large organization may require an excessive effort to control ordinary operations.

SIZE AND SENSITIVITY TO DEMAND. Large size may also create homogeneity of service when different neighborhoods prefer different levels of service. With individual town libraries each separately financed, communities that want higher levels of service can collect higher levels of taxes to pay for them. Communities wanting lower levels of service can enjoy lower taxes. It is even possible that competition among the towns creates some incentive for efficient service.[5] Differentiation of service and taxes among the towns allows the local public sector to match more closely the tastes for services of different citizens than a large homogeneous system. The efficiency gain from the heterogeneity of services might be estimated by examining the variation in expenditure on library services among the towns in the Boston area. It may also be the case that citizens can have a more direct hand in governing their library with more smaller libraries than with one large system. Certainly there are more library board members per capita the more independent systems there are. The advantages of smaller libraries in meeting variations in local demand must be balanced against the possible cost advantages of economies of scale from having a larger system.

The evidence presented in chapter 2 found that while library use seems unrelated to the size of the organization, the larger library systems seem to operate somewhat fewer hours per week and maintain somewhat smaller stocks per capita. These findings suggest that organizational diseconomies may be important for the large public library systems surveyed. One might expect that central library services would be a greater burden for smaller systems, and therefore that smaller systems would tend to have a somewhat larger proportion of their public service staffs engaged at the central library. In fact, no statistically significant association was found between system size (population served) and the relative commitment to a central facility. One might expect large economies of scale in technical services, but automation may be reducing the comparative advantage of a large system in ordering, cataloging, and processing. There is little evidence indicating that large economies of scale exist in public library systems, at least among the large systems surveyed.

SIZE AND SPILLOVERS.   The existence of spillovers may also influence the choice of size for a public library system. A spillover occurs when a service is rendered at no charge to a patron without receiving some tax flow. Normally we think of the benefits of a public service accruing to the residents of a jurisdiction who pay the taxes to support the services. While the political process used to decide on a level of taxes and services may be imperfect, the possibility of sensible decisions will be enhanced if both the benefits and the costs of the services are borne by the same people. If, however, a substantial amount of the benefits of a service accrue to persons who are not residents and who do not bear any of the costs for the services, then a local political process may tend to reduce services. If a substantial fraction of the benefits of a service accrues to persons who do not bear the tax price of the service, then the effective cost of providing services to those who do pay is increased.

If one grows berries attractive to birds, one may have to grow a lot of berries for the birds in order to get some for oneself. If a service spills over, the level of expenditure required to achieve a particular level of service for local taxpayers will be higher than would be necessary if there were no spillovers. If the higher effective price dominates, then the locality may actually cut expenditures rather than try to provide more for the birds. If a target level of service is to be sustained, however, the locality may have to increase services in order to keep a given level available to local taxpayers. The net behavioral effect on local expenditure decision is unclear.[6]

For public libraries, the spillovers occur when services are used by persons other than local taxpayers. Slavet, Bradbury, and Moss suggest that about half of the use of the Boston Public Library Research Division is by persons who do not reside in Boston. Cowing and Holtmann find about the same rate for the Binghamton Library.[7] Nonresident use, however, need not represent a spillover. Employers pay local taxes and may value the public library services for their employees even if the employees are nonresidents. For example, a publishing firm may want its editors to use the public library in researching manuscripts, or employees of a financial firm may use a business reference service. More generally, an employer may value the services of the local public library as a fringe benefit for workers even if the employees are not residing in the city. Thus, an employer's property tax and other local business taxes may finance library services for some nonresidents; not all nonresident use should be counted as spillovers. It is conceivable that local merchants view the public library as a community service to customers, including non-residents, or, more commercially, as a traffic generator. Thus, it is possible to view library services to nonresident shoppers as being supported by the tax payments of merchants.

Previous studies of spillovers have not distinguished nonresident employees and shoppers from other nonresident users, and therefore probably substantially overstate the degree of spillovers of public library services. Nevertheless, spillovers may be important for libraries, especially when one jurisdiction provides services not available in nearby jurisdictions. The main problem probably concerns the central library service provided by a central city system in a metropolitan area where suburban library systems provide little or no central library services.

If spillovers are an important problem in the provision of public library services, three tactics might be entertained to deal with them, one of which is organizational. The first is the most radical: *consolidate* the library service in an area and finance the library on a metropolitan basis. A metropolitan public library service will have much less spillover because most of the people who use the service will live and work within the enlarged jurisdiction. This approach has the advantage of not requiring detailed knowledge of the spillovers. Its disadvantage is that each local area will get about the same level of library service rather than allowing some areas to choose high levels of service with high taxes while others choose lower taxes and services. Also, larger organizations may be more difficult to manage. The existence of metropolitan library systems probably reflects in part a concern with spillovers.

A second approach to dealing with spillovers is to *tie intergovernmental transfers to the level of spillovers*. A state might give aid on the basis of net spillovers among jurisdictions such that the system with larger net spillouts would get higher levels of state aid than the system with low levels of net spillouts. This solution allows small systems to persist but may require careful assessment of the actual spillovers, otherwise systems will exaggerate the spillouts in order to increase state aid. Several states, including Massachusetts and Pennsylvania, give state aid to the largest libraries as regional resource centers, reflecting in part the spillovers. Usually only the very largest libraries are recognized in this way and so existing intergovernmental transfers are only an approximate response to the spillover problem. Intergovernmental transfers will be discussed more thoroughly later in this chapter.

A third solution to the spillover problem is the *levying of fees* to classes of users for whom no tax funds have been received. The library card might be given without charge to residents, to persons employed in the jurisdiction, and to patrons of local merchants. Other nonresident users might be charged for their card. The advantages of this approach are that it is inexpensive to administer, since most libraries control access to library services with a card system; the charge is directly related to the levels of spillover; and the organization of the library is unaffected. The disadvantage is that the marginal cost of an additional user may be well below the charge and so the denial of use to persons unwilling to pay the charge may reduce the net social benefit generated by the library. Many public libraries deny borrowing privileges to nonresidents as a way of reducing spillovers. Fees will be discussed in more detail later in this chapter.

The choice of the size of the public library system depends on three main factors: first, on the advantage that larger-scale organizations have in specializing functions and sharing central services (e.g., cataloging); second, on the disadvantages that a very large organization has with consequent homogeneity; and third, on the degree of spillover of services to nontaxpayers. Given these conflicting factors, it is difficult to make a definitive statement about the appropriate size of a public library system. The best that can be hoped for is the following: if spillovers are unimportant, or are offset by intergovernmental transfers, or are dealt with by fee systems, then smaller library systems may be desirable in order to allow different communities to choose the level of service they want and to avoid the large overhead costs of operating a large system.

AUTONOMY.   Given size, a second organizational issue concerns the degree of autonomy of the library system. At one extreme, a library can be a regular division of a local, general purpose government. In this case, funds may come from the general budget, subject to mayoral and council approval, in competition with other government functions like police departments. The chief executive of the library may serve at the pleasure of the mayor or city or county manager. At the other extreme, a library may be independently chartered, with the ability to levy its own property tax. The library's jurisdiction need not be coterminous with any other local government. The library may be operated by a board either elected or appointed by several different local elected bodies, say a county commission and several city councils. Thus, the board cannot be dominated by any one elected official or group. These extremes define the range of autonomy specified in the organization of different public library systems. Among 31 large public library systems, 28 have library boards; 24 of these appoint the chief executive of the library. Nine of the library systems have some earmarked tax support, 2 of which have no library board. Among the 8,500 or so public library systems across the country, 586 are special purpose library districts.[8]

One advantage of the autonomous organization is that the library's budget is not conditioned by events elsewhere in the city government. A severe winter will not draw off library funds for snow-shoveling and pothole repair. Another advantage is that the independent library board can become more expert in library operations than a typical city council member or budget officer. The disadvantage from a social point of view is that library affairs may be little subject to review by elected officials. The autonomous library with an earmarked tax source may feel little pressure to economize.

The library department of city government will be quite sensitive to the tastes of elected officials. Budget increases may be difficult to come by, and so there is at least the potential for incentives for economizing. Of course, the elected officials may have little knowledge of libraries and so the concern for keeping budgets tight may not induce desirable changes in library operations. Moreover, the elected officials of a general purpose government may trade one service off against another. The library budget then may not be independent of the political power and apparent demands of other agencies.

I suspect that the fiscal instability of public libraries results in part from the semiautonomous organization of many libraries. The library executive hired by a library board may have little ability to deal with a cantankerous mayor and council. The board itself may be too politically weak to bring much pressure to bear on a council, and the library executive may have little or no political support. The chief executive chosen by a library board for professional librarianship qualities may be ill prepared to fight budget battles. The semiautonomous organization seems to yield professional management and a creditable pace of innovation, but at the possible cost of political inexperience and fiscal instability. Substantiation of this hypothesis is beyond the scope of the present work. Of course, the autonomous library fully supported by earmarked taxes will suffer no such instability.

It is undeniable that special purpose governments, including autonomous library districts, have not fared well with intergovernmental transfers. Federal general revenue sharing is conditioned on the levels of taxes raised and spent by the local general purpose government. Revenue sharing is lower in localities where more functions are performed by special purpose governments. In California, following enactment of Proposition 13, a substantial amount of supplemental state aid went to local general purpose governments. Special purpose governments, including eight library districts, got little aid to offset their loss of property tax revenues. Autonomy has its price.

PRIVATE CONTRACTS. Another organizational possibility is contracting with private firms. The local government can provide for public library services by hiring private contractors to operate the facilities. By periodic reletting of contracts with competitive bidding, the government can be assured of low cost operations. The contracting model has been demonstrated to be very effective in refuse collection.[9] Each firm can have an exclusive territory, thus taking advantage of higher densities for pickups, while competitive bidding keeps cost low. The success of the contracting organizational form depends on the ability to define the important dimensions of the quality of service in the contract specifications so that penalties for nonperformance can be imposed. Moreover, it seems important to be able to rebid, say every three to five years; otherwise, competition has little chance of remaining an effective threat.

Having private contractors perform services holds little promise for public libraries. The quality of library services is too difficult to define precisely in a contract specification. How could type I and type II errors in book selection be defined and measured to form part of a contract reward and penalty scheme? How could the quality of the catalog be specified in a contract? How could the quality of reference services be specified and rewarded? Unless service quality is adequately specified, a contractor facing competitive pressures will seek to reduce quality in order to lower the cost.

The durability of the library facilities and book stock also frustrates contracting. If contracts are to be relet every five years, contractors will inherit facilities operated by others. A retiring contractor can sabotage a newcomer by shuffling the card catalog, reshelving materials haphazardly, and so on. Contracting does not seem to hold much promise for increasing efficiency in public libraries. The New York Public Library has operated branch services in three boroughs of New York City since 1901 under contract with the city. The contractual relationship is so persistent, however, that branch operations are little different from other departments of the city government. The threat of being replaced by another contractor plays no role in the operation of the library.

INTERGOVERNMENTAL CONTRACTING. Intergovernmental contracting is another organizational scheme. The local government can contract with another government to provide public library as well as other services. For example, a suburban county might contract with the central city library system to provide library services, as Allegheny County, Pennsylvania, contracts with the Carnegie Library of Pittsburgh. Or one county may contract with the next, as Nassau County contracts with Jacksonville for library services in Florida. Or a municipality may contract with a county library system for the provision of branch services within the municipality, as some municipalities do in Los Angeles County, California. In the extreme, a municipality can incorporate, and buy virtually all its services via contracts with other governments. This is the plan developed in Lakewood, California, in 1954.[10] Intergovernmental contracts may also be entered by a state government with major libraries to provide regional library services within the state. The Boston Public Library, for example, has a contract with the state government for the provision of various regional library services in Eastern Massachusetts. An intergovernmental contract gives more control than an intergovernmental transfer.

With intergovernmental contracting, an area can get the advantages of scale economies in the provision of the goods while buying just the level of service it chooses. The cost savings of the large organization can be had without the usual homogeneity of service. While intergovernmental contracting may not have the same efficiency effect as competitive bidding among private contracts, an element of competition may arise. The municipality retains the ability to withdraw from the contract and operate its own service. Also, the municipality may have some choice among neighboring governments as potential contractors. It is conceivable that a private firm might become available as a potential contractor, and so experience with intergovernmental contracting may be a step toward private contracting. Nevertheless, the difficulties of specifying the quality of services and of terminating contracts may also be important for intergovernmental contracts, as they are for private contracts.

Public libraries across the country are organized in a variety of ways. New England towns may operate small systems as a regular part of the town government. In Ohio, special purpose library districts may encompass a metropolitan area with services fully supported by an earmarked tax. When an area chooses an organizational form for public library services, it may face tradeoffs between size and autonomy, although the choices will be limited by the nature of local general purpose government. In Nashville, Indianapolis, and Jacksonville, library services are metropolitan because local government is metropolitan. Thus, if a size for a library system is to be other than that of the local government, then a special purpose government may have to be formed and it will be more autonomous than a department of a city government. The great diversity of organizational arrangements for public libraries may suggest that no single organizational arrangement is dominant in terms of efficiency and equity.

Intergovernmental Transfers

The third category of policy instrument is financial assistance from state and federal governments. These governments transfer funds to local governments to use for library activities. Grants may be tied to library use (output constraint), as with the Library Service and Construction Act funds, or left to local government discretion as with general revenue sharing.[11] Grants may be tied to particular expenditures (input constraint) as with funds for construction or for materials acquisition. The amount of aid may be distributed to localities on the basis of applications citing specific projects (local initiative required) or may be distributed automatically as program support on the basis of some formula, for example, per capita. Federal funds can come directly or can be passed through a state agency (pass through). Conditions may be imposed on the recipient (conditional aid). For example, local matching funds may be required for a federal construction grant; maintenance of effort may be required for program aid if the donor wishes to add to rather than displace local effort. Finally, the purposes of the donor may have little to do with the purposes of the recipient (irrelevance of purpose). Federal aid may be for local public works projects or employment and training in order to reduce unemployment. The local government may decide that the library is a suitable vehicle for creating employment. By specifying a point in each of these dimensions, one can define a particular kind of intergovernmental transfer program. For example, state programmatic support to public libraries might give up to fifty cents per capita while requiring the local government to match the state's contribution by 25 percent. The total funds would be spent for acquisition of library materials. The possibilities for creative program design are great.

Municipal officials prefer untied aid, with minimal recipient conditions, or, *a fortiori,* increases in such aid because such aid maximizes their own authority without the burden of raising finance. They can view it as a free good. Increases in such funds give officials more discretion. Librarians, of course, prefer aid tied to library use because they may not fare any better in getting untied aid than they do in getting regular funds. In some cases, librarians may prefer funds tied to materials acquisition because many librarians believe that funds for acquisitions are harder to come by from the local budget than funds for positions. Naturally, state librarians prefer federal funds that are passed through, at their discretion, because such funds enhance their own positions. Program aid is generally preferred to project aid by local governments and libraries because no initiative need be taken locally and because project aid is more easily turned on and off by the donor. Program aid, unlike project aid, usually continues for longer periods. Moreover, in order to get project aid, a library may have to do something it doesn't regularly do, whereas program aid may be used for continuing activities. In short, each participant in the aid game will have a perspective on what constitutes the best form of aid.

How should a pattern of state and federal aid to libraries be designed to achieve equity and efficiency? Apart from the seemingly self-serving advocacy of the different categories of recipients, how are alternative aid programs to be evaluated? This is a difficult question to answer because the behavior of the institutions of local government are not well understood. If we knew that local government tends to be more niggardly with the acquisition budget than with the employment budget, then one might want to design an offsetting system of aid that gives matching aid for acquisitions. (Some state aid in New York is for acquisitions.) The evidence cited in chapter 2 suggests that on average libraries may buy too few new materials. Yet not all public libraries may suffer such a distortion in budget. The budgets of more autonomous libraries may be fungible between materials and staff. A program to fine tune the aid program according to the likely behavior of different kinds of libraries is overcomplicated and probably will be seen as unfair by libraries not in the best situated categories. Moreover, the effort to fine tune aid to a particular purpose may induce undesirable efforts to beat the system. For example, aid limited to acquisitions will induce libraries to load as much of their expenditures on acquisitions as possible, for example, book cataloging and processing costs.

If aid for very specific, finely tuned purposes seems problematic, aid for irrelevant purposes is even less satisfactory. As we have seen in chapter 4, in the late 1970s the New York Public Library is operating too many branches for too few hours. Library service would be improved dramatically if a few branches were closed and other branches opened for longer hours. Yet federal aid for local public works is being used to build a new branch. If the branch is to be operated, given the current budget, hours will have to be reduced at other library facilities, making the library service worse. The Queens Borough Public Library has six new branches that have never opened because of the lack of operating funds. Some 25 percent of the employees of the branch libraries of the New York Public Library were supported by federal Comprehensive Employment and Training Act funds in 1978. If federal constraints on the local use of CETA funds preclude their use by the library, as was threatened in the fall of 1978, library operations could be dramatically affected. These federal aid dollars are worth much less than a dollar to the library because they cannot be used to maximize the value of library services.

Some states use their library aid to encourage reorganization. Maryland gives capitation grants to county library systems. As a consequence, most municipalities have given up their library systems in favor of county services. Since Maryland has active county governments of appropriate size, this change in organization has probably improved library services at modest cost. Yet even here, some municipalities have done without the state aid in order to retain control of their municipal library. In states without active county governments, such an inducement to consolidation of library systems would probably fail.

AID RATIONALES.   The design of intergovernmental aid programs to promote an efficient and equitable public library service is difficult both because planned purposes of the aid may not be met and unplanned results may be forthcoming. Consequently, any aid should be kept simple, with simple goals and limited expectations. We have already discussed one rationale for aid to libraries, namely, spillovers. Where high levels of spillovers are found and reorganization and pricing seem inappropriate, it may be desirable to tie state aid to libraries to the net spillovers. Clearly, such a regime will be superior to a simple capitation grant system if spillovers are important, because capitation grants will go to places with poor services that import library service at the same rate as to places with good services that do a lot of exporting. If states tie aid to measures of spillovers, libraries will have an incentive to respond to all user demands rather than play beggar-my-neighbor. Of course, counting spillovers may be difficult and subject to cheating, and so such a regime may be impractical.

A second possible rationale for aid to libraries sees aid as a substitute for technical support. A state may designate particular libraries as resource centers, that is, lending libraries of last resort within the state for particular subjects. A state may then give an annual endowment for collections development and lending services for such resource centers. Pennsylvania supports four libraries in this way, two of which are public libraries and two of which are university libraries. Some states have made designations without financial support. The point here is that there are real economies of scale in some kinds of library services and it is less expensive and more effective to provide such services collectively, at a regional or state or national level (for different services), than to let each local library stand alone. Evidence cited in chapter 2 indicates interlibrary loan flows are a very small part of library services.

A third possible rationale for intergovernmental aid is fiscal stability. Alphonse Trezza, executive director of the National Commission on Libraries and Information Science, advocates 50 percent state support and 20 percent federal support for public libraries because "libraries simply cannot survive in the long run on the property tax."[12] State and federal program aid can be made somewhat automatic and therefore less subject to sharp turns than reliance on the local property tax, although state and federal aid can also take sharp swings.

The property tax, however, is borne locally, and, except for spillovers, the benefits of public libraries accrue locally. Therefore, the property tax seems to achieve a closer match between taxpayers and recipients of services than intergovernmental aid. The property tax allows the local electorate to influence its level of taxes and the consequent level of services much more than can be achieved with state aid formulas. The property tax is a stable source of revenue for local government, being less variant over the business cycle than income or sales taxes. Reliance on the property tax does put the public library at the sufferance of the local political process. The instability that results from such surveillance may be the cost of having a government service that is responsive to elected officials.

One may question the very permanence and stability of programmatic aid for public libraries. As technologies change, we may want institutions to change to take advantage of them. An institution that must fight for its budget may be more responsive to new opportunities and have less inertia than an institution with assured finance. Therefore, one's view of regular programmatic aid may hinge on how one values stability and permanence versus incentives for change and responsiveness.

The intergovernmental aid is likely to be viewed as given when the local budget is considered, and so local general revenue finance of the library is likely to be viewed as the marginal source of finance. High levels of intergovernmental aid will not necessarily reduce the fiscal instability of the library if the aid is taken as a base, with the last 20 percent of the library budget determined in the same manner as when 80 percent of the library budget came from the local general fund. Aid that requires local matching is an effort to influence the expenditure of marginal dollars from the local general fund, but unless the aid is open-ended (the state or federal government will match whatever the local government spends) the expenditure of the last dollar may be fully local and therefore not influenced directly by the availability of aid. The impact on the state or federal budget of open-ended matching grant aid is uncertain, because the dollar amount of aid is determined by local officials; therefore, higher governments may be more reluctant to create open-ended matching grants than to give capitation grants, where costs can be more precisely anticipated.

Intergovernmental transfers are sometimes advocated on equity grounds. Aid can be more generous to localities with more poor people, or lower wealth per household, or more unemployment, or with any other measurable indicator of deservedness. Such compensatory aid is common with state grants for local education, and plays a substantial role in the distribution of federal community development funds. The case for compensatory aid for public libraries, however, seems weak. Libraries seem ill-suited as vehicles for direct redistribution. While some libraries have undertaken adult literacy and community outreach programs, these are not part of the standard operations of libraries, and could be conducted by almost any agency, including the schools or recreation agency. Moreover, if these activities are the reason for giving aid, then aid could be limited to funding such programs. The support of basic library services would then remain local. The library may have some value as a vehicle for social advancement and as a source of information for citizenship responsibilities. These functions seem secondary, however, to the main mission of public libraries of providing a broad range of materials for a general audience. Thus, equity considerations do not seem sufficient grounds for advocating intergovernmental transfers to support basic library services. If equity were the dominant motive for aid, one would ask why not give the aid directly to the deserving persons rather than to local government in the name of deserving persons?

Intergovernmental transfers are an important, flexible method that higher levels of government can use to influence lower levels of government without actually assuming operating control. As a class, such transfer programs are flawed, however, because the grant programs cannot respond to all institutions or to all the problems of local government. The central problems of operating government services are the lack of information about the value of service and the lack of incentive for good management. Intergovernmental transfer programs, designed as they are in the state or national capital, operate blindly, with little information about local circumstances. Nor do such transfer programs generate information about the levels and values of services. Moreover, the transfer programs do nothing to improve incentives for good management. The flow of aid is seldom conditioned on good performance. The sloppy organization with mistaken priorities will get no less, or even more, aid than the lean organization with appropriate priorities.

The support of public libraries by states is quite varied. Eight states provide no support.[13] Fifteen states simply match federal funds. Among these, Vermont only matched a construction grant. Three others have more complex matching schemes. Another seventeen states distributed some aid on a per capita basis or used an aid distribution formula that took account of population. Two states, Georgia and North Dakota, leave the distribution of state aid to a state board. Hawaii operates public libraries as a state function. Four other states have varied other aid systems that are primarily flat grants to approved libraries or project aid. The above categories are mutually exclusive. Some states have very complex aid systems. For example, New York has flat grants, capitation grants, reimbursement for acquisition up to $0.82 per capita for the part of acquisitions expenditures exceeding $0.40 per capita, aid based on area served in square miles, incentive aid to encourage local sponsors, and direct aid to New York City for research libraries. Six states have aid that tends to equalize support for libraries across jurisdictions or have formulas that take account of need. At least four states have closed end matching aid. State aid to public libraries totaled $127 million in 1977, about $0.60 per capita. The most generous state was Maryland with $2.11 in per capita terms; second was Georgia with $1.46 per capita. Obviously, the level and design of state aid to public libraries vary greatly across the country.

Internal Instruments

What can a public library system do for itself? One possibility is to raise revenues directly from users by charging them fees. A second possibility is to centralize control of the library systems.

FEES.   Libraries bridle at the suggestion that fees have a place in the library. Part of the ethic of the public librarian is making library services as accessible to all comers as possible. Many library systems have "free" in their titles. Free service is a condition of state grants in many states, and the no-charge requirement may be a part of the charter of many public libraries. Thus, the barriers to the use of fees are substantial. Naturally, any community that wants to sustain its public libraries with taxes may choose to avoid many charges, and most do. Nevertheless, following enactment of property tax limitation in California, several libraries responded to substantial budget cuts by introducing fees. When faced with severe cutbacks librarians entertain the introduction of fees.

In contrast, economists recognize that prices play a role in addition to generating revenues. Prices carry information and give incentives. In this case, prices might give potential users signals about the relative social costs of library services versus other methods of getting information and recreation. Prices may also give signals to library managers about desirable levels of service and about the combinations of activities that users most desire. Institutions that depend on prices are presumed to be more responsive to user interests and more efficiently managed. In considering fees, the faiths of the librarian and of the economist are in conflict.

The goal of the following discussion of prices for public library services is neither to convince economists that fees are a bad idea, nor to convince librarians that fees are best for all circumstances. Rather I will discuss the great range of possible fee arrangements and indicate advantages and disadvantages of each. The issue really isn't whether to have fees or not, but rather what kinds of fees in what circumstances.

Most larger public library systems already use fees to good effect. Users are charged for photocopying; coin-operated machines are the norm. The cost of the service to the library is directly linked to each user. The user faces the choice of how much photocopying to undertake relative to taking notes or buying an original version of the material. The photocopying fee reflects the real social cost of photocopying, and so each user makes an appropriate calculation about how much of the service to use. The willingness of users to pay shows the value of the service and so signals to library managers how much service to provide. Charging fees for photocopying clearly improves the allocation of photocopying services in libraries. Users avoid queues, the library avoids the appearance of having too little service. Such fees illustrate the economist's view of prices as signals that improve allocation.

The central objection to fees is the discouragement of casual users of library services when the cost of serving them is minimal. Suppose that recreational and educational use of the public library begins innocently on a rainy day with the use of a children's book, a piece of fiction, or a how-to-do-it book. A pleasant experience leads to a return visit and so happenstance turns into custom. If the casual visitor is discouraged by a fee, will habitual users ever develop? Suppose the library is so uncrowded that the cost of accommodating an additional user is zero. Suppose further that casual users incur other costs greater than the cost of the library service they might use when not discouraged by a fee. For example, suppose they buy books or go to the movies. In this case, charging the fee reduces social welfare. A greater social benefit would be created by allowing the casual user access to the library, because benefits are created but no costs are incurred. In this case, a fee makes the allocation of resources worse.

These two cases illustrate the proposition that fees are neither all good nor all bad. In the case of photocopying, a real cost is incurred by the library by the fact of the use. The copy service has real scarcity value, and so a price reflecting its social cost improves the allocation of resources. In the case of the casual user of the library, no additional costs are created by the fact of use and so any charge to the casual user makes the allocation of resources worse.

Given these two conflicting cases, what can we say in general about when fees are appropriate? First, whenever the library incurs additional costs as a direct consequence of the additional use of the library by a user, a fee reflecting those direct costs is appropriate. Such a fee will ration the scarce resource among potential users. A charge for automated information retrieval may be justified on such a basis because the library typically must pay vendor fees for each search. Unless the user is charged a fee reflecting the real social costs, users will use the automated service even when other alternatives involve lower social cost. When a particular library service is congested, as for example, when a borrower must wait for access to a bestseller, then a fee is also appropriate. When a queue develops, use by one person imposes waiting time on others. Thus there is a real opportunity cost of each use. Four of the thirty-one large public libraries surveyed have paid duplicate collections. Borrowers have the option of paying a rental fee for quick access to a bestseller or a longer wait for feeless access. Thus, a borrower can incur the cost of the fee or the cost of the wait. Our first pricing principle, then, is: when real costs are imposed by the fact of an additional use, resource allocation is improved by a fee that reflects those costs.

Is it ever appropriate to charge a user more than the additional cost directly caused by the fact of the additional user? The answer is yes. Users may be charged any fee up to the value of the benefit the user derives from the service without discouraging its use. While casual users may be discouraged by even a modest fee, many other inframarginal users must place much higher value on the use of the library. For them much higher charges would not discourage use. If each user were charged a fee reflecting the value of the service to him or her, the revenues collected would reflect the total benefit of the library service. If the total revenues thus derived were less than the costs of the library service, then the library should be closed. Users would derive more benefit from keeping their money than they derive from the library. Thus, if the library is worthwhile, total benefit must be greater than total cost. A charge system that imposes a fee on each user according to the respective benefits derived by each user would not discourage use of the library, and would provide a stable source of revenue and give signals to library managers about how much service to provide. Our second principle of pricing, then, is: charge each user a fee less than or equal to the benefit of the library service to each.

The possibility of financing the library in such a way involves applying a fee system that discriminates among different users according to the value of the service to each. The difficulty in developing such a system of fees lies in identifying the value of the library services to different users. How are habitual users to be charged more than casual users? One tactic might be to have an annual card fee with a low fee for the first year and higher fees for subsequent years. Of course, the library must have a method of keeping track of names so that users can't drop out briefly and return at first year rates perpetually. This tactic falls short, however, because some people may be casual users for long periods of time. Another price discrimination tactic might be lower rates for children than for adults.

Another tactic involves creating essentially arbitrary classes of use for the purpose of capturing some of the inframarginal benefits as revenue. While general access to library service is maintained without charge, special services might be made available to paying members. Perhaps Sunday afternoon or Tuesday evening hours might be available only to members. Membership in a business reference association might give priority access to business reference librarians and materials. Cubicles, typewriters, special invitations to cultural events, and priority access to reference services might be made available to members. Similarly, nonresidents might be charged.

Ultimately, the labeling of different groups of users according to their valuation of library services so that different fees can be charged seems too difficult. One might want more substantial empirical information about how many users would actually be discouraged by nominal annual fees. Nevertheless, the general presumption seems to be that the number would be large. Therefore, it would seem to be important to treat casual users differently from others according to the value they place on library services. Given the difficulty of identifying different groups, a public library system supported wholly by fees may reduce social welfare.

A third consideration in the charging of fees is the cost of collecting and accounting for the fees. If money is to be handled, additional clerical staff may be required to handle the funds. Accountants and auditors must be employed to keep track of the funds. Security guards may be required to reduce the chance of robbery. The coin-operated copying machines obviously have minimal collection costs and little security problem. A daily attendance charge, however, might require a clerical and security staff at each location, although coin-operated turnstiles are a possibility. The more complicated the fee scheme, the greater may be the collection costs: a rental fee for each day of use of a book charged out requires calculation and checking. Auditing may be more difficult. Thus, the third principle in designing prices for library services is to keep collection costs low. Fee schemes that might otherwise be appropriate may fail because of the difficulty of collection.

Equity is a fourth concern raised when fees are proposed for public library services. Fees are said to be unfair to the poor. Note, however, that fees are distributionally neutral: the benefits of the service are at least as great as the charges, and the distribution of well-being among individuals is unchanged by the fees. The distributional effect of tax supported libraries depends both on the distribution of benefits and the distribution of the burden of the tax. The evidence on library use presented in chapter 3 tends to indicate that higher-income adults use the library more than lower-income adults. For children, the opposite is the case. Overall, adult use dominates. Feeless service, then, supported by a proportional or regressive tax, tends to worsen the distribution of well-being across income groups. That is, higher-income groups achieve a net gain. Only if the service is financed by a strongly progressive tax will feeless service tend to enhance the well-being of lower-income groups more than that of higher-income groups. The incidence of the burden of the property tax is subject to lively debate, but the most recent evidence suggests that it may be roughly proportional.[14] In this light, feeless finance does not dominate a system of charges on equity grounds. Note that a price discriminating fee structure might recognize the lower-value, more casual library use of many lower-income families and so charge them less. Discriminating on the basis of income, however, may be difficult to enforce.

The ideal fee structure for a public library system, then, would always charge at least marginal costs, but never more than the benefit derived by the individual user. Systems that involve low collection costs may dominate. Fees are as desirable on equity grounds as most local taxes. If the public library is to be fully supported by fees, a discriminatory price structure is most desirable. Low fees or free services will be provided to casual users who place a low value on library services while higher fees are charged to inframarginal users who place a high value on the service. No easily administered basis for such discriminatory charges is at hand, and so local tax support for general library services continues to be the dominant financial vehicle.

Given these perspectives on the potential for fees, what fees are most appropriate in public libraries? Most public libraries impose a daily fee for books not returned by the due date. Among thirty-one large systems surveyed, the modal fee for adult materials was five cents per day, from a low of two cents in St. Louis County to a high of ten cents in five systems, including Boston, New York, and Hennepin County. Lower fees are typically imposed on children's materials. The purpose of fees is to encourage prompt return of materials. The quality of library services is enhanced by such fees. Of course, the effectiveness of the overdue fees depends in part on the library's zeal in tracking down overdue materials. The important point here is that libraries are accustomed to using fees on overdue books to improve the quality of library service.

Some libraries routinely charge for photoduplication and interlibrary loan services, because the library itself must bear direct costs for each use. Some libraries are providing access via terminals to commercial computer-based bibliographic reference services. When these services must be supported by the library, it is reasonable to expect that the costs directly incurred in the individual user's behalf will be charged to the user. Such charges ration the costly service among users according to the value each user places on it. Users will seek out less expensive alternatives when they exist. Thus, such fees play a valuable allocative role.

A general daily rental charge per item for the use of any library materials seems the least satisfactory for materials not in high demand. The library incurs little extra cost in allowing such circulation; no other library user is likely to be inconvenienced if the material is not available, and so such a charge will probably discourage library use that involves little cost.

A daily entrance fee suffers much the same problem. Unless a facility is crowded, an additional visitor will add little cost to the operation of the library, will not inconvenience other users much, and so imposes little extra cost. Of course, if a facility is crowded, an entrance fee may appropriately discourage the casual visitor from using the library as a warm place to snooze or a study hall. This, in effect, would give priority to visitors who want to use library materials.

A better system when general library facilities are uncrowded would be an annual membership fee or a card fee. Once the fee is paid, the casual use of facilities and borrowing materials would not be discouraged. Thus, the use patterns of the library are likely to be less affected by an annual fee than by a per use or visit fee. Also costs of collecting the fee will be lower with an annual fee. Of course, an annual fee will discourage the first-time casual rainy-day visitor who is not certain what a library provides.

Currently, public libraries that have memberships make them voluntary. Members receive newsletters and invitations to special events. Voluntary membership fees would be a small part of total revenues, but may provide some discretionary funds for special purposes. Some libraries form private, nonprofit subsidiaries to receive and disperse contributions so that the funds can be kept separate from government funds. Voluntary fees serve a different function than when significant services are only available to fee-paying customers.

Public library services can be improved by the judicious use of fees. Institutional arrangements that treat fee income like taxes and parking meter income by integrating them in local general revenues discourage the generation of fee income; library services probably suffer as a consequence. Some libraries use fees to good effect in rationing the use of services with high marginal costs. More libraries could probably do so. Given the low marginal cost of general library services and the difficulty of enforcing discriminatory prices, library service would be provided at too low a level if no general revenue tax support were available for public library services.

CENTRALIZED MANAGEMENT. In addition to exploring possible methods of increasing fee income, many public library systems may be able to help themselves by centralizing their management. Most library systems that predate 1950 have substantially decentralized forms of management. That is, each branch has substantial operational autonomy. Each branch manager may expend considerable effort in book selection and presentation, in designing control systems, and in laying out operations. Such management takes a great deal of skill to be done well. The best branches are well run, while some branches are mismanaged. Each is a unique operation, although affiliated with the system.

Many of the innovations described in chapter 5 make it possible for the management and control of branch libraries to be substantially centralized. The skill level required of branch managers can be substantially reduced and the average quality of branch management can be increased at lower total cost. In part, the changes are somewhat like those between the decentralized management of Howard Johnson's Restaurants and centralized control of MacDonald's, although the changes in branch banking may be even closer.

With a sophisticated circulation control system, a library system manager can monitor patterns of use at each branch by detailed subject and user characteristics. Requests for materials, and queues, can also be observed, and the information can be used to evaluate the profiles that guide the book approval program. The performance of different vendors providing approval services can be compared with respect to the speed of service and type I and type II errors in selection. Cataloging and processing services can be purchased from vendors on a contract basis. Multiple copies of the microfilm of the system catalog, with branch locations of materials indicated for each item, can be placed in each branch facility. Perhaps antitheft systems and self-charge-out systems can be integrated; such integration would reduce the number of branch personnel and the skills required of them. Overdue notices, circulation records, and cardholder records can all be done by computer in a central facility. Telephone inquiries can be directed to a central staff that is especially trained and equipped for this service. The centralized service I am describing relies on data processing systems to generate management information to monitor operations. More formal rapid feedback is used to measure the success of decisions, and successes are rapidly used to improve service throughout the system. The responsibilities of central managers would be much greater, while the responsibilities of unit managers would be much less, than under a conventional system.

No public library system in the country operates under a centralized management system as just described. Of the thirty-one systems visited, management of the St. Louis County Library is probably closest to the ideal described. I suspect that many special libraries are also capable of operating more in this fashion. The advantage of such a management system is a more uniform, higher quality service at lower total cost. With lower cost per facility, more facilities might be justified. There are two disadvantages to such a management style: the cost of developing such a system and the loss of personality and idiosyncracy in individual units. If more centralized management were to develop, the desirable size of the system might increase.

COMPETITORS

The pattern of development of competing institutions may have a substantial impact on the nature of public library services over the next twenty years. A variety of institutions compete with public libraries. The most direct competition is that of school libraries. Historical society libraries and rental libraries represent competition of a different form. With development of fiber optic data transmission and magnetic bubble electronic data storage, a device that would have access to central data storage archives could be produced. This device would be similar to a home television.

A large proportion of the users of public libraries are elementary and secondary school students. School libraries and public libraries both seek to serve this group. Of thirty-one large public library systems, all but three indicated that all high schools in their areas have libraries. The three exceptions indicated that most high schools have libraries. Twenty indicated that half or more of the elementary schools in their area have professional librarians. Only one indicated that there are no professional librarians in elementary schools in their area. Thus, school libraries are a substantial alternative to public libraries for many students.

From the point of view of the public library, school libraries complement public library services. Whereas the school library frequently has a captive audience and can lay direct claim to a student's time, the public library must offer something more if it is to attract students. One thing the public library offers is evening hours. Only ten of the thirty-one large public library systems indicated that any high school libraries offer evening hours. As a system, public libraries typically offer a larger collection of materials. Indeed, it seems common for teachers to give assignments that send students to the public library. That schools have libraries and that students are important clients for the public library does not mean that the public library's services to students are redundant.

The creative tension between school libraries and public libraries is a consequence of the two institutions' serving a large student audience with funds from the same local government sources. Why not let the school libraries do the job? The answer seems to be that the basic mission of the school library, given the close ties to the school day and curriculum, is largely incompatible with serving a diverse audience on a voluntary basis. Why not put public libraries on school campuses? The answer is much the same: the purpose of the public library in serving a broad audience on a voluntary basis does not fit well with the structured day and objectives of the schools. Those places that have had public libraries operated by the school systems have usually separated them. Terre Haute spun off its public library system. Only Kansas City, among large cities, continues to operate public libraries through the schools. When budgets are cut, the stepchild public library suffers more when it is controlled by the school board. Even in rural areas with little or no public library service, school libraries seldom are open evenings, Saturdays, or during the summer. The growth of school libraries does not seem to pose a threat to public support of public libraries.

Private libraries are another alternative to government operated libraries. In twenty-one of thirty-one areas surveyed, local historical societies operate libraries concerned with local history. In ten of the thirty-one areas, local rental or subscription libraries operate. These libraries are small in number and size because of the ubiquity and quality of public library services. If tax support for public libraries declines and public libraries start charging fees, private libraries of a variety of sorts will be expected to develop. Special libraries operated by business firms have grown rapidly over the last twenty years, as noted in chapter 1. The special libraries have narrow and technical focuses not duplicated in many public libraries. The development of special libraries is probably independent of the health of public library services.

Electronic Publishing

A major potential competitor of public libraries may be the telephone company or cable television. An optical fiber can carry many times the information of a single copper wire in the same space and at lower cost. Thus, a home connected with an optical fiber could sustain many video channels and be interactive. That is, a keyboard could be used to request particular items. The Post Office in Britain has introduced a system to subscribers called "Prestel."[15] The system makes the daily newspaper, business statistics, air and train timetables, and an encyclopedia available on request on a home television device. The system also allows users to use the computer for calculations. The user pays for the local telephone call and a few cents per minute of connect time with the computer. Royalties are added for copyrighted materials. The financial feasibility of the system depends on a large number of subscribers buying the reception device and being wired for the service. Fiber optics has dramatically lowered the cost of hookup. Feasibility also depends on the availability of large-scale, low-cost computer storage. The development of magnetic bubble data storage has that effect. The Post Office plans to add 10,000 pages of material per month to its 146,000-page base. The standard fare of the branch public library could easily be introduced to such a system as it grows. Bestsellers are a logical money maker for such systems. How-to-do-its, mysteries, and even children's books may be economically feasible as the system develops. Catalog shopping and interactive instruction may become part of the service. In the United States, cable television companies may expand into this interactive, home information retrieval market.[16] Telephone companies may put their directories on line.

By 1990 electronic publishing may pose a competitive threat to public libraries. The libraries have survived the growth of book clubs in the 1920s, television in the 1950s, and paperback books in the 1960s. While per capita use of the public library has dropped somewhat, the institutions continue to serve a substantial part of the population. Electronic publishing may reshape the services of the public library, but libraries are unlikely to disappear. The public library may come to serve more specialized needs, including business reference services, access to government documents, and services to handicapped persons.

POLICY CONCLUSIONS

The first conclusion is that local tax support of public library services is appropriate. The benefits accrue locally, and so local taxes will cause localities to more closely balance the value of additional service with its cost. The value of good quality local services may well be capitalized into local land values, and so finance of the service with the property tax may be appropriate on equity and efficiency grounds.

The size of the library system should be large enough so that spillovers are small relative to the total services of the system. In practice, the size of the organization is usually limited by the nature of local government in an area. If there is no metropolitan government, a metropolitan library system is more difficult to achieve. As library system management becomes more centralized, somewhat larger systems may be justified. On the other hand, larger systems are unable to have different tax levels for different levels of service reflecting differences in tastes in different communities.

More autonomous library systems may have more professional management. The professional character of the management may be reflected in fairly rapid diffusion of innovation across library systems. The autonomy of the library system, however, may exact a price: political support would most likely be reduced. The fiscal instability of libraries without full earmarked funding may reflect the lack of political success of the professional managers.

Intergovernmental transfers are a weak tool for improving the quality of library services because by their nature they cannot be tailored to the particular circumstance of individual libraries. Some libraries need more books; some need more staff; some need fewer branches; some need more branches; some need better management; some may need to consolidate; some should be divided up. No intergovernmental transfer will induce better management. No easily devised transfer scheme can induce some libraries to consolidate, some to split up, and some to add branches, while others consolidate branches. Of course, all library managers want more money, and intergovernmental transfers seem to be a less difficult route than fighting local budget battles.

Most libraries have fees for some things; a few public libraries are fully supported by fees, and so are public in the eighteenth-century meaning. Most public libraries can make more aggressive use of fees to improve the quality of services. Some libraries turn to more fee income when tax sources are reduced. Bureaucratic rules that do not allow a library to use fee income for its own purposes should be replaced by rules that encourage libraries to seek some fee income by allowing fee income to be added to the library budget.

Most public libraries are managed in a very decentralized fashion. Innovations in library operations seem to make more centralized management possible. Successful centralized management offers the prospect of making a more uniform, higher quality of service available at lower cost. The development of such centralized management tools will take time and effort. The increase in centralized control will be an evolutionary change.

There is a strong case for more aggressive development of national library services by the federal government. The original cataloging services of the Library of Congress are very important to all libraries in the United States and around the world. The development of a sophisticated, reliable, speedy lending library of last resort for periodicals and for exhaustive collections in all subject areas would improve library services nationwide at lower total cost than if private institutions try to produce such results. Leadership in the development of such institutions by the federal government has generally been weak because no federal agency has a clear mandate to develop such institutions.

Finally, libraries may face a competitive threat from electronic publishing and home information retrieval systems over the next decade. While the British Post Office is currently the world leader in this service, American cable television and telecommunication firms are likely to enter the field in a big way. Public libraries may be forced to rethink their mission as electronic competition develops.

Conclusion

Many public libraries have come on hard times. Budgets have been cut radically in many cases, sometimes forcing hours of service to be cut in half, as in New York; sometimes causing acquisitions of new materials to be cut out entirely, as in Los Angeles County. Sometimes budgets are partially restored after a year or two, as in Buffalo. These changes indicate a severe instability in the finance of many public libraries. Such instability hardly reflects radical short-run changes regarding the value of library services. Public interest in libraries hardly seems to fluctuate so markedly from year to year. Thus, the instability of finance must reflect a weakness of the current methods of financing public libraries.

DECLINING DEMAND AND BUDGET DISCRETION

In part the instability may reflect the high level of discretion local budget-making officials, mayors, and councils have in deciding on funding. Apparently, budget levels must be very high before the electorate or the city's creditors will react to force budget cuts. Similarly, severe cuts can be made before electoral reaction will force restorations. Within this wide band, the local budget process can move library budgets up and down with little difficulty. In fact, from time to time the mayor or council may move the budget markedly up or down in order to test the limits of discretionary authority. The discretionary authority reflects the substantial ignorance all participants have of the real social value of the services.

The library is more vulnerable to such swings than other services because a shutdown of the system does not pose immediate threats to life and safety. Teachers, fire fighters, police officers, and sanitation workers each can threaten shutdowns that have immediate widespread effects on the population of a city. The closing down of the fire department or cessation of refuse collection because of budget deficiencies brings immediate and potent public reaction. While public library services are of substantial value, the closing of the library system does not generate the attention that school or refuse collection shutdowns do.

The natural political base for public library services is the middle and upper classes, persons with more education and higher incomes than average. Demographic changes in some central cities may have eroded the political support for public libraries. Lower birth rates may have reduced the demand for library services. If so, these changes may be of long-run character. The library systems need then to make long-term adjustments to take account of the fundamental changes in demand, whether demand is measured directly or via the political process.

In sectors of the economy that depend on prices as signals of values, the adjustment to changing demands would be immediate and gradual. Falling demands would lead to falling prices, leading profit-making firms to stop expansion, and to plan cutbacks. The wide band of discretionary budget authority in the political budgetary process makes immediate reaction to declines in demand unlikely. However, once a reaction begins it may be very severe, because the bottom of the discretionary band may have been falling over a period of years. The location of the bottom of the discretionary range apparently can only be discovered by testing. Thus, initial cuts may overshoot the mark, and partial restorations in later periods are common.

The discretionary band surrounding local political activity may describe not only the level of the budget for an agency, but may also extend to the mix of activities, that is, the operations of the service. Thus, the budget problem is made more severe because the political officials twist the mix of activities in inappropriate ways. For example, the political process may seek to sustain the existence of numerous branches even while hours of service fall below twenty hours per week throughout the system. A higher level of service—that is, services more valuable to the public—could be sustained within the given budget if the mix of activities could be rationalized.

The public library may be more vulnerable to political reversals because of its common semiautonomous character and its usual professional management. While these organizational characteristics may enhance the quality of library services and lead to more rapid diffusion of innovations than is common in other local government services, the cost may be a lack of political success. The manager chosen after a national search and selected on professional criteria may be less effective in building political support for the library. This hypothesis needs more careful testing.

Organization

An organizational response to the instability might be to create fully autonomous library governments fully financed by earmarked taxes. In this way,
the local budgetary process can be bypassed. The difficulty with this arrangement is that the institution may never respond to declines in demand by cutting
back. There is little pressure to economize when the government institution is
fully insulated from budgetary review. Few institutions have such complete
autonomy, however. Unless the earmarked tax provides full funding, the
library will be involved in the local budget. The earmarked revenues will be
taken as given by the local government, and the local contribution will be
fully discretionary.

Grants

Another response to the instability is increased intergovernmental transfers. Such grants are unlikely to be a way out, however. First, state and
federal governments have even more difficulty in identifying the real social
value of a service than local officials. Therefore, the band of discretionary
authority is likely to be even greater than with local government. On the
upside, a whole new grant program, like general revenue sharing, can be
created quickly. On the downside, the program can be terminated just as
quickly. The funding of federal Library Service and Construction Act grants
went through just such a cycle. Federal funds tied to libraries were cut severely when general revenue sharing was introduced.

Second, intergovernmental transfers cannot differentiate aid according to
the local situation. The same aid formulas are applied to all local governments
and all public libraries. A fully autonomous library, fully funded by earmarked taxes and overflowing with materials, will receive the same aid as a
library system in a rapidly growing suburban area where substantial increases
in services are easily justified.

Third, while a limited argument for transfers might be made on the grounds
that benefits spill over outside the individual jurisdictions, in fact, charges can
be imposed on library users who are neither resident nor employed in the
jurisdiction. The benefits of public library services accrue locally, and so the
case for local finance of the services seems sound.

The evidence about library use in table 2.6 suggests that on average library
systems may be twisted toward too few new acquisitions. Library use is
dramatically affected by the availability of new materials. The value of the
additional use may exceed the cost of adding the new materials in many
locations. Many librarians indicated that if they had the authority, they would
cut branches and staff in order to increase their acquisitions budget. Line item
budgets approved by local government prevent many libraries from making
such reallocations. If intergovernmental grants are to be created to benefit

libraries, open-ended matching grants for acquisitions might be more appropriate than other forms of aid. Such a scheme has defects. Libraries may try to load as many expenditures on acquisitions as possible (buy books already cataloged and processed). Moreover, a few libraries may already have large acquisitions budgets, perhaps, in response to state grants for acquisitions. Thus, the intergovernmental grants will not improve the efficiency of all public libraries.

Information

It is possible that the detailed evaluation of library services, such as that presented in chapter 4, will increase the level of information available to the local political process and so decrease the band of discretionary budget authority. In New York, the quality of library services would be dramatically improved by closing some branches and extending the hours of service at the remaining branches. Of course, additional studies by other investigators may be necessary to develop a preponderance of evidence to influence local budget makers.

Fee

Many public libraries have responded to severe budget cuts by seeking more revenue from fees. In some localities, fee revenues pass into the local general fund and so have no effect on the fiscal health of the library. If fees are to help reduce the fiscal instability of public libraries, the fee revenues must be kept by the library, and to some extent treated separately from the budget process. In this case, libraries have more incentive to collect fees and the fees might provide a more stable source of funds. Ultimately, the case for fees flounders on the problem of keeping prices low for casual users of the library while capturing higher levels of revenue from inframarginal users who place a high value on library services. Such price discrimination regimes, similar to those practiced by utilities, may be difficult for libraries to enforce because most library users can disguise themselves as casual users. Therefore, tax funds probably should not be fully replaced by fees. In many areas there are legal prohibitions against the use of service fees, so the possibilities for fee revenues are constrained.

Diversification

The diversification of library services might also be viewed as a response to declining demand. The increased use of audio-visual materials, the expansion of services for handicapped persons, the availability of employment informa-

tion, and the provision of information about government agencies and programs each reflect a major extension of traditional library services. Many
libraries have developed special materials and programs for persons not liter-
ate or whose native language is not English. The development of these ancil-
lary services has had successes and failures. (They are not easily evaluated.) It
is not clear to what extent traditional services have been cut back in order to
fund the new services. The movement to diversify services may be an appropriate response to declining demand if the new services are valuable.

NATIONAL SERVICES

Libraries can benefit from national services to libraries. Research and
academic libraries may gain more from cataloging information services, and
from lending libraries of last resort services, but such services are also valuable to public libraries. Such services are sometimes provided in the private
sector, either as nonprofit service organizations or as profit-making ventures.
By charging higher prices to users who value the service more (e.g., academic
libraries), such services may be sustained at appropriate levels by private
organizations. However, only a federal agency can have legal claim to receive
all copyright materials, and so basic cataloging information can be created
faster and more effectively by a federal agency than by any private organization. Lending libraries of last resort and archival responsibility for old materials in low demand are privately provided in some instances. However,
leadership at the national level may be necessary to organize such systems.

The Library of Congress has not been able to provide this leadership, even
though it receives the copyright deposit materials. The Library of Congress
does not catalog all the material it receives at the present time, and is not
developing exhaustive collections of materials in all areas of knowledge. The
National Libraries of Agriculture and Medicine play appropriate roles in their
subject areas, but many other areas of knowledge are not so well treated.
Other research libraries do not have access to the copyright deposit materials
or the materials the Library of Congress receives on international exchange.
Thus, exhaustive collections development in specific areas is more costly for
other institutions. Consequently, there are gaps in the nation's archive of
library materials.

In addition, the Library of Congress does not provide a very effective
lending service for other libraries. Its lending service is slow and its holdings
incomplete. Such lending is not its primary responsibility.

Overall, then, it seems that national institutions that serve libraries can be
improved. Leadership by the Library of Congress or new institutions created
for specific functions, such as a National Periodical System, may be appropriate. A nationwide system for ensuring exhaustive collections development
in all subject areas seems to be appropriate. These national services should
enhance the quality of most library services in the nation.

TECHNOLOGY

The revolution in electronics is influencing public libraries now. Computer based catalogs, circulation control systems, and serial and book ordering, are rapidly being adopted by larger public library systems. The computer is having an evolutionary effect on libraries. Early systems are replaced by later systems, often before the early system was in use by all libraries. The systems in place now will continue to improve. While on-line systems are now relatively rare, many of the functions seem likely to move on line as processing costs decrease.

The increased importance and sophistication of computers may affect the way the library systems are managed. While computer based systems are justified initially because they lower costs for achieving particular levels of service, they have a byproduct of generating management information. The resulting management information system can describe circulation and use patterns in substantial detail by location. Requests for materials can be monitored. Delays in acquisition and cataloging can be examined. The length of the queue for various materials will be known. Central library system managers can use this information to evaluate alternative acquisition, cataloging, and processing systems. Changes in hours and in quantities of acquisitions can be evaluated relative to changes in use. In this way, the management of a library system may become substantially centralized, and the number of professional librarians necessary to operate an ordinary branch system reduced.

The evolution of electronics, however, may offer substantial competition to branch library services. The post office, telephone companies, cable television firms and other telecommunication firms may develop home based systems that allow users to request particular information. Such systems give home users direct access to computer-based information files. The telephone directory may be put on line. Encyclopedias, newspapers, bestsellers and how-to-do-it books may be available on such systems in the near future. In short, much of the information available in an ordinary branch library may become available on request on the home television screen. As this new industry develops, public libraries will probably face further declines in demand.

Public libraries have faced substantial competitive threats in the past. Book clubs, radio, and mass market paper backs have each performed services that at least some consumers have preferred some of the time to those of branch libraries. Yet the traditional library services have persisted and continue to be of value. Further adjustments will be necessary as electronic publishing comes of age.

Appendix

A

Library System Data

Data from thirty-one of the largest public library systems in the United States are analyzed in chapters 2, 3, and 5. The thirty-one systems were selected in the following way. The fifty largest public library systems, measured in terms of population served, were identified from the *American Library Directory*.[1] A letter to each inquired about basic facts and requested an annual report. An effort was made to interview all the library systems that responded to the initial request. Hawaii and Seattle were excluded because of interview costs. Los Angeles, Oklahoma City, Louisville, and Baltimore declined to be interviewed within the time period available. Information about the Dallas Public Library was acquired by telephone and mail; the other thirty systems were visited by the author or an assistant. The interviews took place in the early spring of 1978. While the group of thirty-one systems is not a random sample of the largest public library systems, they do represent a preponderance of such systems. While these systems serve a large number of people, most public libraries are much smaller. The systems included here are a more homogeneous group than public libraries in general are likely to be. The focus on large public library systems was necessary because of the limited number of interviews that could be attempted. Tables A.1 through A.4 report detailed information concerning each system.

Table A.I. Library Activities

City	Locations (per 100 square miles)	Book-mobiles	Branch Hours (per week)	Volumes Acquired (per capita)	Titles Acquired	Volumes in Stock (per capita)	Staff (per capita)	Public Service Staff	
								Main	Professional
Boston	58.70	3	40	.141	90,811	1.99	.68	.56	.46
Brooklyn	84.29	0	44	.102	26,127	1.46	.34	.27	.40
Chicago	34.91	0	60	.116	33,100	1.28	—	—	—
Cleveland	51.39	2	41	.273	31,574	3.73	.78	.45	.39
Dallas	4.99	3	42	.155	31,250	1.94	.49	.58	.31
Denver	20.95	2	40	.156	13,992	3.31	.46	.28	.49
Houston	5.52	4	54	.150	21,148	1.52	.43	.33	.48
Milwaukee	13.57	3	53	.279	21,771	3.30	.60	.43	.36
Minneapolis	28.30	1	40	.184	21,414	3.35	.70	.57	.30
New Orleans	4.92	2	47	.063	10,763	1.27	.31	.49	.23
New York	65.57	2	22	.108	26,184	1.07	.32	.17	.40
Philadelphia	40.09	2	41	.112	17,531	1.56	.35	.32	.36
San Antonio	0.80	5	68	.105	11,543	1.24	.17	.51	.52
San Diego	7.39	1	49	.119	10,155	2.10	.40	.43	.38
San Francisco	60.22	1	39	.181	17,642	2.28	.53	.41	.49
Metropolitan									
Atlanta	5.09	4	55	.164	9,384	1.62	.36	.43	.44
Birmingham	1.52	5	45	.061	6,910	1.50	.21	.50	.36
Buffalo	5.10	4	40	.147	29,000	2.70	.25	.49	.52
Cincinnati	8.92	3	50	.124	19,928	3.45	.39	.39	.48
Indianapolis	6.05	4	44	.133	11,239	1.59	.39	.36	.45
Jacksonville	1.44	1	50	.097	10,023	1.93	.30	.49	.33
Nashville	3.00	3	50	.072	6,492	1.09	.26	.45	.54
Pittsburgh	2.61	5	36	.039	12,600	1.28	.24	.43	.31
Sacramento	2.30	4	69	.173	18,993	1.71	.34	.18	.23
Suburban (counties)									
Contra Costa	2.35	1	60	.155	8,141	1.62	.37	.25	.35
Fairfax	4.19	2	57	.220	16,798	2.90	.69	.16	.27
Hennepin	4.81	2	40	.250	8,451	3.15	.60	0	.34
Montgomery	3.60	3	61	.296	6,709	2.51	.63	0	.50
Prince Georges	3.17	5	45	.096	8,416	2.27	.48	0	.53
St. Louis	2.34	23	72	.127	12,000	1.49	.33	0	.12
San Diego	0.86	2	40	.120	8,966	1.04	.29	.15	.16

Table A.2. *Library System Characteristics*

City	Population (in thousands)	Percent Adults Who Are High School Grads	Percentage Population Growth— 1960–1970	Own Net Expenditures (per capita)	Intergovernmental Expenditures (per capita)	Annual Recruit Librarian Compensation (per 40-hour week)	Government Department = 1
Boston	641	54	−8	425	76	16,286	1
Brooklyn	2,602	32	−1	619	581	16,926	0
Chicago	3,367	44	−5	421	120	26,278	1
Cleveland	751	37	−14	205	87	14,559	0
Dallas	844	54	24	168	24	13,640	0
Denver	515	62	4	275	132	13,693	0
Houston	1,232	52	31	707	34	14,859	1
Milwaukee	717	49	−3	434	246	17,437	0
Minneapolis	434	58	−10	159	55	16,662	0
New Orleans	593	42	−5	231	123	13,511	1
New York	3,306	48	−1	619	581	16,670	0
Philadelphia	1,949	40	−3	369	255	14,845	1
San Antonio	773	43	31	191	155	10,584	0
San Diego	697	66	22	133	61	14,865	1
San Francisco	716	62	−3	779	152	15,763	1
Metropolitan							
Atlanta	615	66	9	444	199	11,834	1
Birmingham	645	47	2	200	129	14,452	1
Buffalo	1,113	50	5	368	330	18,409	1
Cincinnati	924	51	7	439	125	15,410	0
Indianapolis	792	55	14	343	148	11,704	0
Jacksonville	529	52	16	207	199	13,543	1
Nashville	448	51	12	297	101	10,543	1
Pittsburgh	1,605	55	−1	305	168	13,799	0
Sacramento	632	66	26	455	280	14,796	0
Suburban (counties)							
Contra Costa	558	68	37	556	220	13,275	1
Fairfax	455	79	65	362	155	15,392	1
Hennepin	526	77	46	155	180	16,687	1
Montgomery	523	80	53	159	226	15,463	0
Prince Georges	661	67	85	352	148	15,851	0
St. Louis	951	61	35	283	85	10,287	0
San Diego	661	64	44	200	157	14,237	1

Table A.3. Library Use

City	Circulation (per capita)	Cards (as percentage of population)	Interlibrary Loan		Loan Period (in weeks)	Renewal = 1	Weeks Wait
			In	Out			
Boston	3.71	74	200	23,000	2	0	8
Brooklyn	2.43	24	492	1,970	3	1	3
Chicago	1.96	20	920	6,225	3	1	3
Cleveland	3.64	NA	NA	7,954	3	1	4
Dallas	4.53	40	1,688	NA	3	1	8
Denver	5.77	59	1,587	13,946	3	1	8
Houston	4.00	55	4,201	21,698	2	1	3
Milwaukee	4.19	53	1,002	12,260	3	0	1
Minneapolis	5.79	NA	958	44,588	4	1	
New Orleans	2.20	29	2,688	3,896	3	1	3
New York	2.42	34	1,399	1,099	4	0	10
Philadelphia	2.88	30	666	10,248	3	1	6
San Antonio	2.97	42	879	6,013	2	1	4
San Diego	5.90	42	997	1,688	4	0	26
San Francisco	3.77	28	1,000	3,000	3	1	1
Metropolitan							
Atlanta	4.47	35	NA	865	4	0	12
Birmingham	3.02	15	498	26,400	2	1	7
Buffalo	4.17	34	3,766	9,610	4	0	
Cincinnati	5.46	38	188	6,130	3	1	2
Indianapolis	4.68	28	334	2,072	4	1	
Jacksonville	3.68	27	931	5,011	3	1	3
Nashville	3.24	32	424	5,487	4	0	2
Pittsburgh	1.75	19	2	25,000	3	1	2
Sacramento	6.31	NA	NA	NA	3		
Suburban (counties)							
Contra Costa	5.43	NA	13,170	14,206	4	1	
Fairfax	10.88	61	848	2,492	3	1	
Hennepin	8.62	34	12,022	2,572	3	1	
Montgomery	9.75	45	5,959	3,293	3	1	
Prince Georges	5.60	NA	6,188	7,852	4	1	5
St. Louis	6.70	25	762	3,940	2	1	6
San Diego	4.43	NA	5,803	9,034	4	0	20

Note: NA = not available.

Table A.4. *Data for Selected Labor Variables: 1978*

City	Recruit Librarian Salary	Hours Worked Per Week	Fringe Benefit as Percent of Salary	Collective Bargaining = 1	Residency Required = 1
Boston	$11,400	35	25	1	1
Brooklyn	11,220	35	32	1	0
Chicago	12,324	37.5	NA	0	1
Cleveland	11,606	37.5	17.6	0	0
Dallas	12,288	40	11	0	0
Denver	11,928	40	14.8	0	0
Houston	11,700	40	27	0	0
Milwaukee	13,623	40	28	1	1
Minneapolis	13,182	37.5	18.5	1	0
New Orleans	9,852	35	20	0	1
New York	11,220	35	30	1	0
Philadelphia	11,598	37.5	20	1	1
San Antonio	8,820	40	20	0	1
San Diego	11,892	40	25	1	0
San Francisco	12,610	40	25	1	1
Metropolitan					
Atlanta	10,907	40	8.5	0	0
Birmingham	12,043	40	20	0	1
Buffalo	12,391	35	30	1	1
Cincinnati	11,854	40	30	0	1
Indianapolis	10,544	40	10.9	0	0
Jacksonville	12,312	40	10	1	0
Nashville	9,168	40	15	0	1
Pittsburgh	10,834	38	21	0	0
Sacramento	12,646	40	17	1	0
Suburban (counties)					
Contra Costa	10,620	40	25	1	0
Fairfax	12,752	40	20.7	0	0
Hennepin	13,906	40	20	0	0
Montgomery	12,410	40	24.6	0	0
Prince Georges	11,888	37.5	25	0	0
St. Louis	9,000	40	14.3	0	0
San Diego	12,168	40	17	1	0

Note: NA = not available.

Appendix

B

‍

Introduction to Statistical Methods

THE ROLE OF STATISTICS

This appendix briefly describes some basic statistical measures and techniques. The value of statistics lies in their ability to refute hypotheses. Hypotheses that are not subject to statistical checks remain just theories. Hypotheses that flunk statistical checks are likely to be discarded. Hypotheses that have withstood a variety of statistical tests are more credible than those that are not so tested. Statistical results carry more weight when they have been replicated by a variety of investigators using different sources of data and somewhat different statistical procedures. Thus, statistical evidence becomes more convincing as it cumulates. In general, statistics are one kind of evidence for decision makers; they inform judgment, but they never replace it.

MEANS AND STANDARD DEVIATIONS

The simplest statistics summarize a single piece of information. For example, how many facilities do public libraries operate per 100 square miles of territory they serve? (See table 2.1.) The actual number of branches and area served will differ from system to system. Consequently, it is appropriate to state an *average value, a value that represents the central value for the sample* of libraries for which information is available. The arithmetic mean is used for this purpose throughout this work. For all thirty-one library systems observed, the mean "locations per 100 square miles" is 17.39.

The mean value shows a central value for the group. One might also want to know how representative the mean is of the group. All the libraries might have very nearly the same number of facilities per 100 square miles or they may be quite different. One measure of the dispersion of the individual values for "locations per 100 square miles" is the standard deviation. *The standard deviation measures variation within the group.* (The variance, another measure of dispersion, is the square of the standard deviation.) For a well-behaved pattern of values, about 68 percent of the actual values will be within one standard deviation on either side of the mean; about 95 percent will be within two standard deviations of the mean. From table 2.1 we find that the standard deviation for "locations per 100 square miles" is 23.28. Since all the library systems have at least one location we know that all of the values of "locations per 100 square miles" are greater than zero. One standard deviation above the mean is about forty locations per 100 square miles: about 68 percent of the systems have forty or fewer locations per 100 square miles of service area. This suggests a very wide dispersion of individual values around the mean: the mean is not very representative of the group because of the great differences among the systems.

One might then ask: is the diversity simply random or are the differences in "locations per 100 square miles" systematically related to easily observed characteristics of the areas served? One possibility is that there are strong differences between central city, suburban, and metropolitan systems. Sorting the group into three subgroups makes it possible to compare the means and standard deviations. The mean for city systems (32.11 in table 2.1) seems to be quite different from that for metropolitan and suburban systems (4.00 and 3.05, respectively). However, there is substantial variation within each subgroup as indicated by the standard deviations for each. Are the subgroup samples likely to be random differences or are the differences systematic? The ratio of variation among the sample means to the variation within each group is a statistic with a known probability distribution, called an F-distribution when the subgroups are random. That is, *the probability that a purely random assignment to groups will yield any given ratio of between-group to within-group variances is known.* This F-statistic for differences in "locations per 100 square miles" across city, metropolitan, and suburban systems is 8.74. (Large values of F indicate statistically significant differences.) This value would occur from a random draw from a uniform population with a probability of less than 1 percent. That is, the city, metropolitan, and suburban values for "locations per 100 square miles" seem to reflect a systematic difference among the three types of library systems. In contrast, there seem to be no systematic differences in bookmobiles and volumes in stock per capita because the values of the F-statistics are very likely to occur from a randomly drawn subgroup from the same basic population. There seem to be no systematic differences across geographic type for these variables.

The classification of systems as city, metropolitan, or suburban is somewhat arbitrary and gives little clue as to why systems choose different numbers of locations or other inputs. Moreover, the simple three-way classification ignores important differences within each subgroup. For example, the library systems face important differences in the cost of labor. Are differences in labor cost associated with differences in library inputs, say locations per 100 square miles?

CORRELATION AND REGRESSION

Correlation

The most direct method of looking for an association between two variables is called correlation. If high labor costs and a large number of locations per square mile tend to be found together, then these two variables are positively correlated. If high labor costs tend to be found with fewer locations per 100 square miles, then these two variables are negatively correlated. If the two show no systematic associations, then they are uncorrelated. Because the probability of particular values of the correlation coefficient for two random uncorrelated variables occurring is known, probability statements can be made about correlation coefficients. Correlation coefficients in table 2.2 are labeled with asterisks when there is a low probability that the two variables being examined are independent.

The simple correlation, however, associates only two variables at a time. The library system's decision about the number of locations may be influenced by a variety of factors at once. For example, an area that has had rapid population growth may not have had time to build all the branches that it may be planning to build. If the lag in branch development due to high population growth were controlled for, then the influence of labor cost differences might appear.

Regression

Multiple regression is a method used to examine the influence of an independent or explanatory variable, like labor cost, on a dependent variable that we are trying to explain, like locations per 100 square miles. The multiple regression systematically controls for the influence of other independent variables, like population growth in the area and the total population served. In this way, the regression coefficient on labor cost reflects the influence of labor cost, given the values of the other variables in the regression. The coefficient on each independent variable in the regression shows the influence of the variable associated with the coefficient, given the values of all the other variables.

Each independent or explanatory variable in the regression has a coefficient associated with it. The coefficient is interpretable in the units of the explanatory variable as it influences the dependent variable. For example, a $1,000 increase in labor cost (explanatory variable) is associated, on average, with 2.842 additional locations per 100 square miles (dependent or variable being explained), other things equal (see table 2.4). Each of the other coefficients in this regression have similar interpretations. A library system with 100,000 more population has, on average, 1.1 more library locations, other things equal.

The coefficients are estimated, subject to statistical error. Just as the mean may represent a group very poorly (as indicated by the size of the standard deviation), so also may the regression coefficient represent the association between variables poorly because of the substantial variation or randomness of the actual values being summarized. A *standard error* can be calculated for each coefficient; the standard error is a little like the standard deviation. The *ratio of the coefficient to its standard error has a known probability distribution, called a t-distribution.* If the absolute value of the t-statistic (coefficient divided by its standard error) is large, the probability that the association is due to simple randomness is small. A t-statistic close to zero indicates that the observed association is very likely to be the result of simple randomness. The t-statistic for labor cost in the "locations per 100 square miles" regression in table 2.4 is 1.626, a relatively small value. The observed association between labor cost and locations may well be simply random. The t-statistic for the coefficient on population growth is -1.8: there is less than a 10 percent chance that this association is the result of randomness. Therefore, we conclude that there is a statistically significant negative association between population growth and the number of locations per 100 square miles.

EVALUATING REGRESSIONS. The evaluation of a multiple regression can involve several steps. First, one might question if all the appropriate independent or explanatory variables are included in the regression. If important explanatory variables are omitted, the estimated coefficients may be subject to unknown bias. When the number of observations in the group is small, however, only a small number of coefficients can be estimated. The inclusion of irrelevant variables may weaken the statistical findings.

Second, one might question if the signs of the coefficients are appropriate. If a positive sign is expected but a negative coefficient is found, one may have less confidence in the results. In some cases only one sign is plausible. In such a case, it is appropriate to take into account the one-sign nature of the variable and apply a one-tailed test. For such a variable, the t-statistic is assumed to be the result of randomness, whatever its absolute value, if it has the wrong sign. For other variables, either positive or negative signs are plausible and so large absolute values of the t-statistic will be an indication of statistically significant systematic relationship, regardless of sign. These are called two-tailed tests.

A third step in the evaluation of regression results is the investigation of the statistical significance of the coefficients. In general, asterisks mark the coefficients that have large t-statistics. A regression with no statistically significant coefficients indicates that we have learned nothing about variation in the dependent variable that is being explained. The bookmobile regression in table 2.4 is an example.

A fourth step is the evaluation of the overall explanatory power of the regression. How much of the variation in the dependent variable is explained by all the independent or explanatory variables taken together? An R^2 statistic is reported for each regression. The R^2 statistic varies between zero and one in ordinary least squares regression The R^2 *statistic indicates the proportion of the total variation in the dependent variable that is explained by the regression.* An R^2 of zero means the regression has explained nothing. An R^2 of one means that the regression has explained all of the variation in the dependent variable: if the values of the explanatory variables were known, the value of the dependent variable could be stated precisely. A second method for evaluating the overall explanatory power of the regression uses an F-statistic. Large values of the F-statistic indicate that the whole regression is unlikely to be the result of simple randomness. The F-statistic for bookmobiles is small. When the probability that F is the result of simple randomness is small, it is labeled with an asterisk.

A fifth step in evaluating a regression is to calculate *predicted values* of the dependent variable using the regression coefficients and the values of the explanatory variables. The *value of each independent or explanatory variable for a particular observation* (library system) *is multiplied by the respective coefficients, and the products are summed.* This is a predicted value for the dependent variable. The predicted value can be subtracted from the actual value to calculate a *residual*. A scan of the residuals (one for each observation) may indicate whether an important variable has been omitted. The residuals may be directly useful in indicating those library systems that have more than the predicted value of locations, and those that have less than the predicted value, given the values of the independent variables. An analysis of predicted values and residuals has not been included directly in this study. The notion of predicted values is important in the discussion of efficiency in chapter 4.

A word of caution about interpreting regression results is in order. Generally, we expect that if one thing causes another, the two will show some statistical association. If increases in labor cost cause library systems to reduce hours of service, we will expect lower hours of service to be found where labor costs are high, other things equal. When such a statistical association is found, we take it as support for the hypothesis. The finding of a statistical association, however, does not demonstrate causation. The association between hours of service and labor cost might well be the result of external forces at work on both. Thus, while statistics can lend support to theories, the statistics can not prove theories correct. However, if statistical associations are not found, the case for a theory may be substantially weakened.

TWO-STAGE LEAST SQUARES REGRESSION. Frequently causality will run both ways between two variables. The amount of circulation from a branch is caused in part by the quality of branch services because library users respond to more books and hours by using the library more. On the other hand, the quality of services is caused in part by the amount of use of the library because the library managers may put more books and hours where they know there is more use of the library. Thus, the simple correlation and regression between say circulation and hours of service will reflect the simultaneous behavior of users and library managers. In effect, both circulation and hours of service are dependent variables.

For policy analysis purposes it may be important to try to estimate the behavioral response of users separately from the choices of the library managers. *One method for separating the behavior of two groups that are making simultaneous choices is called two-stage least squares regression* (TSLS). The first stage is an ordinary least squares regression (OLS) with only one of the dependent variables, for example hours of service, regressed on all of the independent variables. In addition, some variables that may influence the behavior of only one group are included. For example, several independent variables that might influence the library managers' choices about service quality might be included to explain the managers' choices of hours. The predicted values for the dependent variable of the first stage (predicted hours) then reflect the influences of the managers' choices. The predicted values of hours of service from the first stage are used in the second stage, another ordinary least squares regression except that predicted values from the first stage (say, for hours) are used for one of the explanatory variables instead of the actual values. The estimated coefficient of the predicted number of hours is a consistent estimator of the users' response to hours of service. Note that the standard errors, t-statistics, and R^2 for the two-stage regression are calculated using the actual rather than the predicted values of the first dependent variable, and so they do not have the same properties as in ordinary least squares. Generally, two-stage least squares techniques are more successful with larger numbers of observations than are necessary for ordinary least squares. Both ordinary and two-stage techniques are reported in tables 4.4 through 4.7.

DISCRIMINANT ANALYSIS

Discriminant analysis can be used to examine how observations are sorted into groups—for example, adopters and nonadopters of a particular innovation, as in table 5.7. The absolute values of the standardized discriminant coefficients reflect the rank order of importance of each independent variable in sorting the observations into the two groups. *Multiplying each independent variable by its coefficient and summing yields a discriminant score.* A high score means that the observation is predicted to be in one group, say adopters, while a low score puts the observation in the other group. By comparing the predicted pattern with the actual pattern, one can get a heuristic view of the success of the discriminant analysis. A *chi-square statistic indicates whether the overall discriminant analysis is likely to be the result of simple random associations:* statistical significance means that the observed associations are unlikely to be simply random.

SUMMARY

Statistics such as those described have been used throughout this book to explain relationships relevant to public libraries. Decisions about federal policy programs are often based on statistical evidence, including policy decisions toward public libraries.

Appendix

C

Review of Literature on Evaluation of Library Services

Others have analyzed the problem of evaluating library services. Their efforts are reviewed briefly here. First, we review the work by economists, and then that done by operations researchers, and finally that by librarians.

EVALUATIONS BY ECONOMISTS

Several economists have applied benefit-cost analysis to library services. Newhouse and Alexander focused on book selection in the Beverly Hills, California, public library.[1] They assumed that use of library materials represents some fraction of the value of ownership of the materials. Consequently, they suggested that the value of use of library materials is directly related to the purchase price of the materials (art books are more valuable than juvenile books, for example) and that value is directly related to the amount of use. By assuming that the same proportion of users would be likely to buy each type of book if the library copies are unavailable, Newhouse and Alexander estimated a valuation for each category of book and compared the values to the costs of the books. As a result of this analysis they recommended that the Beverly Hills Library buy more expensive, and fewer inexpensive, books.

The Newhouse and Alexander study is valuable because it deals directly with the problem of valuation, but the study has several limitations. Because they were uncertain about how many users would buy books if the library copies were unavailable, the authors were unwilling to state the value of library use; they limited their conclusions to defining the best mixture of book purchases, given the book budget. Of course, the book budget is only one part of the design of a library. Newhouse and Alexander did not deal with the geographic character of public library services—namely, the number of branches—nor did they consider the issue of hours of service.

Hu, Booms, and Kaltrieder used benefit-cost methods to compare mail order and bookmobile services in rural Pennsylvania.[2] The average cost of the bookmobile service was sixty-two cents per circulation, while the average cost of the mail-order service was sixty-nine cents per circulation. The mail-order service was more expensive because of preparation and mailing catalogs. Estimated cost functions revealed that the operating cost per book circulated by the bookmobile service was forty-eight cents; the operating cost of the mail service was sixty cents.

The authors considered five different methods for establishing the benefits of the rural library services. First, they determined how much time users saved ordering books to be delivered instead of actually going to the library. Second, they estimated the additional amount of money users would have spent to buy books if library services were less convenient. Third, the authors asked users what they would be willing to pay for the service. Fourth, they determined at what price books might be rented, if rentals were available. Finally, the authors considered the value of the option to use the service by people who do not use it; that is, the options demand for service. Because asking what users would pay is an unreliable method and because no rental services were in fact available in rural Pennsylvania, to establish the benefit for each service, the analysts summed the time saved, the value of books not purchased, and the value of the options demand for service.

The marginal benefit of rural delivery was calculated to be twenty-nine cents for the bookmobile and forty-seven cents for mail delivery. Thus, while mail delivery yields more benefits per dollar of expenditure than the book-mobile service, the benefits of neither system cover operating costs. The authors concluded that consumers in rural Pennsylvania are better off with the tax saving of visiting the library than with elaborate delivery systems.

The Hu, Booms, and Kaltrieder study is noteworthy because it uses surveys of users and nonusers to develop estimates of benefits. Of course, the study of rural delivery is only tangentially relevant to the design of an urban system.

Other economists estimate cost functions of quasi-production functions without trying to establish values for benefits, but they do not claim to identify efficient levels of service.[3] In the best of these studies, Feldstein estimated cost and circulation functions in 371 cities, using a 1968 Office of Education survey of public libraries.[4] In explaining use, Feldstein recognized that the library activities, branches, hours, and book stock might be shaped by library managers in light of patterns of use. Thus, the simple correlation between use and service level reflects both consumer behavior and managerial choice. While Feldstein used an instrumental variable technique to try to control for the simultaneity, it is not clear what variables were used as instruments. The use of city library systems as units of observation also caused some trouble because no distinction was made between a system with a large central library and small branches and one with a smaller central library and larger branches. Consequently, Feldstein could not develop statistical results to validate the claim that "fewer large branches is preferred to more small branches." Feldstein found that library use is sensitive to the level of service and that expenditures are shaped by local demographics and local government revenue sources.

In an earlier study of the economics of library operations, Black examined expenditure and use in a dynamic context.[5] He recognized that library use would change with changes in population level, income, and wages. Assuming that the efficient level and mixture of services would be determined in response to use in this demographic context, Black emphasized the fact that efficient library service would change with time. Baumol and Marcus considered the changing costs of academic library services, but did not provide an analytic framework.[6] The fact that library costs are rising faster than other costs is not in itself a clue to determining efficiency.

EVALUATIONS BY OPERATIONS RESEARCHERS

In addition to economics, operations research analysts have also studied libraries in some detail. Although Hamburg et al. have surveyed a substantial amount of this literature, they have contributed little to the problem of estimating the valuation that consumers place on library activities. They note that the average rate of return in the private sector is 12.5 percent. "By assuming that the average public library has benefits that exceed cost by 12.5 percent, we estimate the dollar value imputed to an exposure hour."[7]

Operations research analysis appears to offer a better understanding of the production function than the more aggregate methods generally used by economists. In the best example of such work, Morse analyzed the operation of the Massachusetts Institute of Technology library. He used queuing theory to determine the optimum number of multiple copies and a Markov process to predict book use.[8] Morse also considered the optimum length of loan period and the optimum number of reserves. These techniques are readily applicable in many library situations and deserve wide use. However, because Morse studied an academic library and emphasized issues of operation, his approach offers little guidance in making budgetary choices for public library systems.

Raffel and Shisko also used operations research in a study of the Massachusetts Institute of Technology library.[9] The authors asked 283 students and faculty members to allocate a budget over twenty service changes. According to the responses, the authors distinguished two groups of users. The first (mainly students) preferred outside use: more duplicate copies available for loan and longer loan periods. The other group (generally users engaged in research) favored increased acquisiton, a messenger service with the Library of Congress, and department libraries. Using answers to hypothetical questions by relatively uninformed users may not be a reliable analytic technique. Nevertheless, the Raffel and Shisko study represents a creative effort to investigate the valuation of services in the context of an academic library, where the valuation problem is especially difficult.

EVALUATIONS BY LIBRARIANS

Librarians, of course, have also been interested in evaluating library services. Lancaster's comprehensive survey illustrates the strengths and the weaknesses of studies by librarians.[10] Their main strengths are close attention to detail and sensitivity to nuances of service quality. For example, a study conducted by Crowley and Childers assessed the quality of available reference services by asking a set of topical questions during anonymous telephone calls made at random times to public libraries in New Jersey.[11] The authors found that the libraries generally did a poor job of responding to questions that required up-to-the-minute information (recent changes in the President's cabinet, for example). It is easy to see how such surveys might be used by libraries to monitor their own telephone reference services and even to make judgments about the effectiveness of different training methods and work assignments. Another study, by Seymour and Schofield, reported on the use of card catalogs.[12] "Failures" were classified as follows: (1) item in catalog but not found; (2) item in library but not cataloged; (3) item on order; (4) identified item not in collection; and (5) unidentified citation. Clearly, an analysis of the first group of failures might lead to a revision of catalog headings (if inexpensive); failures in the fourth category might give a clue to collections development. These detailed performance studies reflect the librarian's concern with the quality of individual library activities.

Another attempt by librarians to develop performance indicators casts a broader net. DeProspo, Altman, and Beasley, under the auspices of the Public Library Association, propose a more comprehensive data-gathering effort using sampling techniques to describe the user success rate in finding materials (the probability of finding particular items from standard bibliographies in the catalog and on the shelves).[13] A study of the scope proposed by the authors would include consideration of facilities use, reference service, outreach activities, circulation rates, materials available, characteristics of users, and in-library activities. The specific purpose of this proposed method is to develop a broad base of information useful to library management. Clearly, using sampling techniques is a substantial improvement over current data-gathering practice.

The main deficiency of most evaluations by librarians is the lack of concern with costs. Lancaster gives little information about benchmarks for the costs of different kinds of library activity, nor does he suggest how costs might usefully be measured. Even the comprehensive approach proposed by De-Prospo et al. is aimed at improving performance measures; DeProspo et al. give short shrift to costs. Efficiency, however, cannot be defined without reference to costs.

The lack of concern with costs leads librarians into several traps. First, they like to talk about the number of people unserved by libraries. Usually, this means the residents of jurisdictions that have not chosen to build public libraries. But DeProspo et al. broaden the reference:

> Iowa and Minnesota show the percentage of population unserved by libraries, although it is not clear if the figures relate to the lack of a library in a given area or, more important, that a percentage of the population does not avail itself of library service.[14]

The implication seems to be that, whatever the cost and whatever consumers' preferences are, more should be spent on libraries until everyone uses them. Lancaster, only slightly more conservatively, cites the view that libraries should strive to satisfy 90 percent of the population's needs.[15] The notion that the benefits of library services must be balanced against their costs is not reflected in the concept of an unserved population. Moreover, this concept rejects consumer preference as a criterion for judging service levels.

A second trap created by the lack of concern with costs is the application of standards. The Public Library Association promulgated standards for public libraries in 1966, specifying requirements for space, book stock, staffing, training, and so on.[16] The description of a successful public library may be helpful. But the standards seem to suggest that communities that do not choose to buy elaborate library services are not acting responsibly. That some communities have difficulty raising taxes and do not value library services highly, while others want to pay for high levels of service, is easily understandable when efficiency is recognized to account for both benefits and costs and consumer preferences are used as the criteria for judging service. As costs, productivity, and tastes change, the level and mixture of library services that different communities desire also changes. The efficient set of public library activities has changed since 1966 and will continue to change. Since standards are fixed and unresponsive to change, they are not very helpful in evaluating the efficiency of library services.

Finally, a study of efficiency—that is, how benefits relate to costs—should focus on the cost of major library activities. For example, perhaps the most fundamental cost consideration in an urban public library system is how many branches of what size to operate; the second most important issue is how many hours to operate; the third is how many new books to add each year; and the fourth is the size of the central library. These are the major decisions that determine the size of a public library budget and, to a substantial degree, the quality of service. Therefore, these items should be the principal target of evaluation. If the Lancaster survey is any indication, librarians appear to prefer to evaluate catalog use, reference service, information retrieval, and book collection. Lancaster's discussion of the evaluation of library services hardly mentions the number of branches, hours of service, or numbers of books, except to say that more is better.

Notes

CHAPTER 1

1. The history of libraries has been widely studied. General works include Jean B. Wellisch et al., *the Public Library and Federal Policy* (Westport, Conn.: Greenwood Press, 1974), chap. 7; Robert Ellis Lee, *Continuing Education for Adults through the American Public Library, 1833-1964* (Chicago: American Library Association, 1966); *Contributions to American Library History*, ed. Thelma F. Eaton, (Champaign: Illinois Union Bookstore, 1961); and *Library Trends* 25 (October 1976): entire issue. The history of libraries to 1850 and their status then is reported in Charles C. Jewett, *Notices of Public Libraries in the United States of America* (Washington, D.C.: Smithsonian Institution, 1851). This publication seems to be the first survey of libraries in the United States. The contribution of Andrew Carnegie is reported in George S. Bobinski, *Carnegie Libraries: Their History and Impact on American Public Library Development* (Chicago: American Library Association, 1969). The history of federal library policy is reviewed in Redmond Kathleen Molz, *Federal Policy and Library Support* (Cambridge, Mass.: M.I.T. Press, 1976). Information about individual libraries over the last several decades is reported in *American Library Directory* (New York: R. R. Bowker, biennial).

2. The long history of librarians as conservators of the public taste is illustrated by the action of Thomas Bodley, founder of the Bodleian Library at Oxford in 1612. Bodley insisted that the common plays available in every bookstall were unworthy of his library, and so excluded the works of William Shakespeare. This story is related in Louis B. Wright, *Of Books and Men* (Columbia: University of South Carolina Press, 1976), p. 40.

3. Suzanne Frankie, *ARL Statistics, 1975-76* (Washington, D.C.: Association of Research Libraries, 1976).

4. Bernard Berelson, *The Library's Public* (New York: Columbia University Press, 1949), p. 43.

5. Book titles produced are summarized in *The R. R. Bowker Annual of Library and Book Trade Information* (New York: R. R. Bowker, annual). Included are all books enumerated in the publishing trade literature; excluded are government documents and perhaps some books manufactured outside the book trade. A small part of the increase may represent improved reporting in the trade literature.

6. Berelson, *Library's Public*, is the classic source of information about library users. See also *Metropolitan Public Library Users; A Report of a Survey of Adult Library Use in the Maryland-Baltimore-Washington Metropolitan Area*, ed. Mary Lee Bundy (College Park: University of Maryland Press, 1968). A Gallup poll of reading and library use is reported in *Libraries at Large*, ed. Douglas M. Knight and E. Shepley Nourse (New York: R. R. Bowker, 1969).

7. Gallup poll in Knight and Nourse, *Libraries at Large;* Berelson, *Library's Public;* Mary Lee Bundy, "The Metropolitan Public Library Use," *Wilson Library Bulletin* 41 (May 1967): 950-61; Forrest L. Mills, "Trends in Juvenile and Young Adult Use and Services," *Library Quarterly* 33 (January 1963): 58-69.

8. Joseph E. Stiglitz, "The Theory of Screening, Education, and the Distribution of Income," *American Economic Review* 65, no. 3 (June 1975): 283–300.

9. *Census of Governments, 1972* (Washington, D.C.: U.S. Government Printing Office, 1974), vol. 4, 5, table 8, p. 30.

10. Aaron Wildavsky, *Budgeting, a Comparative Theory of Budgetary Processes* (Boston: Little, Brown, 1975), pp. 114–16.

11. Council on Library Resources, *Twentieth Annual Report 1976* (Washington, D.C.: Council on Library Resources, 1976). The current state of the effort is discussed in *Library of Congress Information Bulletin,* 17 June 1977.

12. National Commission on Libraries and Information Science, *Annual Report '75/'76* (Washington, D.C.: National Commission on Libraries and Information Science, 1977). The proposal is discussed more fully in Alphonse F. Trezza, "Toward a National Periodicals System," *Special Libraries* 68 (1977): 7–12.

13. *The Bowker Annual of Library and Booktrade Information* (New York: R. R. Bowker, 1975).

14. Richard R. Nelson, *The Moon and the Ghetto* (New York: Norton, 1977), p. 124.

CHAPTER 2

1. The survey was conducted by interview in 1978. Most of the information reflects the latest fiscal year for which information was available in February 1978. The fifty largest public library systems in the country in terms of population served were identified by the listing in the *American Library Directory*. The thirty-one were selected on the basis of replies to a letter asking for preliminary information. Several libraries that replied to the letter declined the personal interview: Los Angeles, Oklahoma City, Baltimore, and Louisville. Two libraries had to be excluded because of interview cost: Hawaii and Seattle. While the interview group is not a random sample, it does include over half of the largest public library systems in the country. See appendix A for list.

2. The assignment of library systems to groups may be a little more difficult than it would seem. Dallas and Houston are served by a city library but the cities encompass large areas of what would be suburbs in other metropolitan areas. The Milwaukee Public Library serves some limited area outside the city on a contract basis. Perhaps it should be called a metropolitan library. Many of the service areas do not match the political jurisdiction. Nineteen municipalities in Jefferson County do not participate in the Public Library of Birmingham and Jefferson County, Alabama. Two municipalities in St. Louis County, Missouri, have independent libraries. Takoma Park is a municipality that is partly in Montgomery County and partly in Prince Georges County, Maryland; it does not participate in either library system.

3. Library acquisition policy will also be concerned with issues of quality and taste. The Free Library of Philadelphia captured national attention for its refusal to stock the Nancy Drew stories on grounds that the stories do not meet the Library's quality standards. Public libraries may differ in their willingness to acquire Gothic novels. The interview survey did not pursue this issue.

4. Maintenance and security personnel are more difficult to compare because such services are frequently performed by contractors or by other agencies of government. Thus, the library budget may not reflect the full cost of maintenance and security activities.

5. In most libraries, a certified librarian has a master's degree in library science. American Library Association certification required a master's degree in 1951. Some libraries use librarians with bachelor's degrees in much the same way as others use master's degree holders. We have classified personnel as professional according to the job labels used in the library system. There has been some movement toward paraprofessional librarians. The interviews did not pursue this issue.

6. Bernard Berelson, *The Library's Public* (New York: Columbia University Press, 1949).

7. Kathleen F. Feldstein, "The Economics of Public Libraries" (Ph.D. diss., M.I.T., 1977).

8. One might like to control for the simultaneity of library activities and use. More library services may be offered in areas where people value library services more highly. Greater levels of use may induce higher levels of hours, books, and locations. Chapter 4 deals with this simultaneity directly. In the cross system study, the sample size is too small to use the instrumental method to control for simultaneity.

9. An elasticity is defined as the ratio of the percentage change in one variable to the associated percentage change in another. In this case, a 10 percent increase in volumes acquired per 1,000 population is associated with a 3.2 percent higher circulation, other things equal.

CHAPTER 3

1. The expenditure information from libraries is from the author's survey. The comparison of expenses across library systems may be a little misleading because some library budgets exclude capital, building maintenance, or fringe benefit expenses.

2. Standards for library schools, first set in 1925 and revised in 1933, recognized both bachelor's and master's degree programs in library science. In 1951, the American Library Association adopted *Standards for Accreditation* specifying that accredited librarianship programs would be at the master's level. In 1975, there were 58 accredited schools in the United States and 7 in Canada. In addition, there were about 316 other recognized training programs with course work short of the master's level. These programs were oriented primarily toward state certification of school librarians. See *Encyclopedia of Library and Information Science,* vol. 1 (New York: Marcel Dekker, 1968), p. 277.

3. Some persons who hold positions as librarians may have received librarianship training in bachelor's programs before the American Library Association specified that only master's degree programs could be accredited. The Houston Public Library reported a substantial number of librarians with only bachelor's degrees.

4. Carol L. Learmont and Richard L. Darling, "Placements and Salaries 1977: The Picture Brightens," *Library Journal* 103 (July 1978): 1339–45. The mean salary for all new librarians was $11,578. Public libraries on average pay somewhat less than academic, school, or special libraries.

5. Malcolm Getz, *The Economics of the Urban Fire Department* (Baltimore: Johns Hopkins University Press, 1979), chap. 5.

6. Learmont and Darling, "Placements and Salaries."

7. Columbia University opened the first library school in 1887.

8. Learmont and Darling, "Placements and Salaries."

9. Malcolm Getz and Yuh-ching Huang, "Consumer Revealed Preference for Environmental Goods," *Review of Economics and Statistics* 60 (August 1978): 449–58.

CHAPTER 4

1. A recruit professional librarian has an annual salary of about $11,220 and works a thirty-five-hour week in New York. Fringe benefits are about 30 percent of base salary. These figures imply that a recruit librarian costs about $8.00 per hour. The $44.56 per hour of library service suggests that the observed marginal costs of additional hours of public service are well above the extra cost of an additional librarian for a single hour.

2. The relationship between stock and cost can be explored by relating costs to square feet and square feet to stock. The number of square feet in a facility is regressed on the stock of materials:

Square feet = 6633.29 + 0.029 juvenile stock + 0.024 adult stock
   (3.647)   (0.187)   (0.233)
   + 2.200 record stock $R^2 = 0.07$ $n = 59$
   (2.192)

The numbers in parentheses are t-statistics. Among the neighborhood branches, there seems to be little relationship between the stock and space. For the whole system, the relationship is stronger. The number of square feet in the facility is related to maintenance and security costs:

Maintenance cost = 5249.0 + $1.29 square feet $R^2 = 0.70$
              (4.554)   (11.80) $n = 59$

The marginal maintenance cost of $1.29 per square foot plus the approximate annual lease value of $5.00 per square foot suggests an annual space charge of $6.29 per square foot. Because the link between stock and space seems so weak among neighborhood branches it is not possible to relate the estimated space costs to the stock cost.

3. The average cost for an adult hardback book, including library discounts, was $7.09; for juvenile hardback the average price was $4.16. The average price for an adult paperback was $1.98; for a juvenile paperback, $1.26. About 28 percent of library acquisitions are paperback. Processing, including ordering and cataloging, adds an average of 34 percent to the cost of the materials. The processing costs on paperbacks are much lower than for hardback books. These figures confirm the estimate of $7.31 for the average new addition to stock.

4. Joseph P. Newhouse and Arthur J. Alexander, *An Economic Analysis of Public Library Services* (Concord, Mass.: D.C. Heath, 1972).

5. Bernard Berelson, *The Library's Public* (New York: Columbia University Press, 1949).

6. Kathleen Foley Feldstein, "The Economics of Public Libraries" (Ph.D. diss., M.I.T., 1977).

7. Hazen and Sawyer, Inc., "Revised Nine Month Report: Area Waste Treatment Management Planning" (New York: Department of City Planning and Department of Water Resources, 1978).

8. The seven marginal branches are: Mott Haven, West Farms, Woodstock, and Francis X. Martin Regional in the Bronx; and 125th Street, Seward Park, and George Bruce in Manhattan.

CHAPTER 5

1. Joseph Newhouse and Arthur J. Alexander, *An Economic Analysis of Public Library Services* (Concord, Mass.: D. C. Heath, 1972).

2. From 7 June 1970, to September 1971, 25 nonfiction titles appeared on the *New York Times* bestseller lists, with a mean length of stay of 19.84 weeks. During the same period, 25 fiction titles appeared with a mean stay of 24.04 weeks.

3. Charles A. Goodrum, *The Library of Congress* (New York: Praeger, 1974), chap. 3.

4. Brett Butler, Brian Avery, and William Scholz, "The Conversion of Manual Catalogs to Collection Data Bases," *American Library Association Library Technology Reports* 14, no. 2 (March/April 1978): 109.

5. Municipal Library Department, City of Dallas, "Long-Range Plan for Public Library Service" (Dallas: Dallas Public Library, 1977), p. 103.

6. Butler, Avery, and Scholz, "Conversion of Manual Catalogs," p. 172.

7. Ibid.

8. Ibid., p. 150.

9. The speed of availability of Library of Congress cataloging has improved dramatically with the MARC tape system. For pre-MARC experience see S. Elspeth Pope, *The Time-lag in Cataloging* (Metuchen, N.J.: Scarecrow Press, 1973), p. 128.

10. *Library of Congress Information Bulletin* (17 June 1977).

11. F. W. Lancaster, *The Measurement and Evaluation of Library Services* (Washington, D.C.: Information Resources Press, 1977), pp. 19–72. Included is a review of the literature on the evaluation of catalogs.

12. Butler, Avery, and Scholz, "Conversion of Manual Catalogs," p. 172.

13. Josten's Library Service Division, "Book Lease Plans" (Burnsville, Minn.: Josten's, 1978).

14. Richard D. Bingham, *The Adoption of Innovation by Local Government* (Concord, Mass.: D.C. Heath, 1976), pp. 138–40.

15. See Edwin S. Mansfield, *Industrial Research and Technological Change* (New York: Norton, 1968), pp. 133–54, and Malcolm Getz, *The Economics of the Urban Fire Department* (Baltimore: Johns Hopkins University Press, 1979), chap. 6, for a more complete discussion of the theoretical underpinnings of the shape of the adoption path.

16. Each library system was asked when it began using a particular technique. In this way, the year when any particular fraction had been adopted could be identified. Unfortunately, not all libraries that had a practice in use could indicate when the practice had begun. The number of library systems using a technique but not reporting a year of adoption is reported in the last column of table 5.5. In determining the year when 50 percent adoption is reached, these libraries are assumed to be among the first half who adopt. Given the gaps in information, it is not possible to report a specific sigmoidal curve of the diffusion paths.

17. Getz, *Urban Fire Department,* Chap. 6.

CHAPTER 6

1. "Save the Libraries," *Christian Science Monitor,* 22 January 1979, p. 24.

2. "Prop 13 Ill Wind for U.S. Libraries," *Christian Science Monitor,* 5 March 1979, p. 10.

3. Frank Levy, Arnold J. Meltsner, and Aaron Wildavsky, *Urban Outcomes, Schools, Streets and Libraries* (Berkeley and Los Angeles: University of California Press, 1974).

4. The gap in collections development that occurred during World War II caused major research libraries to parcel out among themselves responsibility for exhaustive collections development by subject area. The resulting Farmington Plan associated particular major libraries with particular subjects for exhaustive collections development and last resort lending responsibility by major subject area. The scheme had no federal support, however.

5. Charles W. Tiebout, "A Pure Theory of Local Expenditure," *Journal of Political Economy* 64 (October 1956): 416–24.

6. Alan Williams, "The Optimal Provision of Public Goods in a System of Local Government," *Journal of Political Economy* 74, no. 1 (February 1966): 18–33; F. Trenery Dolbear, Jr., "On the Theory of Optimal Externality," *American Economic Review* 62, no. 1 (March 1967): 90–103; William C. Brainard and F. Trenery Dolbear, Jr., "The Possibility of Oversupply of Local 'Public' Goods: A Critical Note," *Journal of Political Economy* 75, no. 1 (February 1967): 86–90

7. Joseph S. Slavet, Katharine L. Bradbury, and Philip I. Moss, *Financing State-Local Services* (Concord, Mass.: D. C. Heath, 1975), pp. 69–71; Thomas G. Cowing and A. G. Holtmann, *The Economics of Local Public Service Consolidation* (Concord, Mass.: D. C. Heath, 1976), pp. 79–91.

8. *Census of Governments, 1977,* vol. 6, 3, State Payments to Local Governments, Table 7 (Washington, D.C.: U.S. Government Printing Office, 1979). The 586 special purpose library districts are in twelve states; 237 are in Indiana, 91 in Illinois, 78 in Kentucky, 50 in Missouri, 42 in Ohio, 37 in Idaho, 17 in Washington, 11 in Kansas, 8 each in California and Iowa, 4 in Nevada, and 3 in Florida.

9. John Quigley and Peter Kemper, *The Economics of Refuse Collection* (Cambridge, Mass.: Ballinger, 1975).

10. Robert L. Bish, *The Public Economy of Metropolitan Areas* (Chicago: Markham, 1971), pp. 85–91.

11. Redmond Kathleen Molz, *Federal Policy and Library Support* (Cambridge, Mass.: M.I.T. Press, 1976).

12. "Prop 13 Ill Wind," *Christian Science Monitor*, 5 March 1979, p. 10.

13. *Census of Governments, 1977*, vol. 6, 3, State Payments to Local Governments, Table 7.

14. Henry J. Aaron, *Who Pays the Property Tax? A New View* (Washington, D.C.: Brookings, 1975).

15. "Pages of News on TV Screen," *Christian Science Monitor,* 28 March 1979, p. 2.

16. Scott R. Schmedel, "Video Frontier: TV Systems Enabling Viewers to Call Up Printed Data Catch Eye of Media Firms," *Wall Street Journal,* 24 July 1979, p. 40.

APPENDIX A

1. *American Library Directory, 1976–77* (New York: R. R. Bowker, 1978).

APPENDIX C

1. Joseph P. Newhouse and Arthur J. Alexander, *An Economic Analysis of Public Library Services* (Lexington, Mass.: D. C. Heath, 1972), chap. 2.

2. Teh-wei Hu, Bernard H. Booms, and Lynne Warfield Kaltreider, *A Benefit-Cost Analysis of Alternative Library Delivery Systems* (Westport, Conn.: Greenwood Press, 1975).

3. Haynes Carson Goddard, "A Study in the Theory and Measurement of Benefits and Costs of the Public Library" (Ph.D. diss., Indiana University, 1970); University Microfilm #70-26,923. Peter James Stratton, "Public Libraries: Their Structure, Use and Cost of Service Provision" (Ph.D. diss., Northern Illinois University, 1977); University Microfilm #77-03,809.

4. Kathleen Foley Feldstein, "The Economics of Public Libraries" (Ph.D. diss., Massachusetts Institute of Technology, 1977).

5. Stanley W. Black, "Library Economics," in Douglas M. Knight and E. Shepley Nourse, eds., *Libraries at Large* (New York: Bowker, 1969), pp. 590–99.

6. William J. Baumol and Mattiyahu Marcus, *Economics of Academic Libraries* (Washington, D.C.: American Council on Education, 1973), pp. 41–63.

7. Morris Hamburg, Richard C. Clelland, Michael R. W. Bommer, Leonard Ramist, and Ronald M. Whitfield, *Library Planning and Decision Making Systems* (Cambridge, Mass.: M.I.T. Press, 1974), p. 33.

8. Philip M. Morse, *Library Effectiveness: A Systems Approach* (Cambridge, Mass.: M.I.T. Press, 1968).

9. Jeffrey A. Raffel and Robert Shisko, *Systematic Analysis of University Libraries: An Application of Cost-Benefit Analysis to the MIT Libraries* (Cambridge, Mass.: M.I.T. Press, 1969).

10. F. W. Lancaster, *The Measurement and Evaluation of Library Services* (Washington, D.C.: Information Resources Press, 1977).

11. R. Crowley and T. Childers, *Information Services in Public Libraries: Two Studies* (Metuchen, N.J.: Scarecrow Press, 1971).

12. C. A. Seymour and J. L. Schofield, "Measuring Reader Failure at the Catalogue," *Library Resources and Technical Services* 17 (1973): 6–24.

13. Ernest R. DeProspo, Ellen Altman, and Kenneth E. Beasley, *Performance Measures for Public Libraries* (Chicago: Public Library Association, 1973).

14. Ibid., p. 23.

15. Lancaster, *The Measurement and Evaluation of Library Services*, p. 166.

16. Public Library Association, Standards Committee, *Minimum Standards for Public Library Systems,* 1966 (Chicago: American Library Association, 1966).

Bibliography

Aaron, Henry J. *Who Pays the Property Tax? A New View.* Washington, D.C.: Brookings, 1975.

American Library Directory. New York: R. R. Bowker biennial.

Baumol, William J., and Marcus, Mattiyahu. *Economics of Academic Libraries.* Washington, D.C.: American Council on Education, 1973.

Berelson, Bernard. *The Library's Public.* New York: Columbia University Press, 1949.

Bingham, Richard D. *The Adoption of Innovations by Local Government.* Concord, Mass.: D. C. Heath, 1976.

Bish, Robert L. *The Public Economy of Metropolitan Areas.* Chicago: Markham, 1971.

Black, Stanley W. "Library Economics." In *Libraries at Large,* edited by Douglas M. Knight and E. Shepley Nourse. New York: R. R. Bowker, 1969.

Bobinski, George S. *Carnegie Libraries: Their History and Impact on American Public Library Development.* Chicago: American Library Association, 1969.

Bowker Annual of Library and Booktrade Information, The R. R. New York: R. R. Bowker, annual.

Brainard, William C., and Dolbear, Jr., F. Trenery. "The Possibility of Oversupply of Local 'Public' Goods: A Critical Note." *Journal of Political Economy* 75 (February 1967): 86–90.

Bundy, Mary Lee, ed. *Metropolitan Public Library Users; A Report of a Survey of Adult Library Use in the Maryland-Baltimore-Washington Metropolitan Area.* College Park: University of Maryland Press, 1968.

———. "The Metropolitan Public Library Use." *Wilson Library Bulletin* 41 (May 1967): 950–61.

Butler, Brett; Avery, Brian; and Scholz, William. "The Conversion of Manual Catalogs to Collection Data Bases." *American Library Association Library Technology Reports* 14 (March/April 1978): 109.

Council on Library Resources. *Twentieth Annual Report 1976.* Washington, D.C.: Council on Library Resources, 1976.

Cowing, Thomas G., and Holtman, A. G. *The Economics of Local Public Service Consolidation.* Concord, Mass.: D. C. Heath, 1976.

Crowley, R., and Childers, T. *Information Services in Public Libraries: Two Studies.* Metuchen, N.J.: Scarecrow Press, 1971.

DeProspo, Ernest R.; Altman, Ellen; and Beasley, Kenneth E. *Performance Measures for Public Libraries.* Chicago: Public Library Association, 1973.

Dolbear, Jr., F. Trenery. "On the Theory of Optimal Externality." *American Economic Review* 62 (March 1967): 90–103.

Eaton, Thelma F., ed. *Contributions to American Library History.* Champaign: Illinois Union Bookstore, 1961.

Encyclopedia of Library and Information Science. New York: Marcel Dekker, 1968.

Feldstein, Kathleen Foley. *The Economics of Public Libraries.* Ph.D. dissertation, Massachusetts Institute of Technology, 1977.

Frankie, Suzanne. *ARL Statistics, 1975–76.* Washington, D.C.: Association of Research Libraries, 1976.

Getz, Malcolm. *The Economics of the Urban Fire Department.* Baltimore: Johns Hopkins University Press, 1979.

——— and Huang, Yuh-ching. "Consumer Revealed Preference for Environmental Goods." *Review of Economics and Statistics* 60 (August 1978): 449–58.

Goddard, Haynes Carson. *A Study in the Theory and Measurement of Benefits and Costs of the Public Library.* Ph.D. dissertation, Indiana University, 1970.

Goodrum, Charles A. *The Library of Congress.* New York: Praeger, 1974.

Hamburg, Morris; Clelland, Richard C.; Bommer, Michael R. W.; Ramist, Leonard; and Whitfield, Ronald M. *Library Planning and Decision Making Systems.* Cambridge, Mass.: Massachusetts Institute of Technology Press, 1974.

Hazen and Sawyer, Inc. "Revised Nine Month Report: Area Waste Treatment Management Planning." New York: Department of City Planning and Department of Water Resources, City of New York, 1978.

Hu, Teh-wei; Booms, Bernard H.; and Kaltreider, Lynne Warfield. *A Benefit-Cost Analysis of Alternative Library Delivery Systems.* Westport, Conn.: Greenwood Press, 1975.

Jewett, Charles C. *Notices of Public Libraries in the United States of America.* Washington, D.C.: Smithsonian Institution, 1851.

Josten's Library Service Division. *Book Lease Plans.* Burnsville, Minn.: Josten's, 1978.

Knight, Douglas M., and Nourse, E. Shepley, eds. *Libraries at Large.* New York: R. R. Bowker, 1969.

Lancaster, F. W. *The Measurement and Evaluation of Library Services.* Washington, D.C.: Information Resources Press, 1977.

Learmont, Carol L., and Darling, Richard L. "Placements and Salaries 1977: The Picture Brightens." *Library Journal* 103 (July 1978): 1339–45.

Lee, Robert Ellis. *Continuing Education for Adults Through the American Public Library, 1833–1964.* Chicago: American Library Association, 1966.

Levy, Frank; Meltsner, Arnold J.; and Wildavsky, Aaron. *Urban Outcomes, Schools, Streets, and Libraries.* Berkeley and Los Angeles: University of California Press, 1974.

Library of Congress Information Bulletin, 17 June 1977.

Library Trends 25 (October 1976): entire issue.

Mansfield, Edwin S. *Industrial Research and Technological Change.* New York: Norton, 1968.

Mills, Forrest L. "Trends in Juvenile and Young Adult Use and Services." *Library Quarterly* 33 (January 1963): 58–69.

Molz, Redmond Kathleen. *Federal Policy and Library Support*. Cambridge, Mass.: Massachusetts Institute of Technology Press, 1976.

Morse, Philip M. *Library Effectiveness: A Systems Approach*. Cambridge, Mass.: Massachusetts Institute of Technology Press, 1968.

Municipal Library Department, City of Dallas. *Long-range Plan for Public Library Service*. Dallas: Dallas Public Library, 1977.

National Commission on Libraries and Information Science. *Annual Report '75/'76*. Washington, D.C.: National Commission on Libraries and Information Science, 1977.

Nelson, Richard R. *The Moon and the Ghetto*. New York: Norton, 1977.

Newhouse, Joseph P., and Alexander, Arthur J. *An Economic Analysis of Public Library Services*. (Concord, Mass.: D. C. Heath, 1972).

"Pages of News on TV Screen." *Christian Science Monitor*, 28 March 1979, p. 2.

Pope, S. Elspeth. *The Time-lag in Cataloging*. Metuchen, N.J.: Scarecrow Press, 1973.

"Prop 13 Ill Wind for U.S. Libraries." *Christian Science Monitor*, 5 March 1979, p. 10.

Public Library Association, Standards Committee. *Minimum Standards for Public Library Systems, 1966*. Chicago: American Library Association, 1966.

Quigley, John, and Kemper, Peter. *The Economics of Refuse Collection*. Cambridge, Mass.: Ballinger, 1975.

Raffel, Jeffrey A., and Shisko, Robert. *Systematic Analysis of University Libraries: An Application of Cost-Benefit Analysis to the MIT Libraries*. Cambridge, Mass.: Massachusetts Institute of Technology Press, 1969.

"Save the Libraries." *Christian Science Monitor*, 22 January 1979, p. 24.

Schmedel, Scott R. "Video Frontier: TV Systems Enabling Viewers to Call Up Printed Data Catch Eye of Media Firms." *Wall Street Journal*, 24 July 1979, p. 40.

Seymour, C. A., and Schofield, J. L. "Measuring Reader Failure at the Catalogue." *Library Resources and Technical Services* 17 (1973): 6–24.

Slavet, Joseph S.; Bradbury, Katharine L.; and Moss, Philip I. *Financing State-Local Services*. Concord, Mass.: D. C. Heath, 1975.

Stiglitz, Joseph E. "The Theory of Screening, Education, and the Distribution of Income." *American Economic Review* 65 (June 1975): 283–300.

Stratton, Peter James. *Public Libraries: Their Structure, Use and Cost of Service Provision*. Ph.D. dissertation, Northern Illinois University, 1977.

Tiebout, Charles W. "A Pure Theory of Local Expenditure." *Journal of Political Economy* 64 (October 1956): 416–24.

Trezza, Alphonse F. "Toward A National Periodicals System." *Special Libraries* 68 (1977): 7–12.

U.S., Bureau of Census. *Census of Governments, 1972*. Washington, D.C.: U.S. Government Printing Office, 1974.

———. *Census of Governments, 1977*. Washington, D.C.: U.S. Government Printing Office, 1979.

Wellisch, Jean B.; Patrick, Ruth J.; Black, Donald V.; and Cuadra, Carlos A. *The*

Public Library and Federal Policy. Westport, Conn.: Greenwood Press, 1974.

Wildavsky, Aaron. *Budgeting, a Comparative Theory of Budgetary Processes*. Boston: Little, Brown, 1975.

Williams, Alan. "The Optimal Provision of Public Goods in a System of Local Government." *Journal of Political Economy* 74 (February 1966): 18–33.

Wright, Louis B. *Of Books and Men*. Columbia: University of South Carolina Press, 1976.

Index